now difficult to remember the surprise, the whiplash of excitement, produced by this 1953 *Tosca* and *Lucia* and the Cetra recording of *Traviata*.

Though Callas had not sung for twelve years – she had last sung (really sung) on 5 July 1965 at Covent Garden – she was alive. And suddenly we were told she was dead. I wanted to talk about her because for me there was no difference. Callas was alive, Callas is alive. I wanted to tell her story. Perhaps in order to understand myself better. Callas, a life. Dates, roles, names. Tracing a wild path from height to height, from beginning to end, till the last scene on the last day. '*Avanti a Dio!*' Tosca leaps, the curtain falls and Callas is silent. Hers was one of the shortest careers ever, a perilous balancing act, a stunt on the flying trapeze, theatre in all senses of the word, a voice in a thousand that even the most inexperienced opera-goer will always recognize. All this I wanted to say in a few short weeks – to talk about her life in the heat of my emotion.

Perhaps Callas's life is simply a love story which we have turned into a legend.

Did she really at seventeen or eighteen decide to be the greatest singer of her time? Did she really play the records of Claudia Muzio and Rosa Ponselle, the greatest singers of their time, over and over to herself – promising herself that she too in time would sing Bellini and Verdi as no one had ever sung them before? Was the description of a plump little twelve-year-old with black plaits listening to *Lucia di Lammermoor* and teaching herself airs from *Carmen* true or false? Perhaps it is all a legend created with hindsight.

But if it were after all true? If the golden legend – red and gold, the colours of the curtains and boxes of La Scala – were a true reflection, the mirror of her life? Or if Callas's life, in the end, was moulded to fit the flamboyant twists and turns of the legend? If we want to believe it, then everything falls into place. Callas *was* the infant prodigy who won radio talent contests in New York or Chicago. During the war years in Greece she *did* work night and day on Rossini and Donizetti with a teacher who grasped her genius. She *did* place her singing, her art, her voice, her blind desire to recreate opera, above all else. And in order to succeed she sacrificed everything, accepted everything. To become the greatest singer, the greatest tragic actress, she surrendered to a destiny which she had chosen quite as much as it had chosen her.

And so Callas suddenly seems to be the heroine of an opera created by her and for her. A woman alone, lost in a man's world, where men demand that women sing and look beautiful, that they reach the heights and make them weep, even if it kills them. A world in which men – Pygmalions burning their Galateas for their own delight – build, mould, decide, order, arrange. In which a woman is expected to be self-effacing and servile (after all she is adored, isn't she?). Callas accepted all this. The weariness and the pleasure, the applause and the catcalls, the jewels, the sleepless nights, the insults and the photographers, the possessive hand of a man, the breaking voice, the mornings of anguish, the stagefright. All this, because it was the price she had to pay to become what she had to

Callas as Tosca

INTRODUCTION

I was in Venice. The previous day we had been eating fried squid near the Fenice, and once again I felt sorry that I had never been there. It was in this theatre, a few days after Christmas 1947, that Callas had made her début in *Turandot* and *Tristan*. She was twenty-three, I was ten. Six years later I had discovered her first recordings and been dazzled by them. Then we set off for Strà to visit the Villa Pisani and see the *Apotheosis of the Pisani Family* – the splendour of Tiepolo bursting from the four corners of a pale sky, and above a woman with bare arms leading a youth towards a scene representing the theatre of the world. But we saw nothing of all this. Earthquakes in the Friuli region had caused several deaths and the Villa Pisani was closed for repairs. We had to make do with a walk in the gardens. As we drove back to Venice V. slipped a cassette into the tape deck and Callas's voice rang out – Callas in the second *Tosca* of 1964. Her confrontation with Scarpia, her defiance of death, death. Gently Callas kills, and dies for it.

That evening I caught the train, the last remnant of the Orient Express, and it was when I reached my flat in Paris that I learned of Callas's death. There was a message by the telephone: 'A.D. rang to talk to you about Callas's death.' At that moment, I remember, I began to cry. Perhaps a nervous reaction, perhaps no more than that. I picked up the telephone to call A.D. – whom I do not know well but who shares that love we so often feel for certain faces, certain voices, certain women. We spoke briefly. Then I hung up quickly to listen to the recording of *Macbeth* I had brought back from Venice.

J. d. O. arrived at ten in the morning. 'Callas is dead,' she told me but there was nothing I could say. Someone rang and asked me to write an article about her straightaway, and still there was nothing I could say. People rang again, later the same day, two or three days after. Rashly I had promised to write a biography one day for a publisher I did not know. He reminded me of this. I had been thinking of writing about Wagner ('Folly,' Callas-Violetta would have cried). I had been to Bayreuth – Chéreau's production, Boulez's conducting, the beauty of Gwynneth Jones as Brünnhilde, the noble figure of Donald McIntyre as Wotan, there was so much to be said. But suddenly, on the spur of the moment, again without really thinking, I came out with, 'Why not write about Callas?'

Remember her first recordings. I was sixteen. *Lucia, I Puritani, Tosca* – I could scarcely believe it. How could such music exist, when opera for me meant Mozart, perhaps Wagner, at most Verdi? And then one's first *Tosca*, the first cries of '*Mario, Mario*' off-stage in those already slightly tremolo, quivering accents like nothing one had ever heard before. It is enthusiasm, which had always been more or less boundless but was now sharpened and redirected, I was left with an aching feeling of what we had missed during the five years of dwindling activity towards the end of her operatic career and the dozen of almost total silence before her death. This book quite admirably reflects this sense of gradual deprivation which overcame many of us as Maria sang less and less and of total loss when we heard of her death.

Lord Harewood

FOREWORD
BY LORD HAREWOOD

When Maria Callas died on September 16 1977, it was obvious that biographies would proliferate. During her life, there had been two or three excellent books about her art and her records and one or two others about her activities seen from rather personal angles. But a biography, setting out the facts and the theories, the rumours and counter-rumours, had not been truly attempted.

Now we have one which is at the same time judicious and involved, but which by no means excludes the excitement and awe natural to the opera fanatic. Monsieur Rémy has gathered together the facts with care and whenever I can check from first-hand knowledge, he has got it exactly right – although my own experience of a later performance of *Andrea Chénier* and the public's reaction to the heroine was quite different from what he reports on the first night; Callas was not only marvellous but the public loved her – though she told me of the earlier reaction against her and ascribed it mainly to opera politics.

There is good, interesting and I think accurate evaluation of the Press's insistence on typecasting her as an inconsistent, temperamental prima donna who frequently turned towards the shrew, and just as good an assessment of how much of this was built up on prejudice, which looked for facts to justify theory, and how much justified by that inherent energy which primarily searched for perfection through unparalleled depths of preparation but found other outlets in a total rejection of what she found alien – which sometimes included Press 'persecution'.

What I particularly like is the way Monsieur Rémy has not just described a storm-tossed career but rather attempted to define two opposing lines, one descending and the other ascending, running through it: its 'fated' element, by which the seeds of every failure could be discerned in every triumph; and the gradual shift of emphasis from Maria Meneghini Callas as the greatest Italianate prima donna of her day to Callas as world star. These lines were evident at the time though easier to spot afterwards, and they were just as apparent in private life as in public performance. If, as I believe, Callas narrowly succeeded in resisting corruption by the ballyhoo which surrounded much of her career, this was surely evidence of some inner grace because the temptation was not so much constantly around as positively flaunted by Press and flatterers alike.

Just before I read this book, I was preparing quite an extensive talk on this greatest of operatic artists and, in an effort to make an assessment and to put first-hand impressions and her vast recorded repertory in some sort of perspective, I had read much of the published material and listened again to most of the records. Quite apart from a rekindling of my

Lord Harewood and Callas

7

CONTENTS

Foreword by Lord Harewood / 7

Introduction / 9

Chapter One / 13
EARLY DAYS (1923-1947)

Chapter Two / 37
A STAR IS BORN (1947-1951)

Chapter Three / 65
THE CONQUEST OF LA SCALA (1951-1954)

Chapter Four / 87
PRIMA DONNA ASSOLUTA (1954-1959)

Chapter Five / 137
THE QUEEN WITHOUT A KINGDOM (1959-1963)

Chapter Six / 161
THE DEATH OF THE SWAN (1964-1965)

Chapter Seven / 171
TU, IN QUESTA TOMBA (1966-1977)

List of Callas's roles / *185*

Discography / *189*

Library of Congress Cataloging in Publication Data

Rémy, Pierre Jean.
  Maria Callas.

  1. Callas, Maria, 1923-1977. 2. Singers—Biography.
ML420.C18R45   782.1'092'4 [B]   79-28301
ISBN 0-312-51448-4

MARIA CALLAS

A Tribute

Pierre-Jean Rémy

Translated from the French by Catherine Atthill

ST. MARTIN'S PRESS, NEW YORK

For André Tubeuf,
without whom this book would never have been written

MARIA CALLAS
A Tribute

be: a slave to her singing and to those who wanted her singing and created it – impresarios, conductors, husbands, critics, lovers, opera directors and above all her public, we who devoured her. She closed her eyes and surrendered.

Round and round in the whirlwind – even if it is only a wind machine rustling veils and curtains – move the roles she was to become, like shadows or great white ghosts. The victims, the madwomen who people librettos and the world's opera houses. Lucia de Lammermoor, Anne Boleyn, La Sonnambula. . . A victim, she was Iphigenia before she ever sang the part. Deserted, she was Traviata, attacked, insulted, spurned, for a few notes flung in her face at the end of the third act. She was violent and proud, Tosca who killed for love and in the end died for love. She was seen as a sorceress, as Medea, when really she was Norma, a vestal, the custodian of a sacred art, a superb tradition which she had rediscovered, the woman who at the last moment will not raise her hand against those she has loved, choosing once again to die alone.

This is the Callas we must seek out in the thousand and one episodes of her 'scandalous' daily life, and in the full story of a voice. Never have two lives been so intricately intermeshed as the life of this woman and the life of her voice. From New York to Athens, Athens to New York, Venice, Milan, London, Paris, Callas was the butt of gossip columns, the 'tigress', the 'capricious prima donna'. Gradually she climbed the ladder of success, she reached the top and stunned the world, becoming in the end the most famous singer in the world. But her voice, the day-by-day chronicle of her singing, its ups and downs, her triumphs and her disasters, are part of the same story. When she came on stage and her voice rang out we waited for her arias in *Norma* or *Tosca* – 'Casta diva', 'Vissi d'arte' – with bated breath – would she live up to her legend? Just as in the press we followed with morbid curiosity her travels in Greece on Onassis's yacht, or saw her haughtily slam the door in the photographers' faces.

The story of a woman and the story of a voice. The sublime moments, the depths of anguish. But it is also the story of a woman and a voice selfishly enslaved by us men from the start, by all of us – opera directors and members of her public. And so it is the story of a woman, a voice and a group of men around her, pestering, snapping, wearying and in the end covering their faces at the kill.

Why Callas? Because she recreated opera. Because she revived an art of singing which had been forgotten or neglected for years. And because she was the first to realize that opera is theatre too. Because beyond Callas as a vocal phenomenon, beyond her musical sense, her timbre, and the colours of her voice, there lay a tragic actress who – like Wieland Wagner just a few years before – set opera on a new road, who showed that there was something else.

After Callas, opera will never by the same again.

EARLY DAYS
(1923-1947)

It all began with a series of journeys between Greece and America, as if from the start neither the Kalogeropoulos family (Callas, as they became in New York) nor Maria could make up their minds whether Europe or the New World was the best place to make a career. These ships ploughing their way across the Atlantic and the Mediterranean, with Maria even then unable to settle down, are aptly symbolic – already she was restlessly in search of something more.

The first crossing was in 1923. A middle-class couple, the wife Evangelia and her husband Georges, a pharmacist, with their first daughter, decided to try their luck in New York. This was the first journey out, and Maria was born six months later. Fourteen years later Evangelia changed her mind. In May 1937 she returned to Greece alone, with her two daughters, her ambition now to turn her daughters Jackie and Maria into great artists. This time we know the name of the boat – the *Saturnia*. In 1945, with the war in Europe at an end, Evangelia's dream came true: Maria had become a real singer. Now it was Maria's turn to leave for New York to try her luck. She sailed from Piraeus on the *Stockholm* in September. On the quayside her teacher Elvira de Hidalgo kissed her goodbye, but warned her that Italy, not America, was where she should make her career. Maria did not listen; two years later she was back, on the *Rossia,* the last of these ships. In New York she had met with snubs and disappointments, but now she had a contract in her pocket. A few weeks later, on 6 August 1947, she was at last to make her début in the Arena at Verona before twenty thousand spectators. Elvira de Hidalgo, her teacher, had been right. Italy was the place for her career.

But let us go back to that first journey from Greece to New York in 1923.

It was summer. The weather was fine, the sky blue above the Greek islands. Evangelia and Georges, off to seek their fortune in America, had no intention of breaking all links with their Greek homeland. They were simply looking for something else in life. There was a considerable difference in their ages and they did not get on at all well. Evangelia would describe Georges sourly as a butterfly flitting from place to place. They had also just suffered a great sorrow with the death of their second child, Vassilios, during a typhoid epidemic. Vassilios had been the son of the family; there was an older daughter, Cynthia, later known as Jackie, but for the Kalogeropouloses a son was a son, and his loss was mourned bitterly. Then Georges began thinking to himself – why should his family scrape a bare living in Greece when the world was so vast and there was every chance of doing better elsewhere? So Georges Kalogeropoulos, pharmacist in the Pelopennesian town of Meligala, sold his business without consulting his wife and decided to emigrate. Evangelia did not know they were leaving Greece until the day before they sailed; she followed her husband full of bitterness and resentment, for she was pregnant and the journey was bound to be tiring.

The Kalogeropoulos family landed in New York on 2 August 1923, the day on which the death of President Harding was announced. Harding was not particularly popular but flags were flown at half mast in the port and the boats sounded mournful blasts on the hooters.

The couple settled down quickly. Although Georges was not able to start his own business at once he was still a pharmacist, and Evangelia organized and decorated the apartment they rented on Long Island. They recreated Greece as best they could with icons and a few carpets and waited for the expected arrival of their new baby. It was midwinter – a blizzard raging, white streets, traffic jams, when Maria Callas was born on 4 December 1923 in the hospital on 106th Street, New York, a little Greek girl in New York. Evangelia was longing for a son to take the place of Vassilios, the little king carried off by illness, and for four days she refused to look at her daughter. But after four days she started to love her. Maria's life began and Evangelia devoted herself to her daughter – like Norma, Bellini's priestess, who could not bring herself to kill her children either.

In New York the couple and their two daughters led the life of Greeks adjusting as best they could to their new existence. After a few months on Long Island they were able to move to a central district, to Manhattan itself. In 1927 Kalogeropoulos was finally able to start his own drugstore, in a Greek quarter of Manhattan. Evangelia lavished her attentions on the children because she had nothing else to do, except quarrel with her husband. Meanwhile Maria Anna Cecilia Sofia had already begun to eat everything she could lay her hands on. And this is where the legend begins, a baby-pink legend at this point which shows Maria stuffed with food and never satisfied, wolfing and gobbling, and holding out her hands for more. But everyone likes a baby who eats well, so she was fed to bursting point. The fat baby grew into a fat child, a fat girl and eventually the 'elephant who would like to sing Butterfly', in the idiotic words later attributed to Rudolph Bing, general manager of the New York Met. 'When she wanted cookies she would stand up in her cot. . .' Evangelia is at great pains to explain that she was an ideal mother. And so Maria Kalogeropoulou – now Maria Callas since her father had decided to take a more easily pronounceable name in America – grew fatter and fatter as she grew up.

Now the loving memories of those who knew the little girl and are eager to show that they of course immediately guessed. . . 'At the age of four she would listen enthusiastically to the family pianola,' Evangelia recalls. While her mother busied herself in the kitchen, the little girl would play on her hands and knees in the living-room. A photograph shows her with round cheeks, huge, black eyes filling half her face and a delightful fringe. Another photograph, this time of Maria Callas twenty years later in Venice as Princess Turandot, links up with the image of her

as we remember her – marvellously childlike and, though plump, magnificently beautiful. The little girl crawled about on the carpet brought from Meligala, among the icons and the embroidered cushions, using her hands to work the pianola pedals which she could not reach with her feet, listening ecstatically.

'Or records.' The inevitable legend of the infant prodigy, a chubby little Mozart with a golden voice, a girl Menuhin who was to become a singer. More memories from Evangelia, now Evangelia Callas. She bought recordings of operas, *Faust, Mignon, Lucia* and the two little girls – for Cynthia too was a prodigy according to her mother – sang along with Rosa Ponselle, the greatest singer of the day at the Met, then at the height of her glory, whose recordings brightened the Callas's family life.

Family life? Not really. According again to the legend created by Evangelia – though on this point her evidence is confirmed by others – Georges Callas was opposed to his wife's and daughters' interest in music from the start. Eventually he even tried to forbid the singing and piano lessons which Evangelia wished them to take. He did not see how they could spend so much money on frivolities during a depression, especially when he, a new American, had been forced to sell his own drugstore and become an employee again. Poor Georges Callas, now a pharmaceutical salesman, protested vigorously. Evangelia struggled to pay for her children's musical education with money she saved herself. 'Two dollars a lesson, four times a week,' she boasts.

If there was anything miraculous about Maria Callas's childhood, it was her mother's extraordinary foresight. She saw beyond appearances and sensed her younger child's gifts. What was amazing was her relentless dedication to developing these gifts. She decided that her two daughters would be artists, or better still stars, and she was willing to sacrifice everything for their joint vocation. Initially Maria, like Cynthia, took only piano lessons, but she had already started to sing. She listened to records. Another fond memory, perhaps elaborated with hindsight, describes how one afternoon the whole family were sitting round listening to a live broadcast of *Lucia di Lammermoor* from the Metropolitan Opera. The leading singer bungled the mad scene. And Maria, then aged ten, complained vociferously about this awful sound. The rest of the family made fun of her, asking what she knew about it. But even at that age she proudly insisted that she was right, that Madame X, prima donna at the Met, had sung it wrong, but that she, Maria, could sing it properly! The stream of memories continues. She would sing airs from Italian opera or popular melodies to anyone willing to listen. *La Paloma* for example, a sickly Argentine air all the rage in the thirties. Maria would sing it all day long with the windows open while passers-by gathered in the street below to listen.

We see her now. Black hair framing her face and falling to her shoulders, a rather slow gaze. She is sitting at the piano, accompanying herself as she sings arias from *Mignon, Oberon,* or *Carmen.* 'At ten, she already knew almost the whole of *Carmen!*' Her mother watched over her, her father fumed. They had to change apartments to save money and moved to a cheaper neighbourhood, but Evangelia only became more hopeful. Her daughters would succeed where she had failed.

They embarked on radio talent contests, the competition circuit, the mistaken path of public appearances, since as far as Evangelia was concerned this was the only road to success. Maria Callas, from the age of eight or ten, was the object not only of care and attention, but also of pressure and persuasion, bullying or sheer exploitation, on the part of a possessive mother, impresarios, agents, husbands. . .

'She won a fine wrist watch in a radio contest. . .' Her mother is in ecstasy. Because, dressed in an organza frock with pink and white flounces, Maria stood on the stage of a New York cinema, converted into a music hall, and murmured *La Paloma* to a hallful of jealous mothers muttering 'My daughter can do that!'

But the little girl soon put the cheap watch away in a drawer with her other trinkets and went back to her piano or sang another popular song. Meanwhile Evangelia continued to feed her sweets, cakes, anything. Her voice needed nourishment. She was fat and she was shortsighted. From a very early age Maria had poor sight and wore thick-lensed glasses without which she was lost. But in spite of all this something could be made of her! And so, a myopic smile on her lips, Maria would strike up the same song again on another stage, in another cinema, like a wise little monkey. Later she would make a painful admission. 'I don't bear a grudge, but a child should not be deprived of its childhood. My mother was in too much of a hurry.' Or another bitter remark, when surrounded by fussing admirers: 'There should be a law against that kind of thing . . . A child treated like that is worn out before its time. . .'

Bitterness, resentment and poisoned memories – Maria Callas remembered her New York childhood without pleasure. Despite the flounced frocks, the impeccable ringlets and the big satin bow à la Shirley Temple on top of her head, she felt ugly, with fat arms, pudgy legs in neat white ankle socks, round glasses giving her a moon-faced look, and a dose of acne, the result of her mother's dietary whims. 'There should be a law against that kind of thing. . .'

Malibran, born Maria-Felicia Garcia – daughter of the great Garcia, one of the most famous tenors of his day – did her vocal exercises to the accompaniment of kicks up the backside and perfected her runs with the help of blows and slaps before she was twelve years old. That was in Paris in 1820. A hundred and ten years later in America little had changed. Maria was stuffed with titbits, because a good voice needs plenty of fat to develop properly, as everyone kept saying, and she was dragged off to seedy contests to learn to overcome her nerves by appearing in public. She could also learn genius – at an even higher cost.

Suddenly the legend becomes loathsome and everything we hear about Callas sounds laughable and absurd.

The second journey was the return journey to Greece. In 1937 the relationship between Evangelia and Georges Callas worsened to the point where they could no longer stand one another, and they decided to split up. Georges Callas was making only a meagre living and everything was very expensive in America, whereas in Greece the mother and daughters could live quite royally for the same amount. Besides, making a success of two infant prodigies like Jackie and Maria in New York was an enormous undertaking. There were thousands of fond mothers convinced that their offspring was unique. Old films of America in the thirties show clips of these obsessive women shepherding a little boy or girl in front of them, destined they declared to become another Mickey Rooney or Deanna Durbin one day. In the streets of Rome and Milan, Anna Magnani, doll in hand, was playing the same game – *Bellissima!* Evangelia Callas had enough common sense to see that in the circumstances for Maria Callas or her sister to become a child star was a daydream; she decided simply to turn them into artists.

Hence their return to Greece.

Georges and Evangelia separated by mutual consent. He agreed to continue working for them in his own drugstore, or for someone else. She would work for the glory of her children in her native Greece. Jackie went on ahead a few weeks earlier and in May 1937 a Chilean steamer, the *Saturnia,* set off for Greece. Evangelia describes it all in her book – the voyage of mother and daughter with their three canaries, their seasickness and Maria's performances in the captain's saloon. 'She refused to sing at mass on Sunday but when she was asked to sing at the captain's soirée, for the first-class passengers. . .' This is vaguely unpleasant, even grotesque, but it cannot be left out.

Maria entered the saloon dressed as a child, with an Eton collar, a thick fringe, her face made up and powdered, and the thick glasses which she laid at her side to play the piano. The captain and his guests were waiting. Maria had her audience. Quite self-assured, filled with the energy which always gripped her when she found herself on stage, the little girl broke into *La Paloma.* Everyone clapped. The *Ave Maria* which followed was a success, the *Habanera* from *Carmen* a triumph. Maria plucked a carnation from a vase and with a provocative flash of her eyes – though here perhaps, imagination is running away with us – threw it to the captain, Carmen to Don José. The captain raised the carnation to his lips and gave the little girl a doll in return. 'To my Maria who had never played with dolls.' Evangelia Callas's cry of triumph – her daughter had never been a child like the rest.

For a child who had known only the streets of New York, the

classrooms of the public school at the corner of Amsterdam Avenue and 188th Street and the sleazy cinemas-cum-music halls of the Bronx or Brooklyn, the sudden discovery of Greece in those days must have been a breathtaking revelation. All the ancient myths still lived on in picture-postcard landscapes; in the shadow of the Parthenon all the old familiar clichés fell into place. After the concrete of Washington Heights this land of orange trees in bloom seemed a promised land, and the Callas girls revelled in it. 'The warm scents of the Greek spring floated in the air,' as Evangelia described it with unexpected poetry.

The first thing mother and daughters did was to change their name back. Callas was short and sounded almost American – in America. But back home they took their own name again, just as they took up again with their uncles, aunts and young cousins. Evangelia Callas soon resumed the sonorous Greek syllables of her real name, Kalogeropoulos. The whole of the Dimitriades family, Evangelia's family, was there on the platform of Athens station to welcome her and Maria after their landing at Patras. Jackie was there too. They were reconciled with Greece and with the past. Every month Georges, still Callas, sent a hundred dollars from America to the newly returned exiles. Life could begin again.

Life, or a young singer's years of apprenticeship. So far we have spoken ironically of Maria Callas the child, the singer, the infant prodigy. Certainly the unhappy little girl, fussily dressed, shown off by her mother in front of every available audience, must have been a bit ridiculous. Certainly her mother's single-minded determination to turn her daughters into stars seems almost demented. It is difficult to be completely serious when remembering the baby's cookies, the little girl's sweets, her spotty cheeks, the bow in her hair – despite more romantic memories of her organza or organdie frocks.

But in Athens during 1937 and 1938 all this changed. The little girl was growing up. She still had spots and puppy fat, but her voice – the voice which had been recognized in her – was about to explode. She was just fifteen and over the next ten years, until she first received the applause of the Arena at Verona, this voice was to blossom and develop. From now on the story takes a serious turn; for the time being anecdotes take second place. Her elder sister continued playing the piano and Maria sang.

Mother and daughters moved first into the Dimitriades family home, a stone's throw from the Parthenon. It was a large baroque building, all stairs, imposing capitals and potted plants, with kitchens larger than the largest bedrooms. A real Callas décor created by Visconti. Everyone in the household sang, played an instrument or loved music. Pipitsa and Sophia, the aunts, had pleasant voices and Ephtemios, one of the uncles, was the first to recognize Maria's real talent. The whole family lived, worked and ate together. Maria spent a great deal of time in the kitchens, eating everything she could. Her mother tells us that she was particularly fond of fried eggs and an extra fattening type of spaghetti which they had invented together. The Kalogeropoulos-Dimitriades household again held that great voices were made of mountains of pasta and pounds of rahat-loukhoum. However, very soon cracks appeared in the family relationships and Evangelia moved to a large modern apartment on Patission Street where Maria really began work.

First Evangelia tried to place her daughter, as she now realized she had a treasure on her hands. They took advice and gave auditions. Ephtemios Dimitriades had given his opinion, but they still needed to hear the experts' views. The famous Greek bass Nicola Moscana listened to Maria and was amazed at her talent. Soon an audition was arranged with Maria Trivella, a plump little soprano without a great past, who was a good teacher and worked at the National Conservatory. She was enthusiastic and immediately took Maria on as a pupil.

There were two reputable music schools in Athens at the time – the Athens Conservatory, a highly respected institution which produced the country's leading opera singers; and the National Conservatory, less well-known but with less stringent entrance qualifications. In 1937 the first turned Maria down because she was not yet sixteen, but by lying about her age she managed to get accepted by the National Conservatory in early 1937. She was now about to begin serious study.

Little need be said about Maria Trivella, for posterity will scarcely remember her name; yet it was with her that Maria Kalogeropoulou discovered her real voice. Her first teacher immediately realized the enormous potential of her pupil whose register, still ill-defined, already seemed extraordinarily open – she sang Carmen, Donizetti's Lucia and Santuzza in *Cavalleria Rusticana* with equal ease. She embarked on a course of intensive lessons and vocal exercises. It was in *Cavalleria Rusticana* that Maria made her first stage appearance in 1938 when she was sixteen. Mascagni had written his opera in 1889 and until a few years ago an astonishing recording, conducted by the composer himself, was still available from HMV. Like *Pagliacci* it began with a kind of prologue. Mascagni, his voice trembling with emotion, addresses the audience and tells them what they are about to hear. If it is symbolic that Callas later made her first appearance at Verona in the role of a singer, the Venetian La Gioconda in Ponchielli's opera of the same name, it is just as remarkable that the first role she ever played on stage was Turridu's jealous mistress. A woman older than her lover, who when deceived by him betrays him to the wrath of a cuckolded husband. The husband stabs Turridu to death in their Sicilian village one Easter morning. As the organ and the choir ring out, Maria becomes a vengeful, passionate fury, the first of the wronged women, marked by fate, bearing death like a black cloak. All her life she swung between these two extremes – the victim and the tigress. But the tigress – Santuzza, like Medea – is also a victim.

Today when we hear Callas's voice on record in these notes of bottomless despair shivers run down the spine. What was it like for those who heard Maria Trivella's pupil that day in 1938? Perhaps at first they saw only a tall, fat girl lost on a stage without her spectacles. They could not know of the lava boiling beneath her placid exterior, and there is no one now who can tell us about that first evening. Soon another woman

21

teacher took the place of Maria Trivella and played a decisive role in making Maria Callas what she became.

Elvira de Hidalgo was a great Spanish singer, a well-known teacher, who fell in love with Greece and was to find herself trapped there by the war. Soon it would be 1939 and, after an unsuccessful initiative by the Italian forces, the Germans occupied Athens and invited the Italian troops to share the delights of occupation with them as brothers in arms. Unable to return to her own country, with even less chance of getting to America, Elvira de Hidaldo – a singer who had performed all over the world and had come to Athens for one season only – was obliged to teach at the Conservatory for the whole of the war. When she heard young Kalogeropoulou it was a revelation. Despite Maria Trivella's lessons, her voice still had little polish. Elvira de Hidalgo described 'cascades of sound, not yet fully controlled. . . I listened with my eyes closed and imagined what a pleasure it would be to work with such metal, to mould it to perfection.'

From then on the most marvellous understanding developed between the famous soprano, now past her prime, who had sung with Caruso and Chaliapin, and the awkward young girl. Later we shall see how two men at least 'made' Maria Meneghini Callas. Before that two women had 'made' Maria Kalogeropoulou Callas – her mother, with her ruthless approach and Elvira de Hidalgo, a female Pygmalion, who found her own happiness as her pupil's voice emerged. They embarked on a course of hard work as partners and friends. 'I began to take lessons with her from morning to night,' Callas recalled in 1970. 'I would start with her at ten in the morning, we stopped at lunchtime usually for a sandwich and continued until eight in the evening. I would never have dreamed of going home earlier, for the simple reason that I would not have known what to do there!' In her heyday Maria Callas had second thoughts about some of her passions, and doubted the value of some of her friendships and loves. But the name of Elvira de Hidalgo was always for her a synonym for hard work, devotion and almost filial piety. Everything her mother had failed to give her, and more, she found in Elvira de Hidalgo.

However Hidalgo's primary aim was to teach singing, and Callas's account of her lessons twenty years later shows the vital part the Spanish singer played in her career. It was with her that Callas learned to work recklessly, to sit up all night learning scores. Above all it was with her that she discovered and came to love the composers and roles, at that time forgotten by other singers, with which she was to make her name.

Maria Trivella had begun to create an instrument, but Hidalgo was to turn it into a matchless tool. From the start Hidalgo admired the raw material of the voice at her disposal when Maria gave herself up to her, body and soul, voice and art, but she was also immediately aware of its defects.

Maria's register has been mentioned. It was immense, ranging from a smooth, agile coloratura to the warmest, most wide-ranging, of dramatic sopranos, like Norma, Leonora in *Il Trovatore* and Isolde. Between these two extremes she was equally at home as a light soprano (Rosina in *Il*

Barbiere) or lyric soprano (Tosca, Aida). In 1960 Olivier Merlin, critic of *Le Monde,* remarked that she really had three voices, 'an upper voice at the back of the throat, a middle voice not always perfectly stable, and a lower voice with tremolo.' Her defects were equally important, and were of two kinds. First those that could easily be corrected with work and exercises – a certain roughness of sound, an inadequate control of volume – in short, a wealth of vocal material which tended to break its bounds and which above all needed careful placing. Then there were defects which were more difficult to eradicate because they sprang largely from the nature and range of the voice itself. Callas sang as if she had three voices, three registers. The problem was that between each of these voices – between the upper and middle register, and again between middle and lower – there was a break, a dangerous hiatus when passing from one tone to the next in these registers. These were gaps which vocal exercise alone could never fill. Here again constant work on the voice, and exercises to reduce the gaps gradually, were needed. That, and supreme musicianship combined with incomparable dramatic sense to make the listener forget the flaws. Callas really only managed to eliminate these gaps when her voice had passed the stage of maturity and when fatigue had softened the intensity of each register.

Anna Bolena

Elvira de Hidalgo understood all this perfectly. She also realized that people might quite simply not like her pupil's voice. Some of Callas's most fervent admirers (the composer Virgil Thomson, for example) admitted frankly that her voice could be ugly and uneven. One writer, a keen follower of the prima donna at the height of her career and in love with her like all the rest of us, was not ashamed to confess that the first time he heard her, in the 1953 recording of *Lucia di Lammermoor,* he hated her, and gave the records away because he disliked them so much. When Elvira de Hidalgo came upon the unformed, baroque gold of young Maria Kalogeropoulou's voice, she must have sensed that she was dealing with a very rare phenomenon.

To protect this amazing metal Hidalgo gave Maria her first piece of advice – to confine herself to the light roles in the repertory for the time being, to stick to the light, clear, flexible coloratura register and to explore fully the area of genuine *bel canto,* at that time neglected. In due course her voice would develop and she would be able to consider other roles.

Recognizing Callas as the heir to a lost tradition was Hidalgo's triumph. When Rossini, Bellini and Donizetti wrote *Armida, Norma* or *Lucia di Lammermoor* between about 1810 and 1840, operas suited to singers like Pasta or Adelina Patti, they invented a new style of singing in which everything was subordinated to an extremely difficult melodic line with elaborate ornamentation which each singer usually adapted as he or she pleased. This style of singing required a generally light voice which could adapt to all the difficulties encountered in a composition whose aim was to play tricks with the voice. These roles, or others like Rossini's *Il Barbiere,* Bellini's *Il Pirata* or Donizetti's *Anna Bolena,* called for the 'beautiful singing' which is the essence of *bel canto.*

With Verdi from 1850 onwards, and more particularly with Berlioz (though his influence was slight), all this changed. The voice and the singer were expected to be far more expressive and the variations between the extremes of the vocal register became far more important. The composer wanted more than *bel canto* – he wanted his music to speak, to express. The *verismo* operas of the end of the century – Puccini, Leoncavallo, Giordano – pushed these tendencies to the limit, using and abusing the voice's potential to simulate emotions ranging from the spoken word to a sob. First they used singers trained in the old school who still regarded musical sense as more important than expression, but then came several generations of singers who unawares deliberately sang badly, perhaps for the sake of expression, but above all for volume and effect. The early twentieth century was a time when the art of pure singing reached its nadir.

With few exceptions (notably *Lucia di Lammermoor*) operas which demanded genuine *bel canto,* requiring a light, flexible voice, disappeared from the repertoire. In the great opera houses of the world, Bellini and Donizetti were consigned to the stock room, together with the technique of *Medea, Anna Bolena*'s cap, the golden sickle from *Norma*.

For hours, months, years, Elvira di Hidalgo made her pupil study this forgotten repertoire. She firmly ignored any hints of a mezzo voice and for the time being made Maria forget all about her heavier or more dramatic roles. Maria had sung an aria from Weber's *Oberon,* 'Ocean, thou mighty monster', for her audition. Now Hidalgo told her not to look at it again for twenty years. Perhaps, beneath the molten gold of this voice, she recognized the fragility of the upper register, the strain which over the years led to stridency, the vibrato which soon became so difficult to control. Elvira di Hidalgo's most important contribution was her success in persuading Callas during her studies in Athens to stick to one type of singing. Maria was to have her fill of this style – 'I was like a sponge, ready to soak up everything,' she said later, a vivid image for the way she breathed, drank, gorged herself on the music.

Her heart and mind were filled with the heroines of *bel canto* – Rossini's astute young girls, Bellini's fragile virgins, Donizetti's broken-hearted queens. As she had a prodigious memory, she only had to hear a tune once to know it. When lent a score she could read it overnight and reproduce it to her teacher the next morning, having (almost) learned the role. She was obsessed by vocal runs, finely chiselled high-lying phrases, ornamental figures. Anna Bolena, Norma, Maria Stuarda – she devoured the music with an insatiable appetite for *bel canto*. As Elvira di Hidalgo loved these *bel canto* heroines in the same way, the two women developed a kind of shared life, a sense of complicity in their music. Yet the older woman realized that her pupil was more than the ideal Donizetti heroine that she, the teacher, was creating like a marvellous plaything for herself. Hidalgo never meant Maria to sing only these roles and this repertoire, though for the time being they were the best suited to her talents. She knew Maria could do much more besides.

By her choice the teacher made her pupil a splendid gift – a vast, unjustly neglected, repertoire which Maria Callas would have at her fingertips when the time came. When the singers of the world were still churning out Tosca, Butterfly, Traviata, at most Lucia, Maria Callas was to emerge with some unbelievable trump cards up her sleeve – Elvira in *I Puritani*, Medea, Norma. That, together with a voice, was the finest present imaginable. And so Maria, whose mother had forced her hand at the beginning, now made up her own mind – with Hidalgo – to become the greatest singer in the world.

However the understanding between teacher and pupil went beyond this. Elvira de Hidalgo quickly discovered the hidden treasures of Maria's personality beneath her stodgy exterior. She began to tackle the outward appearances, determined to draw the butterfly out of its chrysalis, to create Callas as we knew her – the Callas of those superb photographs from the 1954-55 season. Hidalgo, like a real mother, perhaps like the mother Maria had never really had, taught her to stand and move, to throw out her chest, and throw back her shoulders. Later Visconti took over, but it was Hidalgo who told her what to do with her hands hanging limply at her sides. She taught her how to dress to her best advantage. Maria was still strapping, but instead of being lumpy and awkward, she became self-assured, with a firm and imposing bearing and a direct gaze. She learned how to walk across a stage without her spectacles as if she could see. Elvira de Hidalgo shaped and moulded her. Gradually Maria began to look like herself.

Meanwhile in her daily life she met real singers and heard all the students at the Athens Conservatory every day, with Elvira de Hidalgo to point out the strengths and weaknesses of their voices to her. She drank it all in: the Spanish soprano was creating a new woman as well as a voice.

It is easy now to see why Maria gradually moved away from her mother and why her mother resented it. In her memoirs – to return to the level of anecdote again – Evangelia Callas complains bitterly. She dared not criticize Elvira de Hidalgo's role, but she felt she was losing her child. She noticed that Maria was becoming proud, eager for fame and money and, worst of all, that she was rude to the servants. The girl who was to make her début at Athens Opera was very different from the fat child who had arrived in Greece three years earlier. Quite simply, Maria had become a singer.

She had already appeared in public in 1940 at a gala concert given by the school. The programme included arias by Verdi, from *Un Ballo in Maschera* and *Aida,* and Maria had her first success. A few months later she sang *Suor Angelica,* one of the three operas of Puccini's *Il Trittico.* The role was not the kind of thing Elvira de Hidalgo had in mind, but the work was put on by the Conservatory and Maria Kalogeropoulou, now the school's star pupil, could not fail to shine in it.

These were only student performances, but in November 1940 Maria suddenly appeared on stage at the Athens Opera in Suppé's *Boccaccio,* an operetta rather than an opera, in which she had only a small part. But she was applauded and praised, and accepted as a proper singer at the outset of her career. She was seventeen and her sudden success went to her head. All her old grievances were revived against her mother and even against her sister, prettier than her so everyone said and, she believed apparently with some justification, the favourite. 'Maria had definitely grown plump,' her mother comments, 'but she needed weight to support her voice. Singers rarely have the figures of models. . . Later she blamed me because she was fat and ate too much; it was to compensate because I neglected her.' From now on Maria looked with a critical and unforgiving eye on those who had turned her into the clumsy girl she had been before all Elvira de Hidalgo's tact, delicacy and affection set her free.

Meanwhile it was wartime and the war too played a vital part in Maria Kalogeropoulou's destiny.

Much has been said about the Kalogeropoulos family's life in Athens during the troubled years from 1940 to 1945. Stories and memories, some pleasant and even amusing, others rather less so.

Mme. Callas has of course explained that she and her daughters were in touch with the Resistance. One of Callas's hagiographers, following Evangelia, has described in detail how the family sheltered wanted political prisoners and members of ELAS (the armed wing of the Greek resistance) and even fugitive English pilots. One story tells of a secret hiding place behind a cupboard or a linen room, police inquiries, a search the day after some airmen had left, the fear and trembling, the sudden relief. If the authorities had found what they were looking for it would have meant the firing squad, according to Evangelia, and the end of Maria Callas. On another level there were the hardships and shortages of war. Poor Maria continued to eat as much as she could of the scarce food supplies – a scanty diet of stewed tomatoes and inferior spaghetti – sharing the plight of all who had to suffer the miseries of occupation. Then there was the black market and trips to the countryside to bring back supplies, not to mention the horsemeat people ate to get their teeth into something. It is amazing that in spite of everything Maria did not lose weight.

There is another side to the story. The true story. The theatres reopened after a very short time, and General Speidel, brother of Speidel of NATO, a patron of the theatre and commander of the German occupying force in Greece, encouraged the arts. Mario Bonalti, a colonel in the Italian artillery and a very proper soldier, it was said, took the Kalogeropoulos family under his wing. There are also more improbable rumours, like the story which appeared in *Die Welt* in 1970, claiming that Maria was directly under the protection of the P.K. (the *Propaganda Korps,* the non-combatant wing of the German army responsible for reporting on military operations and for propaganda in occupied countries). A certain Friedrich Herzog is said to have got Maria's career off to a good start.

These are only malicious rumours which belong with the thousand and one other reasons invented after the event to explain Callas's success. However the war certainly did mark an important and dazzling departure in her career. In July 1941 the Tosca at Athens Opera was suddenly taken ill. The curtain went up on Maria Kalogeropoulou.

First the gossip and hearsay, as usual. Elvira de Hidalgo took the initiative in suggesting her pupil as a last-minute stand-in. The Italian connection played its part and Maria was accepted. A costume suitable for this seventeen-year-old matron was quickly made, a hat placed on her head, a long cane – very 'Directoire' – in her hand for elegant effect. She was pushed on to the stage. Fifteen years later the first really spiteful little anecdote was put about to complete the picture. It was said that she had scratched the face of the sick prima donna's husband when he came backstage to prevent her appearing in his wife's place, or that she had slapped a stagehand or lighting technician who dared to bet within her hearing that she would not last the evening. And so she went on stage with a black eye. Malicious gossip, no doubt, but it cannot be ignored. The mere fact that it occurs so early in the supposedly true account of her career makes it part of the character emerging before our eyes – Maria Callas, *prima donna assoluta,* but the tigress too.

However the circumstances surrounding this performance of *Tosca* are irrelevant compared with Tosca herself. On 4 July 1941 an unknown singer aged seventeen appeared on the stage of Athens Opera with the Greek tenor Antonio Delendas and scored a triumph. It was reported with enthusiasm in the P.K. chronicle, by Friedrich Herzog, in the *Deutsche Nachrichten in Griechenland.* This article apparently opened all doors to Callas.

Imagine this young Floria Tosca crying out her love and hate, the singer playing the part of a singer in love and burning for revenge. '*Come la Tosca nel teatro . . .*' It has been said so often that few roles suited Maria Callas's personality as well as the heroine of Victorien Sardou's play adapted by Puccini and his librettist. The story of a great singer in love with a painter in Rome at the time of the anti-liberal reaction, when Bonaparte's name meant freedom. Mad with jealousy, Floria Tosca unwittingly betrays her lover to Baron Scarpia, the cruel chief of police who dominates the opera. When Scarpia tries to take her by force or make a deal with her – her liberty and her lover Mario's if she will give herself to him – she pretends to agree to make it easier to kill the man she hates. But Mario dies all the same and Tosca too chooses death, leaping into space from the battlements of the Castel Sant'Angelo in the most spectacular of all operatic suicides.

Yet Callas, as we are constantly told, did not like the role. Her thirty or so performances of it in half a dozen countries from 1950 onwards – her last *Tosca*s in Paris, the last London *Tosca* – and the recordings will be discussed in due course. All we need say here is that together with Traviata, it was her most sublime incarnation, the role which remains most clearly in the memory. More than *Norma,* far more than *Lucia.* Not just because Tosca is a tigress driven wild by love and death, but because over the years Callas brought all her musical and theatrical skills to her singing of the part.

It is a pity we cannot compare the cries of savage pleasure uttered by the seventeen-year-old Floria Tosca/Callas at Scarpia's death in Athens in 1941 with Callas's performance in 1953, when in full possession of her powers, or with Callas in 1964, an artist above all else. The passionate response of this young girl discovering the excitement of the theatre and the madness of murder must have been unforgettable. Imagine her 'Vissi d'arte' – her appeal to Scarpia in the second act, 'I lived for art, I lived for love,' the aria which seems to symbolize Callas – a smoothly flowing cantilena sung by a strong young voice, only just beginning to flower.

This is what we should remember about the Athens *Tosca* of 1941; the rest hardly matters. And when Maria Kalogeropoulou leapt from the ramparts of Castel Sant'Angelo in the last act she found Elvira de Hidalgo waiting in the wings. A career without precedent in the history of the twentieth century had just begun.

'The beginning of h professional career a programme for th 1942 Athens Tosc; *signed by Callas in 1960*

The first steps in her career were taken under the auspices of her friendship with the Italian authorities. Later, with her usual bitterness, Callas recalled how her mother had paraded her in front of audiences of Italian soldiers who gave her sweets in return for all the arias she could sing. True or false? – half and half, but the truth hardly matters. Maria sang and was admired. In those dark years you could not choose your audience. The important thing for a beginner was to be heard. There was a war on, but the public listened and the press wrote about her performances of *Tosca* as well as her concerts. A 'magnificent dramatic soprano voice', she had 'electrified the audience'. The Athenian critics went into raptures about this discovery, praising her sure dramatic sense, her astonishing musicianship.

When Athens Opera finally engaged Maria Kalogeropoulou on a permanent basis for a fee of 3,000 drachmas, it was the natural outcome of her Spanish teacher's efforts. If only for this reason, Elvira de Hidalgo's stay in Greece had not been in vain. And this was just the beginning. Next season Maria Kalogeropoulou sang *Tosca* some fifteen times, this time officially, not as an understudy. 1942 marked the beginning of her professional career.

She could only go forward. A year later she again appeared in a series of performances of *Tosca,* and then rather surprisingly in *The Land of Smiles* by Franz Léhar, though there are no reviews of this. Maria Kalogeropoulou figured in all the lists of principal soloists. In 1944 she appeared in four works with Athens Opera, two of which deserve special mention. We need not dwell on *Cavalleria Rusticana,* in which she sang Santuzza for the last time here, or on a modern opera by Manolis Kalomiris, *O Protomastoras (The Builder)* in which she had a small part.

Tiefland on the other hand is more interesting. It is a work by Eugène d'Albert, popular in Germany and first performed in Prague in 1903. A singer of the stature of Emmy Destin appeared in it when it opened at the New York Metropolitan in 1908. It is a sombre *verismo* story of love and death in a rural setting. Martha, the mistress of a rich, grasping landowner, falls in love with a shepherd. In the end the shepherd kills the landowner who has humiliated Martha and returns to the hills with her. Maria took the part of Martha, a noble, tormented figure like so many of the lost heroines she was later to play. The opera was clearly put on to please the Germans, and this may have been one of the reasons for the accusations levelled against Maria once the war was over.

But young Callas did not just sing the second-rate music of Eugène d'Albert. On 14 August 1944 in the theatre of Herod Atticus in Athens, *Fidelio,* Beethoven's only opera, was performed for the first time in

Greece with Callas as Leonora. Here we are concerned with historical fact.

Think about this Leonora. The war was ending. A few months later the German forces would be routed, Valhalla destroyed, the Reich at an end. The Italians had surrendered a year before. *Fidelio* is the opera of hope and love – of conjugal love, the love of liberty and liberty itself. For love, Leonora disguises herself as a man and gets into the prison where her husband Florestan lies, to save him from political oppression, from injustice and death. Everyone who has heard it has shared the same emotion in the first act, when the chorus of prisoners – pale living shadows, walking dead, rising one by one from the bowels of the prison – sing, filled with hope, of their joy at breathing the open air again. When René Maison, an exiled Belgian, Kirsten Flagstad, another exile, and Bruno Walter, driven from his home by absolute evil, took part in it, on those evenings at the Met in 1941, all communicated the same fervour, preserved for us on a rediscovered record.

And Callas's Leonora in occupied Athens in 1944? The ambiguity of a voice singing of love, hope and a final glimpse of liberty, a voice which the press of the occupying forces was the first to acclaim. An ambiguous occasion, but the evidence which survives thirty years later all conveys the same enthusiasm for a dazzling technique.

Yet Callas never again sang Leonora's *Abscheulicher,* or her moving call, which in a few bars combines all Beethoven's genius with the most beautiful phrase ever written for the female voice:

'*Komm, Hoffnung, lass den letzten Stern/Der Müden nicht erbliechen.*' ('Come Hope, let not your last star/be eclipsed by despair!')

A few bad photos are all that remain of this Callas in Athens in 1944. It is tempting to read into the curious gaze of the singer standing between the German conductor Hans Hörner and the Errol Flynn-like Pizarro of Evangelios Mangliveras a sense of disquiet or uncertainty. But Callas herself had nothing to say about that August evening when she sang of love and hope in the midst of those who had tried to kill liberty and murder hope throughout Europe. Her mother describes how the next morning a German officer tried to kiss her because she was Maria's mother, but she nobly refused 'because you are an enemy.' Better to invent our own rather different memories – Callas-Leonora in 1944, an ambiguous symbol of liberty, but of what kind?

For the times were about to change. Two months after *Fidelio,* Athens, like the rest of Greece, fell into the hands of the partisans. A few days later the British Army disembarked at Piraeus. During the weeks which followed, there was panic among those who feared the spectre of communism, but foreign machine guns and the Greek police banished the red scare in only two years and brought the noble peace of camps and prisons to the whole of Greece. We are back in the realm of opera, with Posa, Rodrigo in Verdi's *Don Carlos,* and his magnificent reply to Philip II who has spoken of peace and order: but ' *la pace del sepolcro*' – the peace of the grave. Before this shadow fell on Athens there were a few weeks of terror for the well-to-do, among them the Kalogeropoulos family. Evangelia describes with a wealth of detail her family's anti-communist deeds. Patission Street was once again a haven for victims of the new terror, including this time no less a person than a former Minister of the Interior, General Dourentis. Her daughters, she tells us, ran great risks and once again there were the shortages, the black-marketeering and a meagre diet of spaghetti.

Soon, happily for these good people, silence fell, the silence of the grave, and the communist movement was bloodily crushed. In Patission Street they could breathe again – what a lucky escape they had had. . . Because Maria Kalogeropoulou had played too active a part during the last season of the occupation, her contract with the Opera was not renewed. In fact Callas's talent and above all her overwhelming personality had aroused so much jealousy among her colleagues and even the Opera administration that they seized the first excuse to get rid of her. Not a purge, just a reorganization.

By now it was July or August 1945. As Maria was born in America she still had an American passport, but the American consulate warned her that in these troubled times she was in danger of losing her American nationality. Suddenly she realized that there was nothing else for her in Greece, and that New York was only a few days away by ship. Her father was still there, and perhaps a real international career. After one last concert to raise money for the journey, one last appearance as Laura in *Der Bettlelstudent,* a second-rate operetta by Karl Millöcker, she left on the *Stockholm* one fine September day in 1945. Maria Kalogeropoulou left Greece. Maria Callas was returning to America.

Elvira de Hidalgo had taught Maria that – for the time being at least – she should regard herself as a light soprano or coloratura, that she should sing Bellini and Donizetti and above all that she should spare her voice, lest its dark brilliance lose its flexibility. But what did Maria sing at Athens Opera? Santuzza, Tosca, Leonora and a part in Kalomiris' *O Protomasturas* which even Evangelia Callas could see almost broke her daughter's voice. From the outset of her career, because of her tremendous range, Maria Callas forced her voice. She sang Leonora at the age of twenty-one, an astounding stroke of genius, but vocal madness. Some fifteen years ago, Anja Silja, the outstanding soprano from Berlin who transformed the august temple of Bayreuth with her youth, enthusiasm and eagerness to try everything, discovered what it cost, and she was not twenty-one. But Callas wanted to become the greatest singer in the world and she could not resist temptation.

During the years they had spent together Elvira de Hidalgo had warned Maria that though she could learn to sing in Greece it was to Italy that she must go to become a great and world-famous singer. Above all, not to America, where the machine for making reputations also delighted in flattening them. But at twenty-two Callas knew what she wanted, and that was one thing – to go back where she came from. America might mean American soldiers, chewing gum and silk stockings, but it also meant the Metropolitan Opera.

If Maria was leaving behind the two women who had foreseen what she was one day to become, only one was on the quay at Piraeus to see the *Stockholm* leave. Elvira de Hidalgo had come right to the boat; Evangelia had not been invited to the lunch given by the mayor or to the leave-taking at the harbour. But both mother and teacher had reason to feel bitter. One was losing her daughter for ever. Callas felt nothing but resentment and sorrow for her childhood with her family and her mother. The other was losing the greatest voice she had ever met in her teaching career, raw material which was rich, young and alive, but which was already slipping away from her, disregarding her advice.

Looking forward to success: as Leonora in Il Trovatore

Callas's second stay in America, after her first spell of thirteen years there, was not a happy time for her. Almost a star, a prima donna at the Athens Opera, she suddenly found herself alone, unknown and without plans in New York. After her great expectations during the last years of the war it was a brutal let-down.

It was September. It is easy to picture this large young woman stepping down on to the wet quay, bundled up in a coat which did not really suit her, despite Elvira de Hidalgo's efforts to make her dress a little better. In her pocket she had a hundred dollars which her father had sent a few weeks before, and that was all. She was not expecting to be met. She went through the customs, the entry formalities to the United States which took longer then, even with an American passport. Suddenly a slight, modestly dressed man of about sixty, came up to her and asked if she knew a Maria Kalogeropoulou among the passengers. Maria burst out laughing – this man was her father. She had decided not to look him up, since she had come to think of him as a good-for-nothing, the image her mother had forced on her. But father and daughter fell into one another's arms; Maria had a roof over her head, a bed to sleep in and a father again. For better or for worse, they decided to struggle along together. When Evangelia joined her daughter a year later, she came to live with them – but in her daughter's room, she insisted, living with her husband only as a sister – in a small apartment in the Greek quarter near Thirtieth Street. A disreputable quarter, Mme. Callas complained, no doubt regretting the bourgeois comforts of Patission Street. Maria, however, settled down and made the best of it. She decorated her room, hung a few pictures and set off in search of adventure. New York was hers.

Studios, impresarios, professional singers, amateurs, chance acquaintances, long waits, unsuccessful auditions. New York soon crushes the hopes of those who set out to devour it; instead it devours them, or indifferently ignores the flood of people eager to conquer it. Anyway, who cared about a fat, twenty-two-year old girl who wanted to sing *Aida?* Singers, directors, studios, impresarios – the doors were closed. Then waiting-rooms, the day-long hopes of a meeting and the tiring return to a shabby apartment. Yet it would have taken much more than that to discourage Maria Kalogeropoulou.

First she changed her name again. Goodbye to the resounding Greek syllables of her official surname. Back in America with her father she became Maria Callas. She was back in the land of plenty, of silk stockings and chewing gum, in America which had scarcely known hardship and suffering, Callas, an American again, began to eat hamburgers, cheeseburgers, bacon and eggs and pancakes with maple syrup. A diet like that from breakfast onwards worked wonders for the morale. It set you up, filled you with hope in search for the great part which would make your name. And opera meant Toscanini and the Metropolitan. Maria Callas launched an attack on these two strongholds.

She began by meeting the great Giovanni Martinelli who had appeared almost every season at the Met for more than thirty years. He was an old hand and an extraordinary man. He had sung in the Italian première of Puccini's *La Fanciulla del West,* and had played more than forty roles in the Italian repertoire in New York. Even now his records are astonishing, a light voice, with superb musical sense and technical skill, in the most unbridled of *verismo* operas. Towards the end of his career he even sang *Tristan* with Kirsten Flagstad. To Maria Callas he seemed a demi-god. He listened to her carefully and without committing himself told her that she sang very well but needed more lessons. Too bad, she would have to try elsewhere.

Nicola Moscona was not a demi-god. He was the famous bass Maria had met in Athens when she first arrived in Greece. However in New York he was more reserved. He tried to avoid a meeting and finally refused to give an opinion. In fact he was afraid to waste the small amount of influence he had with Toscanini on a young singer who had not yet proved herself in New York. Checkmate again. Throughout her stay of just under two years Callas never managed to meet Toscanini. Worse that that, without knowing her, Toscanini soon became her enemy since he always energetically defended Renata Tebaldi in the quarrel between the two singers which became such a delight for gossip columnists. It needed a dramatic reconciliation – when Maria theatrically offered the old maestro the most beautiful of the red carnations which were showered on the stage at La Scala on the evening of *La Vestale* – before Toscanini would finally applaud her.

But during those lean years in New York this triumph was still far way and Toscanini was an impregnable fortress. One by one, often unfortunately with second-rate singers, he was making those famous recordings of operas – *Falstaff, Otello, Aida, La Traviata, Un Ballo in Maschera* – which are still some the finest examples of the art of conducting an opera. Meanwhile Callas, in her wet mackintosh, plodded around in the rain.

Suddenly like a bolt from the blue came an unbelievable event in the life of any singer – one of the most magnificent refusals ever. Edward Johnson, General Manager of the Metropolitan Opera, finally gave her a long-awaited audition and immediately offered her a contract – *Fidelio* and *Madame Butterfly,* no less. Of course this unknown young singer, suddenly offered two leading roles in two important repertory productions by the Met's manager, would smile ecstatically, her heart thumping, and sign eagerly without bothering to read the contract. But Maria Callas was no ordinary beginner, and her reply to Edward Johnson was incredibly 'no'. She refused to make her début at the New York Metropolitan at the age of twenty-three as Leonora and Butterfly. Open-mouthed, Edward Johnson took back his contract, folded it up and put it in his pocket. Unabashed, Callas explained. She would willingly sing *Aida* or *Tosca* if asked. This must have been too much for the General Manager of the Met, who retired from the international opera scene fairly soon afterwards. Maria Callas resolutely waited another eight years for her New York début.

But this was not just a whim and Maria had good reasons for refusing. The *Fidelio* on offer was to be sung in English and even in New York it seemed absurd not to sing Beethoven's music in the original German (even though surprisingly she later recorded the Venice *Parsifal* in Italian). And at thirteen and a half or fourteen stone, Callas was simply not willing to make an exhibition of herself as the fragile, fifteen-year-old heroine of *Madame Butterfly*.

So Maria immediately returned to the routine of meetings and auditions. But now that she had closed the doors of the Metropolitan, New York had nothing else to offer. However there was one interesting and hopeful project in sight, and one that appeared to offer a degree of certainty.

Some time after her arrival in New York, Maria Callas had met a strange couple who had much in common with the intriguers of Italian comedy who crop up again and again in the careers of great writers and artists. Go-betweens and fixers, they are always there. In *Der Rosenkavalier* they are called Annina and Valzacchi and spy on Octavian and Sophie for Baron Ochs whom they quickly betray in turn. In New York they lived on Riverside Drive and were called Louise Caselotti and E. Richard Bagarozy, known as Eddie.

Louise Caselotti, after an unsuccessful career as a soprano, had appeared in Hollywood musicals before settling down in New York as a singing teacher, or rather a coach, accompanying singers in their exercises and rehearsals. Her husband Eddie was a lawyer interested in the theatre in general, and opera in particular. He was also no doubt susceptible to Maria's charms. The three of them had an idyllic relationship, and saw each other every day: each morning Maria worked with Louise and she often dined with them both in the evening.

It might never have developed into anything other than a rather stormy relationship had Eddie Bagarozy not suddenly decided to throw up his career as a lawyer and become an impresario. Together with another fairly well-known Italian agent, Ottavio Scotto, he embarked on an apparently exciting venture, with the purpose of bringing European singers to the United States. To do this Bagarozy and Scotto decided to revive the Chicago Opera and create a new permanent company for it, to be known as the United States Opera Company.

The list of singers who agreed to take part in this undertaking was impressive. It included one of the three greatest Wagnerian tenors of his day, Max Lorenz, the superb Siegfried at Bayreuth during the war years, Hilde and Anny Konetzni from the Vienna Opera and a handful of new talents like Mafalda Favero, Galliano Masino and above all the young bass Nicola Rossi-Lemeni who reappears throughout Callas's career. The first project was to be a series of performances of Puccini's *Turandot* with what was to be the sensation of the year – Maria Callas's début. She was to sing the very taxing role of the formidable princess of the three riddles, for whom love means death to those who dare to love her. The first performance, twice postponed, was finally planned for 27 January 1947 and the cast assembled by Bagarozy was already rehearsing under the Italian conductor Sergio Failoni. With an impudence which equalled her eagerness for success, Maria preferred to sing a role which enhanced her glory among strangers in Chicago, rather than a second-rate *Fidelio* at the Metropolitan!

In the excitement of the last days the ensembles received their final rehearsals, the finishing touches were put to the extraordinary duet in the last act unfinished at Puccini's death and completed by Alfano, a run-of-the-mill composer of the *verismo* school, with an unexpected flash of genius. Mock-Chinese costumes were made for Maria. The box office opened. Then suddenly Bagarozy threw in the sponge. Alarmed by this influx of foreign singers, the American chorus-singers' union – and heaven knows, the chorus in *Turandot* is all-important – demanded a financial guarantee which neither Bagarozy nor Scotto could provide. Their scheme fell apart; and they just managed to organize a last-minute concert to raise funds for the European singers' return tickets.

Maria's American adventure was over. Elvira de Hidalgo had been right: New York had nothing to offer. Meanwhile the young singer had made friends with Nicola Rossi-Lemeni; they decided to delay their departure a few weeks, then a few months, and her luck changed. Rossi-Lemeni, who was to sing in Verona the following summer, introduced her to Giovanni Zenatello, artistic director of the Verona Festival. Zenatello was in New York looking for a Gioconda to sing in Ponchielli's opera and was hesitating between the great Zinka Milanov, one of the most beautiful Leonoras in *Il Trovatore* of all time and a stunning Aida, and Herva Nelli, then Toscanini's favourite singer. However Zenatello listened to Nicola Rossi-Lemeni's protégée and it was a revelation to him. Callas was to sing at Verona the following August.

Now Maria could leave America. She had not made her name there, but she had a contract in her pocket, and a début in the famous Arena at Verona was a very great honour. On 13 June 1947 the *Rossia* weighed anchor with Rossi-Lemeni and Maria Callas on board. They were happy and that very day Maria had signed a contract with Bagarozy, who for 10 per cent of her fees was to be her sole agent and 'promote her career'. Poor Callas at the dawning of her career could not know what a hornet's nest she had stirred up as she smilingly kissed Bagarozy on both cheeks.

But this time she had made the right choice between Europe and America. Her real life was beginning.

La Gioconda
(opposite)

Chapter Two

A STAR IS BORN
(1947-1951)

Only those who have seen an *Aida* or *Trovatore,* or in this case *La Gioconda,* in Verona can really imagine the scene. The open space of the Arena is lit by blazing floodlights. The applause is deafening – twenty-five thousand people, cheering the high notes, welcoming the chorus, going mad as the prima donna makes her entrance. Verona is everything Italian opera stands for – night-time, music and the human voice, the extravagant display of the crowd, an occasion of supreme bravura. To sing on a clear midsummer night in Verona a singer needs the lungs of an ox, the strength of a navvy and a throat made of steel. From down below, dwarfed by the lights, by the interplay of sound and light, the voice floats up, carried by the perfect acoustics.

Here on the evening of 6 August 1947 Maria Callas, dressed in the splendid costume of the Venetian street singer Gioconda, first appeared before us. The Callas of our memories, now recreated from images and old recordings.

Ponchielli's *La Gioconda* has all the strengths and weaknesses of opera at its most rudimentary, with a plot based on Victor Hugo's drama *Angelo, Tyran de Padoue* – a pretext for the most passionate transports of emotion. Since 1876, when the opera was first produced, several great singers have appeared in it – Caruso, Emmy Destinn, the first Senta in *The Flying Dutchman* at Bayreuth, Rosa Ponselle, of whom more later, and then Callas.

La Gioconda: sheer chance of course, but it seems prophetic that Maria Callas made her début as this singer who, like *Tosca,* dies for love. What is more, the heroine of Ponchielli's opera is in love with a sailor, a sea-captain, who has left her for the wife of a senator. Chance perhaps – but twelve years later who was the sea captain, and a few years after that who was the senator's wife? In *Tosca* the dagger is used to kill Scarpia; La Gioconda stabs herself with it after the dark, despairing cries of 'Suicidio . . .' the famous aria from Act IV, one of Callas's earliest recordings. Sheer chance, this choice of a role which followed her life and voice so closely, but one of those chance events which from time to time gave her life and career a sense of more than random fate.

As she came out into the arena on the arm of Anna Maria Canali who played the part of La Cieca, Gioconda's blind mother, this rather plump young woman was still an unknown quantity. She was limping slightly after spraining her ankle during rehearsals, too short-sighted to see more than a yard in front of her; a beginner, there almost by chance because of an Italian impresario's bright idea in New York. We can only guess what the audience heard that first evening. An interesting voice, as everyone remarked, but above all a voice of extraordinary potential, yet with

tremendous flaws. In particular there were those two breaks between registers which only partially disappeared after ten years of constant practice, vocal exercise and solitary work. The critical listener could find this irritating. Her timbre was uneven, with the strident notes in the upper register which were much criticized later on, though in Verona they were probably not yet very pronounced. They only became a problem later when Callas's voice was damaged by heavy roles sung too soon and its weaknesses were revealed, but these perhaps unpleasant sounds must already have potentially been there. All this is only guesswork of course, but we can get some idea of her interpretation of Gioconda in 1947 from a recording, her first commercial recording, made only five years later.

As soon as she appeared on stage Callas created the character which was to be hers throughout her career. She acted with vibrant, explosive force. In the courtyard of the ducal palace the humble ballad singer repulses Barnaba, the spy who loves her and whom she soon comes to hate. Like Tosca and Scarpia. She expresses her disdain with a hiss of scorn. At the end of the opera she kills herself in front of the man who has bought her, leaving him only her corpse. The effect is spine-chilling. 'Volesti il mio corpo demon maledetto . . .' and you shall have my body. With this harsh cry she immediately and forever became a tragic heroine in the eyes of us, her public and the world. Already she seemed to be the famous 'tigress' of the press ten years later. But she also displayed the utmost tenderness in her duet with the unfaithful sea-captain – a *mezza voce* like no other, breathtaking *pianissimi* floating dreamlike to an impossibly high B flat. Hearing her today, remembering her yesterday, the miracle once again begins to work on us.

Here was a voice to bring the listener to his knees, or so it must have seemed to one listener – a short, rather plump, balding man, greying at the temples, who had been introduced to Maria Callas a few days before by his friend Gaetano Pomari, one of the festival organizers. He made up his mind to offer Maria a life together if she was willing.

'As soon as she opened her mouth,' remarked another even older listener, a handsome leonine figure, 'I recognized an exceptional voice.' He immediately saw what he could make of this voice and this personality – how he could mould the voice and bring the singer into the limelight of the world's theatres.

The first of these two men was Meneghini and he had already fallen in love. The second was the conductor Tullio Serafin who had worked with the greatest singers of the day for over forty years. The two most important figures in Maria Callas's life after her mother and Hidalgo now came on the scene.

First Meneghini, prime target of the press, with their maudlin pity and petty betrayals. This bashful suitor who first met Maria on the evening of her arrival in Verona or the day after was a wealthy industrialist of good family, a confirmed bachelor. He was a member of that provincial bourgeois élite of theatre-lovers and café-goers, moving on the fringes of fashionable society until people gradually forgot that twenty years before he had been regarded as a good match. His respectable career revolved round his flourishing construction business and his elderly, domineering mother. Spoilt and pampered, he spent money freely but always counted the cost. His carryings-on with dancers and actresses visiting the town had gradually earned him the reputation of a portly Don Juan. This did not amount to much in the home of Romeo and Juliet, but so far Signor Meneghini had not been very demanding. Until Callas's tempestous arrival.

When he was introduced to the woman who was so soon to become his idol and the world's – in the Padavena restaurant we are told – he bowed, appearing perhaps more confident than he felt. But something stirred within him. Surrounded by bustling friends and eager waiters, the maître d'hôtel menu in hand waiting for their order, Maria Callas, embarrassed and awkward, must have smiled back. Though later, in front of twenty-five thousand spectators, she displayed the splendid, almost insolent assurance which never deserted her on stage, among these busy people, speculating perhaps on her and on her future, she was ill at ease and uncertain. Giovanni Battista Meneghini, attentive, full of compliments, did all he could to reassure her. Suddenly something happened to her too.

Meneghini

Thirty years later, the question still remains – what was this current that flowed between them, this bond that suddenly brought them together? They seemed so unalike. True, Maria was still just a caterpillar, a large girl in an ill-cut dress, but she knew that one day she would turn into a butterfly – a dazzling butterfly with wings so easily singed. She had travelled, and had friends who were artists, not just starving hopefuls, but real singers like Rossi-Lemeni who had already known success. Meneghini, an ageing provincial worthy, hardly seemed a suitable match for this buxom girl with the New York accent. Yet for both of them it was in a way love at first sight. Perhaps on Maria's part it was based more on reason, on a sudden need for peace and quiet after her American experiences, than on passion, but it was love at first sight nonetheless. Within a few days days she decided to give herself up to this man who offered her a strong, almost fatherly sense of security, and above all a wealth of love and attention. He was also willing to play a radical, apparently decisive part in her career. All Maria had to do was sing; he would do the rest. From 1951 Meneghini officially became her sole agent, and remained so for eight years.

Looking back, Callas's life seems to be a series of surrenders. Violent and passionate, a heart-rending figure, Maria Callas had only one wish – to let herself go. She was constantly seeking and hoping for some external influence to rule her, someone else's will to guide her, the iron fist in the velvet glove to control and direct her for ever – her mother, Hidalgo, Bagarozy, Meneghini, later Onassis or the musical directors of her recording companies. Callas the passionate, Tosca, Medea and Norma rolled into one, was above all Traviata, tormented by her loneliness and by her beauty. A frail heroine who could not take a step unless someone held her hand. Then and only then could she conquer. And we, her adoring public, demanded more and more from her. In the end our selfish admiration, our infatuation, our blind passion killed her, gently but surely.

With Meneghini's arrival Callas had only to sing, and sing she did. The little man and the tall singer were together for more than ten years, a strangely ill-matched couple, presenting a front of married bliss to the world. The papers loved to carry touching photographs and soppy comments. Meneghini became 'Titta' and Callas declared that she would give up her career for him. Titta would listen and smile sweetly – no chance of that, so far as he was concerned, but perhaps this is unkind. He followed her from town to town, concert to concert, opera to opera. Back home of an evening, even in the most luxurious suite of the most luxurious hotel, Maria would cook Titta's favourite dishes, recipes carefully recorded by the newspapers. Meneghini showered her with presents, furs and jewels. A peep into her wardrobe revealed three hundred pairs of shoes according to *Ici Paris* or the *News of the World*. Above all Maria loved the little dog, Toy or another, he had given her. Very soon Titta's presents were bought with money Maria had earned for him, but the headlines and the public stilled cooed fondly over these lovebirds.

Maria and Meneghini did not in fact get married until 1949, just before she left for a tour in Argentina. Before that they moved from hotel to hotel amid general sympathetic approval, apart from the angry gaze of Meneghini's family and his old mother who regarded the Greek-American singer as a mere actress. His mother had always hoped that her dear Giovanni Battista would never marry. The Callas-Kalogeropoulous family were not enthusiastic either. Meneghini was old enough to be Maria's father and they could not understand her infatuation. Evangelia was jealous. Yet however severely we judge Meneghini's part in Callas's life, with hindsight it was certainly he, at the outset, who made her what she became, for better and for worse. If he made a fortune from her voice, in many ways it was he who had moulded and created it. Perhaps damaged and distorted too? Rather we should say that with the demands he placed on her he moulded a character to go with the voice. And this character made the voice, with its weaknesses and flaws, her own, with such magnificent assurance that it is now impossible to imagine what the woman and her voice might have been like had they not been over-stretched by roles she should never have sung.

At first Meneghini kept his business interests, but he became less and less involved and finally relinquished all his commitments to devote himself to Callas. He became her agent, manager and répétiteur. He chose her roles and signed the contracts. Maria never argued; he fixed the fees, and was later much criticized for this. 'You must pay to hear Callas,' jovially he rang up the till. 'This year Maria's fee has doubled,' a shock to Karajan. Maria would meekly lower her eyes and explain that these sordid money matters were nothing to do with her. 'You must see my husband.' By turns jolly, scheming, clumsy and eventually frenetic, Meneghini was a skilful and effective operator, always on the make, like another Valzacchi from Strauss' and Hoffmansthal's *Rosenkavalier*.

But there was more to him than that. Self-interested he certainly was, but he also had a constant sense of amazement and surprise. He could not believe that this woman was his, that she had given herself to him and accepted him as he was. Meneghini revelled in his love. An earthworm in love with a star, and a rather fat little worm at that, but if the star was willing to let him follow in her wake that was enough for him; and it was not too difficult to play prince consort to such a submissive queen. In any case, it was difficult to know who had the upper hand in this partnership, so unnatural that it came to seem natural. Maria meekly lowered her eyes, and for ten years added her husband's name to her own. After her previous name changes, she now became Maria *Meneghini*-Callas. And the provincial businessman, now the princess's prime minister, really was the iron fist in the velvet glove. Perhaps this is what we can never forgive, because it makes him too like us.

On her arrival in Verona Maria Callas met another man who also played a decisive part in the years to come. The old gentleman who remarked when he heard her in the Arena in Verona, 'As soon as she opened her mouth, I recognized an exceptional voice.' Tullio Serafin, Maestro Serafin, a very different sort of man to deal with. Twenty years later Callas said there were 'only two conductors in the world: Serafin and Giulini.' So much for Karajan, Bernstein, de Sabata and all the others she had worked with.

Tullio Serafin

Serafin was born in 1878. He started his career as a violinist and conducted at La Scala from 1909. In 1913 he started the Verona festival. He was above all an opera conductor and his career was linked to all the greatest names in the field. He did much to further the early career of the greatest American singer of the twenties and thirties, Rosa Ponselle. With her he introduced almost forgotten operas which were not revived again until Callas. The New York Metropolitan mounted *Norma, La Gioconda, La Vestale* for her and her alone, a point worth remembering when comparing, as is often done, the careers and voices of Ponselle and Callas, the two *prime donne assolute* of the century. Serafin had also worked with Claudia Muzio, who created twenty or so heroines of post-*verismo* opera, and many other singers who became famous at his side. His wife, Elena Rakowska, was well known as a Wagnerian soprano in both Italy and New York. Serafin himself was an enthusiastic, warm, generous man, with a fine nose for talent. When he first heard Callas in Verona and conducted her in *La Gioconda* it was again love at first sight, the love of immense talent for genius. From then on Callas's career, like Ponselle's twenty years before, was backed up by Serafin's influence, his admiration and his ambition for her. For Serafin it was like rediscovering Ponselle. He wanted to turn Callas into another, different Ponselle, to make her 'La Callas'. Callas described Serafin as 'the first great conductor I worked with. He was my mentor. He knew me before my marriage and between him and me there were always very strong links'. Serafin for his part told Callas, 'Your voice is an instrument which you must study during rehearsals exactly like a piano. But during the performance, forget you have studied. Play with your voice and enjoy it. Express your soul through it.' Callas once again lowered her eyes and listened.

Later, in 1956, Callas quarrelled for a time with the old conductor. She accused him of treachery – of conducting her rival, Antionetta Stella. But their estrangement was short-lived and there are thirteen EMI recordings as living proof to ear and heart of this wonderful partnership. When Serafin died in 1968 at the age of ninety Callas mourned him like a father. A father, a friend, and as she said a mentor.

During this first period of her professional life in particular, until about 1951-52, Tullio Serafin played as large a part as Meneghini in the choices Callas made and her new roles. Overjoyed at discovering this superb young voice, adaptable, disconcertingly instinctive, yet capable of fulfilling the demands of all kinds of roles, Tullio Serafin urged Callas to sing all these roles. Brünnhilde at the age of twenty-five, followed without a break by Elvira in *I Puritani,* an incredible, dazzling tour de force.

Others would say it was suicide.

In this respect, the great conductor, so besotted with his diva, can also be held guilty. If Callas had not followed his advice between 1947 and 1951 she might never have been Callas. But she might have been another Callas for longer. For three or four years the Callas we know pursued a headlong course. She sang everything, and we now know that it damaged her voice. During this period no one bothered about Elvira de Hidalgo's warnings. Her teacher had told her to start with *bel canto* and the coloratura repertoire. Light roles, she must sing light roles! But Callas sang the most onerous lyric and dramatic soprano roles – because she wanted to, because they were suggested to her, because people wanted to see what she would make of them. In a few months Callas's destiny was at stake. In thrall to our dreams, to the men who helped make her what she was, she was bruised and battered before she even began. Those shadowy figures, her two substitute fathers, who so marked her life, had already firmly taken hold.

Callas's career as a whole falls into three parts – three distinct stages in the development of her voice, even of her 'vocal problems', during her singing years. There is ample evidence of each stage, for Callas was recorded more than any other singer of the century. She made numerous 'commercial' recordings, mainly for EMI, but above all there are an unknown number of 'pirate' records or tapes, thanks to enthusiasts, or to radio stations which broadcast her operas live, who recorded many of her interpretations. There are at least six or seven known recordings of *Tosca* or *Traviata,* as many of *Lucia,* and four of *Aida.* Each version shows a different side of her, and step by step, phrase by phrase, we can follow the story of her voice. These recordings make exciting listening. They are usually not available commercially, but can be obtained with a little persistence. All fans know where dealers specializing in pirate recordings are to be found. And so year by year we can follow Callas's development.

Until 1953-54 she sang almost anything and everything that was suggested. The range of parts is staggering. The heaviest roles – Turandot, Lady Macbeth, La Gioconda, Abigaille in *Nabucco,* Isolde, Brünnhilde, Kundry in *Parsifal*. She tackled at random *Aida* and the *verismo* of *Andrea Chénier* and *Fedora*. She excelled in the *bel canto* of *I Puritani* or Rossini's *Armida,* and threw herself into what are rightly or wrongly regarded as the lightest roles – Gilda in *Rigoletto* or Fiorilla in *Il Turco in Italia*. Up to 1954 Maria Callas had not one repertoire but three, covering the whole range of soprano registers.

Then from 1953-54 Callas suddenly abandoned all the roles just mentioned, with only one or two exceptions. She never again sang Armida, Aida or the redoubtable Abigaille. No more Brünnhilde, no more Wagner. She simply could not risk it. Years later she talked of rediscovering Isolde, of making her die an ecstatic death in Paris, Milan or New York; but this was only a dream, when everything else was over.

During this period, which lasted until about 1958, she concentrated on no more than four or five roles, roles she had sung before, usually towards the end of her first period. Tosca, Traviata, Lucia, Norma and Medea. At the same time in a blaze of publicity she tackled several outstanding parts, painstakingly recreating the characters from within – Donizetti's *Anna Bolena,* Bellini's *Il Pirata* and Gluck's *Iphigénie en Tauride*. But these were exceptions, prepared over long periods.

Finally, after 1959, Callas's career took the form it was to have to the end. Concerts, the rare creation of a role for a series of performances – Donizetti's *Poliuto*. But no more *Lucia,* or *Traviata* – 'Addio del passato. . . .' The protean past disappeared and Callas was left with only three roles, like a living statue imprisoned by her own singing. Medea, Norma, Tosca. Cherubini, Bellini, Puccini: perfect control in *bel canto* from the earliest beginnings; incomparable musicianship in *bel canto* from the golden age; and finally, in Puccini's *verismo,* a dramatic sense never matched by any other singer. Her voice had its ups and downs. One evening it would compel absolute admiration, but on another (the 1962 Milan *Medea,* her last) one longed to creep quietly away. This is the sad truth. For fifteen years Elisabeth Schwarzkopf did not sing many more roles on stage – the Countess in *Le Nozze di Figaro,* the Marschallin in *Der Rosenkavalier,* Countess Madeleine in Strauss's *Capriccio* and more Mozart with Fiordiligi in *Così fan tutte* – but her performances were always consistently even and successful, whereas Callas's voice became more a matter of adventure.

The potential for this threefold development of Callas's life and voice was already there that summer evening in 1947 in Verona, when this woman, with her sublime yet fragile voice, met the two men who were to give her and her voice life.

Medea: one of the roles that stayed with Callas almost to the end

From the end of 1947 Maria Callas embarked on the most incredible vocal adventure of the century – the adventure of her life and voice. She had a unique appetite for new roles and for success. In four years, from 1948, she played eighteen different characters one hundred and seventy-three times. Eighteen women who all die or kill for love in the grand tradition of grand opera.

This history of Italian opera is really the story of a few women, always the same ones, since Italian opera as we know it began with Rossini, Bellini and Donizetti. Before them librettos followed a different pattern. There were two sources of inspiration: antiquity for *opera seria*, Neapolitan or Venetian comedy for *opera buffa*. There were of course important female characters in antiquity and in the operas based on it. To take only operas composed during the seventeenth and eighteenth centuries dealing with Iphigenia and Ariadne, there were more than forty-five Iphigenias in one hundred and sixty years and about twenty Ariadnes. There were an equivalent number of pert young heroines, Zerbinettas straight from the pages of Goldoni and his contemporaries. Rosina in Paisiello's *Il Barbiere di Siviglia,* the first *Barbiere,* had plenty of rivals.

With the turn of the century, above all with Donizetti and Bellini, all that changed. Romantic drama and the gothic novel made their impact on the operatic scene, introducing a blend of Sir Walter Scott, unlucky Stuarts and Celtic maidens. Complex stereotyped classical plots in which the main heroine, Iphigenia or Zerbinetta, was just one element, were superseded by a new vision of the heroine as the focal point of the action. These are the dark women of our timeless dreams, victims of our fantasy – Norma, Lucia di Lammermoor, La Sonnambula, Elvira in *I Puritani* — their airy, flowing cantilenas always on the brink of madness, though not perhaps madness in its clinical form.

As the century advanced Violetta in *Traviata,* Mimi, Tosca, and Santuzza in *Cavalleria Rusticana* took over from Bellini's heroines but all bore the mark of the victim. It is this quality which distinguishes the heroines of the golden age of Italian opera from other heroines of our cultural heritage. To suit a particular sensibility these women are all victims, oppressed like Lucia or Traviata, or avenging like Turandot or Tosca. They are the same women whether they raise the knife or offer themselves up defenceless. Tigress or sacrificial victim, they are above all women in love, victims of their love and doomed to die for it. Jealousy is at the centre of their passion; while an audience of men, Serafins and Meneghinis, look on, commenting, demanding, destroying.

These women are very different from the heroines of German opera.

Wife or mother, virgin, sinner yet redeemer, sister, the German heroine, epitomised by Sieglinde in *Die Walküre,* has an unreal, almost mystical aura, whereas the Italian soprano is all flesh and tears. Elizabeth in *Tannhäuser* and Agathe in *Der Freischütz* are really petites bourgeoises from Bavaria or Vienna. Violetta is a bourgeoise too, but she is above all a marked woman, like Elvira, Tosca and all Puccini's heroines. And role by role Callas showed us the living, warm, vulnerable flesh of each of these women, until, her private life and roles inextricably tangled, she came to be identified with the wildest hopes and cruellest disappointments of the women she incarnated. Gradually, opera by opera, until the final silence, the identification became more and more complete and irreversible.

The next four years were an orgy of new roles, culminating, as the dawning star slowly grew into a legendary figure, in Callas's official début at La Scala on 7 December 1951. But immediately after her considerable success in *La Gioconda* in Verona, Maria Callas, her destiny now in the hands of Giovanni Battista Meneghini, spent several weeks without working. It looked as if *La Gioconda* had failed to set anything in motion, for though the press welcomed this new artist Serafin himself was undoubtedly the hero of the occasion. When the lights went down on the Arena in Verona, after a *Faust* in which Renata Tebaldi sang Marguerite, her path thus crossing Callas's for the first time, Serafin took active steps to place his protégée, but nothing seemed to come of it. There was vague but unrealistic talk of a *Ballo in Maschera* in Milan, then nothing more was heard. Maria Callas did not yet have the necessary stature for La Scala. Undeterred, Serafin continued his backstage manoeuvres on her behalf. He talked about her wherever he was conducting, he boasted of his discovery and presented her as 'his' singer, eager as he was to repeat the miracle of Ponselle. Finally Christmas in Venice brought an important step forward towards success. After Verona, another festival.

The first Cetra record includes the *Liebestod* from *Tristan,* recorded by Callas in 1951. It has become a classic, a bible of our emotions. Callas's timbre is clear – clearer than in the usual Isolde – and uniformly regular, with none of those breaks which make purists shudder. There is an unaccustomed sensuality which cannot be dismissed as Italian simply because the recording is in Italian. The orchestra, conducted without subtlety by Arturo Basile, is no match for the warm intensity of this soaring, disembodied voice.

Callas's Venice Isolde probably resembled this recording – a touching, fragile Isolde, quivering with a passion which is mortal from the start. On 30 December and at three more performances in January 1948 Callas had considerable success, singing with a dull Tristan and with two other singers who often appeared again at her side – Fedora Barbieri as Brangäne, Isolde's attendant, and Boris Christoff as King Mark. She repeated this success the following May in Genoa, this time with her friend Rossi-Lemeni as Mark. She sang *Tristan* five times more in Rome in 1950, then never again. All that remains of this role, so unlike everything else we know of Callas, is the extract from the old Cetra recordings.

However the 1947-48 Venice season was not yet over. Callas doffed Isolde's veils to don Turandot's diadem.

Puccini's *Turandot* was the opera Scotto and Bagarozy's company had hoped to put on in Chicago in January 1947. The libretto, by Adami and Simoni, is based on a play by Gozzi, in turn inspired by a tale from the *Arabian Nights*. It is the story of a Chinese princess, the cruel, proud Turandot, who will only give her hand and her kingdom to the prince who can answer three riddles she asks. Those who fail are beheaded. In this splendid piece of chinoiserie, this tale of bloodshed and death, Puccini's music attains a formal beauty and complexity of surprising modernity. And this time we can recognize Callas herself in the role she plays. The stern and terrible empress becomes a woman through love, but she destroys the pathetic, innocent slave Liù who is in love with the man who conquers Turandot.

This is one of the most violent roles in the Italian repertoire. The hardest of all Puccini's characters, as well as the most difficult and demanding vocally. The extraordinary harangue during the riddle scene in the second act preceded by the princess's terrible warning, '*In questa reggia*', and the moments of indescribable gentleness which interrupt her superhuman declarations, can break the most solid voice. The opera was created by Rosa Raisa under Toscanini in Milan in 1926, but it was Tullio Serafin who conducted the first New York performance with Maria Jeritza, another many-sided artist, who created Strauss's *Ariadne auf Naxos* and *Die Frau ohne Schatten*.

In a few months between 1948 to 1949 Callas sang the role twenty-four times. After her success in Venice, the rest of Italy wanted to hear her in the part – Udine, Rome, Verona, Genoa and Naples. In 1949 she sang Turandot four more times in Buenos Aires and then, as with Isolde, she abandoned the role. In Venice she sang not under Serafin but under another equally interesting but less brilliant conductor, Nino Sanzogno. Luckily Serafin was with her when she recorded *Turandot* ten years later for EMI. The result is astounding, though one feels that her brilliantly deployed vocal resources are not what they must have been at the time of the Fenice performances. The 1949 Turandot must have been even more aggressive, darker and less gentle despite the veiled threat in the voice, even in moments of utter abandon.

To continue singing *Tristan* or *Turandot* would have been suicide. At the time of Callas's first Venice appearances Louise Caselotti, who had come over from New York, warned her about this. Though Callas was annoyed and sent this Cassandra back to her husband, a quarrel which was to have bizarre consequences, she took the point. 'I must concentrate on *bel canto*', she remarked; and then did nothing about it.

After Venice came an avalanche of offers. She repeated *Turandot* in the Baths of Caracalla in Rome and then in Verona, recklessly displaying her voice each time. Next came two Verdi operas – *La Forza del Destino* in Trieste, and then, in Rovigo, *Aida*.

47

Despite Callas's regular performances of *Aida* from 1948 to 1953 and three or four complete recordings (including a commercial set conducted by Serafin) which show what she made of the role, Callas never really *was* Aida. She put too much fire and energy, too much intelligence even, into what is scarcely more than a lament without true passion. Perhaps Aida is not really a role at all. With an impossible E flat at the end of the triumph scene, Callas was enthusiastically received in Europe and Mexico, but it is hard to see her as the unhappy slave opposite the formidable Amneris. It is only in the last scene, when she is walled up in a tomb to die with her lover Radamès, condemned because of her, that her last song – '*O terra addio, addio valle di pianti*' suddenly touches us. Her earlier handling of this non-role is forgotten, and instead, as the stones slip into place one by one, as the granite chamber closes in on her, Aida becomes Callas, walled up alive in her own legend. 'Farewell earth, valley of tears. . .'

However, her Leonora in *La Forza del Destino,* a despairing, fated figure, deserves to be remembered by something better than the commercial recording made in 1954 with a worn-out Richard Tucker and a Rossi-Lemeni in poor form. Of all Verdi's libretti, this is the most richly melodramatic. Like *Il Trovatore* it is a Spanish drama of revenge and love. Alvaro, trying to elope with the woman he loves, accidentally kills her father. Leonora's brother Carlo scours war-torn Europe for the murderer. Carlo and Alvaro fight side by side and swear friendship, neither knowing who the other is, until they finally meet in a duel. Leonora's distraught prayer in the last act, when she is living as a recluse, '*Pace, pace, mio dio*', is a great moment of pure yet urgent singing. There may be more sensual or more religious Leonoras, but none is more harrowing than Callas as her brother and lover prepare to kill one another.

Role followed role with dizzying speed and in November 1948 Callas first sang *Norma* at the Teatro Communale in Florence. Fedora Barbieri was Adalgisa and the conductor was once again Serafin, making his dream come true for the second time. After Gioconda, Rosa Ponselle's key role, Callas sang Bellini's druidess, another part on which the great American singer had left her mark. Later it was assumed that the role had been revived for Callas but it had not been long dead, for Ponselle's interpretation was still available to all on record.

In remembering Callas, *Norma* stands for far more than *La Forza del Destino, Aida* or *Trovatore.* It was Bellini's masterpiece, composed in 1831 when he was not yet thirty. There is always more to say about it. The most famous aria, '*Casta diva*' is even said to have influenced the mood of Chopin's Nocturnes. The music glides and floats with a melodic and orchestral richness unequalled in any other opera of the first half of the nineteenth century. The story is of exemplary simplicity. The druidess Norma loves Pollione, a soldier of the Roman forces occupying ancient Gaul. She has had two children by him and keeps this guilty love secret. When she discovers that Pollione now loves Adalgisa, a virgin of the temple, she first thinks of getting her revenge by killing her children, but then decides to sacrifice herself and offers herself as victim in Adalgisa's place. At the last moment Pollione joins her on the pyre.

But *Norma* is far more than a love story, far more even than the music, however divine. It was, as has been said, one of Callas's five great roles. One of the five roles which marked her throughout her career and afterwards just as she marked them. It was the last opera but one she was to sing on stage. Before the final *Tosca* at Covent Garden in 1965 she sang *Norma* in Paris. Callas's airy, floating voice in *Norma* reaches us from the darkness of time, a still, blue night glinting with the pale mistletoe to be cut by the goddess's silver sickle. Norma – her tenderness, her self-sacrifice in love – is the archetypal woman of Italian opera. After *Tosca,* the jealous tigress so magnificently in love, comes this broken-hearted love, willingly offering itself up to the executioner's sword.

Adalgisa is also one of the finest roles in the Italian repertoire. The most famous singers of the nineteenth century appeared in this great role for coloratura, dramatic mezzo. At the La Scala première Pasta and Giulia Grisi sang Norma and Adalgisa respectively. Later they often exchanged roles since voice types were not as rigid then as now. At the end of the nineteenth century one of the last great Normas was Lilli Lehmann, but the most famous in modern times, before Callas, was of course Rosa Ponselle. Ponselle sang the role in 1927, with Giacomo Lauri-Volpi and Ezio Pinza, two of the greatest names in opera, known to us from early recordings, Pinza as an utterly self-assured Don Giovanni.

As Norma at La Scala

The Normas of Callas and Ponselle have often been compared. Ponselle's voice is intrinsically beautiful, her 'Casta diva' unequalled for its ease and for the clarity and uniform beauty of the timbre. The cabaletta which follows is unbelievably light and at the same time infinitely noble. Yet Callas has a colour, a humanity, a lyricism and a love not found elsewhere. Ponselle was not of course the only other Norma. Early recordings of Adelina Patti and Marcella Sembrich have survived, and closer at hand we have Sutherland and Caballé. But Rosa Ponselle was the greatest Norma and Callas moves us more than Ponselle. Callas's first performance of Norma in Florence in late 1948 was one of the key dates of her life, perhaps the foundation of everything that was to follow. She sang the role eighty-eight times in the eighteen years up to 1965 and made two commercial recordings of it (in 1954 with Serafin, Mario Filippeschi and Ebe Stignani, and in 1960, again with Serafin, but Mario with Christa Ludwig as an impressive but controversial Adalgisa and Franco Corelli as a far better Pollione). These records are scarcely less alive than the live recordings (Mexico 1950 and 1952, Rome and Milan 1955, Paris 1965). Callas perfected the character to the point where she could arouse a whole range of complex emotions with equal ease at any performance.

Callas's performances of Norma – far more than her Lucias or Toscas, spectacular though they may be – represent a precise and unique blend of genuine bel canto and the most powerful emotion. With the words 'I figli uccido' as she raises the dagger above her children, her voice trembles; but her musical control never weakens, a sure sign of genius.

Callas's genius. 1948 and 1949 were the years when this budding genius finally blossomed. Still following in Serafin's wake, 1948 ended with a dazzling apotheosis in Venice. A daring tight-rope walker, high above the ground with no safety net, eyes wide open, Callas performed her vocal feats.

This episode did much to establish her reputation as an intrepid singer. Tullio Serafin had booked her some time before to sing in Die Walküre. It was madness for her to sing this Wagner opera, with Brünnhilde's fomidable 'Ho-jo-to Ho!' her long declamations and enormously demanding lyric phrases, but she sang it six times. Though the rest of the Italian cast was undistinguished, she worked on her own role until she was satisfied with it. A foolish undertaking which only earned her glory because of another feat she performed at the same time. She had just started her performances of Brünnhilde when Tullio Serafin asked her at very short notice to replace Margherita Carosio, who was due to sing Elvira in Bellini's I Puritani and was indisposed. Carosio, who had been singing the opera since 1942, was a well-known young soprano. Replacing her was a challenge. There were six days to go before the first night, and no understudy or replacement could be found in such a short time: few singers knew the music of I Puritani, almost forgotten for some years. There had been successful revivals, for example with Caspir in 1933 or Tetrazzini in 1909, but at a time when Italian singing was at a low ebb few sopranos included I Puritani in their repertoire. In any case the tenor's role, created by the great Rubini in 1835, was usually regarded as the most important in this far-fetched story of madness, love and supposed betrayal, with a happy ending in which sanity returns and Stuarts and Cromwellians are reconciled in the middle of the English Civil War. In the circumstances it seemed a total impossibility to find a replacement for Carosio. Maria was called from her hotel room to see if she could by any chance save the situation. She had only just got out of bed, but she performed without a moment's hesitation, and sang Serafin and his hastily assembled friends the aria 'Qui la voce', the only aria she knew from the opera, one she had learned with Elvira de Hidalgo in Athens. When she had finished her listeners looked at one another. She was superb. 'You just need to learn the whole part by 19 January', concluded the delighted Serafin. Callas had the ideal voice for Elvira.

She still had two performances of *Walküre* on 14 and 16 January. Her stay in Venice had begun in madness, but it ended in total dementia. Callas took up the challenge without turning a hair. Allowing herself not a moment's rest between Brünnhilde's calls on stage and Elvira's trills and runs in the rehearsal room, she was a triumphant success. Not since the legendary Lilli Lehmann at the turn of the century – with a hundred and seventy roles behind her and a career of more than fifty years, preserved in a few very old recordings – had there been a soprano capable of singing a work from the *bel canto* repertoire one evening and Wagner the next. It meant forcing her voice into two different moulds with diametrically opposed tonalities and objectives. But with disconcerting ease Callas switched from the highest coloratura to the most wide-ranging dramatic part. Like Lilli Lehmann, Callas was becoming a legend.

First she had to learn the role. She had been well trained for this by Hidalgo, in the days when, 'like a sponge', she could lap up a score, even the most obstinate *bel canto*, in a single night. Conscientious, intelligent and methodical, she was the complete artist, totally equipped for her art. In six days she knew the whole of Bellini's music.

Callas's approach to the part, the way she studied and moulded Elvira's character, is an object lesson for modern singers tackling *bel canto*. It was a modern approach to a style of singing firmly rooted in a classicism which was already out of place in its own time. With Callas, Bellini's most difficult chromatic runs and roulades acquire a musical quality which they had lost and which far surpasses their mere virtuosity. She never infringed the elementary rules of perfect legato which had been developed and perfected by all the great interpreters of Bellini at the beginning of the last century – names like Pasta and Grisi, a legend among lovers of *bel canto*. But into them she breathed a vitality and vibrancy, the achievements of a new style of singing which had finally broken out of the rut of post-*verismo*. For the first time here was a tragic actress singing Bellini, adding just the right touch of emotion to the uninterrupted stream of airy, almost dreamy music, turning technical mastery into a call from the heart, a deeply felt and incredibly moving moment of uncertainty. The last phrases at the end of her 'Qui la voce' in

Act II, the few words '*Vieni a nozze. Egli piange*' and the whole of the cabaletta '*Vien diletto*', with their tenderness, their desperately forced high spirits, are a vocal firework, a dazzling display of emotion.

Callas's performance at La Fenice was a triumph. Her *Puritani* was discussed all over Italy, Europe and America, and opera directors all over the world now knew a new star had been born. From now on Callas showed unswerving devotion to Bellini. And we can still listen again and again to the pirate recording made in Mexico City in 1952 and the EMI recording made by Serafin a year later at La Scala: Elvira in *I Puritani,* or madness at its most tender and sublime, more moving even than the madness of Lucia di Lammermoor.

During these years Maria Callas's life story is a growing list of roles. Her passion for new music and characters now became a way of life.

After *I Puritani,* the landmarks of 1949 were *Parsifal* in Rome in February and her extraordinary Abigaille in *Nabucco* at the Teatro San Carlo, Naples in December. In between, from April to June, came her first international engagement when she sang with Serafin, Mario del Monaco, Fedora Barbieri and Nicola Rossi-Lemeni at the Colón, Buenos Aires.

Kundry in *Parsifal* was Callas's last Wagnerian role, the harrowing figure of the repentant sinner who alone can bring grace and healing. After this, and after five more *Tristans* in Rome the following year, Callas gave up Wagner for ever. The records made from tapes of the Rome *Parsifal* are vocal curiosities of historical and anecdotal interest, but Callas was not by any stretch of the imagination a Wagnerian heroine. Moving though her death of Isolde was, her Kundry, with its unexpected, over-dramatic nuances is surprising rather than anything else. It is even slightly comical – so Callas sang Wagner too, did she? She did, but at a time when she would take on anything. It was one of the delightful absurdities of her career that she made her début at Rome Opera in *Parsifal* – the opera house from which she departed so clamorously ten years later.

Abigaille, on the other hand, was one of her most striking interpretations. The librettist Solera, who wrote most of Verdi's patriotic works, made *Nabucco* a kind of hymn to liberty. It is one of the most interesting early Verdi operas, with soprano and baritone, Abigaille, the terrifying princess, drunk with war and death, and Nabucco (Nabucodonosor), the fallen king, rivals in cruelty. The formidable role of Abigaille, created by Giuseppina Strepponi who married Verdi in 1859, is legendary for the voices it has broken. And whereas Turandot, that other cruel princess, is a completely introverted figure, her evil being the distant evil of China and deep personal traumas, Abigaille is a political character, all her energies directed towards the outside world which she longs to dominate. Love – ostensibly the mainspring of the action and of Abigaille's jealousy for her supposed sister Fenena who has stolen the man she loves – is only a pretext. Abigaille wants to rule the world and the enslaved Jews. Defying her, the oppressed Jews sing the famous chorus '*Va pensiero . . .*' which became the symbol of Italian freedom during the second half of the nineteenth century, a muted or open protest against the Austrian authorities at a time when the initials of Verdi's name stood for Vittorio Emanuele, Re d'Italia.

Maria Callas understood and mastered Abigaille's character from the start. The pirate records made in 1949 are now available commercially, though until only recently they were precious treasures, listened to and recorded on to cassettes as another little bit of Callas. There is an amazing contrast between her entrance in Act I when she finds the two lovers together defying her – a private quarrel – and her political meditation in Act II. Her cry of rage '*Qual Dio vi salva?*' ('What God will save you?'), followed by the terrible, long drawn-out, menacing '*Talamo la tomba a voi sarà*' ('Your tomb will be your bridal couch'), is a burst of terrifying uncontrollable jealousy, the angry outburst of a woman whose pride – as woman and lover – has been wounded. But in Act II, beneath her angry words '*Su me stessa rovina, o fatal sdegno*' ('Upon me hurl thyself, oh fatal anger') she is an inspired prophetess announcing her seizure of power. After the more intimate scale of Act I and Abigaille's confrontation with the couple who have deceived her, comes a declaration of war which carries far beyond the walls of the palace of Babylon, and takes on a universal significance. In Callas's interpretation the jealous, betrayed woman becomes a visionary. Her gradual climb to the heights of rage, culminating in '*O fatal sdegno*', one of the most beautiful cries ever uttered on stage, is not just a dazzling display of her incomparable technique. It is also proof that at twenty-six Callas already had that innate sense of the theatre, that ability to master a role on which she was to base her art fifteen years later – when, her detractors would say, she had nothing else left.

We now hear these stirring sounds as if far removed in time, against an indistinct, crackling orchestral background blunted by the poor quality of the recording. But this 1949 Naples *Nabucco* (with Gino Bechi, the great baritone from the heyday of *verismo,* as Nabucco, and the conductor Vittorio Gui) is more than a unique document – it is one of the great moments of singing of all time.

Nine years later Callas made a studio recording of Abigaille's arias, more sensual with perhaps an even greater attention to the music, but the 1949 records have an inventive and dramatic energy like no other. However, after these performances in Naples, Callas never again sang Abigaille on stage. Even more than Turandot, it was a role which could break a fragile voice for ever.

For Callas was fragile – in health, voice and personality. From a very early age her health had been delicate. The obesity which still afflicted her as Kundry in Rome or Abigaille in Naples was obviously glandular in origin. As a child living with her mother in New York or Athens, Maria had always suffered from tiredness and dizzy spells. As an adolescent and adult her low blood pressure often gave cause for concern and later she suffered quite serious drops in pressure. She was also very susceptible to all kinds of infections, especially severe sinusitis which troubled her towards the end of her career. In late 1950 her slow recovery from a bad bout of jaundice prevented her singing *Don Carlos* in Naples. As early as 1951 she had to interrupt her South American tour, and was too exhausted to give the performances of *Aida* scheduled for São Paulo. Her legs at that time were so swollen that she had difficulty walking. Even before journalists looking for copy began saying she had lost her voice, Callas was almost always in poor physical shape. This explains many of her subsequent refusals to sing, cancellations and moods interpreted as whims.

Besides this, on stage Callas was blind. She was still incredibly short-sighted and without her thick-lensed glasses was lost. Her mere presence in the theatre demanded extraordinary effort and attention from her, as did her movements and gestures as an actress, and her singing. This was a further physical strain on her; though blind she had to act with the same ease and assurance as if she had had perfect vision.

In 1949, between Kundry and Abigaille, she was already showing signs of fatigue. She was certainly doing too much, but this did not stop her undertaking an engagement in Argentina, where she sang *Turandot, Aida* and a triumphant *Norma*. After this she rested, while Meneghini, whom she had married before leaving for Buenos Aires, set up home for them in a flat in Verona. During this period before *Nabucco* she made her first records of the *Liebestod* previously mentioned, 'Casta diva' and arias from *I Puritani*. Later these were reissued as a long-playing record with 'Suicidio' from *La Gioconda* and long extracts from *Traviata*.

Immediately after *Nabucco*, Maria Callas, now Maria Meneghini-Callas on programmes and record sleeves, and apparently in great form again, embarked on a series of new appearances which all added to her growing fame as a star.

First came three performances of *Norma* at La Fenice, Venice, followed by a rapid shuttle between Brescia and Rome, with a repeat of her exploits at the beginning of the previous year in Venice, only this time with travelling as well. In six days she sang two *Aida*s in Brescia and two *Tristan*s in Rome. These were followed with equal success by further performances of *Tristan* and performances of *Norma*, first in Rome, then in Catania, Bellini's birthplace, where she was ecstatically received. Maria was drunk with music and her own success. She was ready to go on and on, and Meneghini pushed her, eager for her voice of bronze and silver to be turned into gold, if she would just sing that little bit more. Contracts were pouring in.

Then unexpectedly, almost accidentally, she was offered a chance to appear at La Scala. Perhaps this was a false start, rather than a real début; but it was a début all the same. In spite of her overnight reputation Maria Meneghini-Callas was still very much a newcomer and she would never have been considered for a leading role at La Scala, the Mecca of Italian *bel canto,* if plans for a Verdi opera had not gone wrong. But fate once again played its part. Renata Tebaldi, installed at La Scala since 1946 by Toscanini, was indisposed and Maria Callas was invited to take her future rival's place in *Aida.* It was the chance she had been waiting for.

Before an impressive audience, which included even the President of the Italian Republic, Callas sang with del Monaco, Barbieri and Cesare Siepi. She expected a triumph, but it was a *succès d'estime*. In Milan triumphs depend on far more than the singer, fine singing, powerful emotion or a beautiful voice; perhaps Meneghini had forgotten to sweeten the all-powerful claque in the gods which dispenses bravos and boos, but is capable too of the most damning silence.

But this silence, broken only by a few lukewarm reviews in the Milanese press, did not discourage Maria. After this false start at La Scala she would not return again until begged to do so. Meanwhile that summer she made the first of three visits in three successive years to Mexico.

A Mexican Violetta

Maria's visits to Mexico City were an important milestone in the history of contemporary opera. She sang eight operas there in three years and all were broadcast on the radio and recorded, some several times, leaving precious evidence of her art in the early years. It was in Mexico City that she first sang *Il Trovatore, Lucia* and *Rigoletto*. She also appeared again as Tosca, a role she had not sung since Athens. The collection of Mexico City records are far from perfect technically, but they contain some incomparable strengths and beauties – the famous E flat held for ten seconds in the triumph scene from *Aida*, the unbearable pain and intensity, never equalled, of Tosca's cry as Scarpia tortures Cavaradossi, *'Non è ver! Sogghigno di demone!'* a perfect blend of musical and dramatic sense. The records form a distinct entity in Callas's career of a kind which never occurred again.

During her first visit in 1950 she sang *Norma* and *Aida* alternately with the tenor Kurt Baum, then *Tosca*, then *Il Trovatore* again with Kurt Baum. The first three we know. *Trovatore* was a new role. But each work marked an important moment in the history of opera. To take just one example: *Tosca*. When the jealous Tosca asks Mario to paint Mary

Magdalen in the church of Sant'Andrea della Valle with eyes as black as her own, *'Ma falle gli occhi neri!'*, there is an extraordinary tenderness, a note almost of amused coquetry, in this thread of a voice murmuring a suggestion which is really more than an order – a long, airy phrase with an innocence never repeated again. Callas's first recorded Tosca, despite the scratchy background noise, the blurred, elusive sound, is a heart-rending performance.

Her *Trovatore* was perhaps the first of her great interpretations of mature Verdi. This opera has always been one of the most popular in the Italian repertoire; the characters in the convoluted, highly melodramatic story are not subtly drawn, but they have a solidity and a rough simplicity which give the work a beauty of its own and ensure its success. Leonora wavers between Manrico, the troubadour she loves, and Count di Luna, the Spanish noble who wants her to be his. She loves only one, but in order not to lose him pretends to surrender to the other. Behind the three stands the stern firgure of Azucena, the witch, burning for revenge, and a curse hangs over the two brothers who do not know who they are. It is reminiscent of Victor Hugo's *Burgraves*. 'He was your brother', cries Azucena at the end of the opera when the Count has had Manrico executed. By then Callas has already killed herself. Her Leonora is very young, full of a beauty perhaps as yet not completely controlled. She used her voice to capacity and was a considerable success. However it was not until a few years later that she made full use of a dazzling palette of colours in the blaze of lyricism heard in *'Tacea la notte'* in the 1956 recording under Karajan. Yet on these pirate records her appeal to Count di Luna's clemency has the intensity, the fervour of a young girl in love. The *Miserere* of the last act with Kurt Baum shows her at the height of her powers and the whole scene – Manrico in prison, Leonora's lament, the chorus of dead souls singing of the final outcome – is a moment of piercing anguish.

But four roles and ten performances in a month, ranging from the technical demands of Norma to the lyricism of Leonora and the dramatic interpretation of a youthful, fiery Tosca, were something of an endurance test. By the end of her stay in Mexico City Callas was exhausted. Her first *Trovatore* on 27 June showed clear signs of fatigue. She also appeared to be increasingly affected by her separation from Meneghini, who had been unable to join her. He alone could encourage or restrain her as necessary and make her spare her resources as she should. She returned to Europe in a state of physical and mental exhaustion, with one wish – to rest in Verona. For three months, from June to September 1950, Callas did not sing. It was one of those periods of silence when she took up the piano again; she loved this instrument, which she played superbly, and often turned to it for comfort. Year by year her love for it grew until it was far more than a hobby.

Towards the end of 1950 she had to take to her bed with a severe attack of jaundice, postponing until 1954 her creation of the role of Elisabeth de Valois in *Don Carlos* and that sombre expression of grief, her appeal to the ghost of Charles V, *'Tu che la vanità. . .'*

The 1950-51 season, the last before Callas's official consecration at La Scala, was characterized by the same search for new roles, the same eagerness to do more and more. Callas, aware that she was being noticed, expended her energies recklessly. She certainly pushed her voice and her health beyond their limits and Meneghini was so enthusiastic about his wife's success that he too seemed to urge her on.

After several more performances of *Tosca* and *Aida* she had her first meeting with another man who was to play a leading role in the years to come. This man had great influence on an important stage in the development and orientation of her art and his name was to become a by-word for a certain kind of beauty and formal elegance: Luchino Visconti.

At that time a number of Roman artists and intellectuals used to meet in Rome as the 'Anfiparnasso' group. These writers, journalists and theatricals, interested by Callas's personality and dramatic sense, were putting on one of Rossini's earliest operas, *Il Turco in Italia,* which had not been performed in Italy or elsewhere for almost a century. Visconti was one of the prime movers of the 'Anfiparnasso' group. He had seen Maria two or three times in roles as different as Norma and Kundry, and he now suggested that she should play Fiorilla, the flighty young wife of the old Neapolitan Geronio in love with the footloose Turk Selim. It was the first time Callas had been offered a comic role. She was persuaded that she could be funny in it and accepted the dual challenge of making people laugh and reviving the comic *bel canto* repertoire. For several weeks Visconti and Callas lived side by side. The prima donna immediately became part of a group of left-wing intellectuals very unlike the singers, conductors and run-of-the-mill producers who had previously crossed her path. It was an improbable and miraculous combination from which opera as we know it emerged. Enthralled, Maria talked and listened. Visconti and his friends were equally enchanted and Visconti promised himself that he would work with her again. This was to happen during the glorious years at La Scala and the dazzling 1954-55 season. But now, for the first time, Callas took part in a production especially designed for her and she much enjoyed it.

The première of *Il Turco* took place on 19 October 1950 at the Teatro Eliseo. The impressive cast also included Sesto Bruscantini, Cesare Valletti and Mariano Stabile, Toscanini's great Falstaff and the sublime Don Giovanni on the first ever long-playing recording of *Don Giovanni.* The conductor was Giannandrea Gavazzeni who was just beginning to make his name as a conductor after more than twenty years as critic and musicologist. Callas was an unequivocal success. Vocally, she worked wonders such as one might expect only from creative artists trained in this kind of technical display. She also demonstrated brilliantly that she could switch from the taxing roles of Turandot or Abigaille to the light, delicate fioriture of Rossini at his lightest without a hint of strain. Four years later, on record and on stage at La Scala, she repeated her performance of Fiorilla with the same ease. An Italian critic at the time was struck by an enchantingly soft E flat perfectly placed at the end of a difficult and very ornate aria. Incredible to think that only a few weeks before the same voice had been singing the impressive, large-scale laments from *Tristan*. Callas was not just a supremely musical dramatic artist. She was also a vocal phenomenon.

After this dazzling display of her powers, Callas took on three new characters, of which one above all others was to give her career a new, tragic dimension – Violetta in *La Traviata*. The other two were Elena in *I Vespri Siciliani* and Euridice in Haydn's *Orfeo ed Euridice*. She also almost sang another role which two years later was to represent an important milestone in her career as a tragic actress – Lady Macbeth in Verdi's opera. But alas, to Callas's regret and ours, this *Macbeth* which would have been so beautiful never materialized. Toscanini was planning a last *Macbeth*, to be given both at Busseto, near Verdi's birthplace, and in New York, and later recorded. Though he did not know her and was in fact rather ill-disposed towards her, he intended to use Callas. But the project dragged on, while Toscanini grew older and his powers declined. Finally the plan fell through and the world never heard the great combination Toscanini-Callas.

But such disappointments are typical of opera. So too are triumphant seasons, gala openings and festivals. The *Maggio fiorentino*, the Florence May music festival, is one of the most famous. Callas was invited to sing at it for the first time on 26 May 1951.

She appeared in *I Vespri Siciliani* with Boris Christoff, conducted by the famous Mozartian conductor Erich Kleiber. She was a subtle, sensitive Elena equally concerned with the dramatic requirements of the plot and with the vocal skills demanded by her role. The plot is extremely far-fetched, though based on historical fact – the massacre of French troops in Sicily during the twelfth century. Scribe, who wrote the text for the Paris Opera in 1955, turned the story into one of those eternal conflicts between love, family loyalty and friendship so dear to nineteenth century opera. Few operas end as absurdly as *I Vespri* which leaves the characters as the massacre is about to begin without knowing who will be killed. Svoboda's sets for Paris Opéra leave them standing on a staircase as the curtain falls. Musically the work is full of superb moments including a bass aria 'O tu Palermo', an exhortation to Palermo by the proscribed Procida, and a cabaletta for the principal soprano '*Vostra fato è in vostra man*'. No one who heard Callas sing this will ever forget it. No other coloratura ever gave Verdi this lightness, this transparent yet solid quality. Her aria in the last act, the famous bolero '*Merce, dilette amiche*', is a perfect example of Callas's art at the height of her powers – both for her deep sense of theatre which allows her to

At La Scala as Elena in I Vespri Siciliani, *in which she appeared with Eugene Conley as Arrigo, Enzo Mascherini as Monforte and Boris Christoff as Procida*

mould and adapt all the *bel canto* techniques of which Verdi here makes uncharacteristic use, and for the superb musical sense which she displays, even when she falters; for example she adds an unnecessary E, manages to miss it and then immediately retrieves it. In this respect the pirate recordings of these four performances from May and June 1951 are a valuable anthology. They illustrate everything Callas had learned from Hidalgo, plus that extra dimension she was acquiring day by day in the theatre, a quality which no other singer of her generation dared to display so freely.

But after a further series of performances of *I Vespri* at the opening of the 1951-52 season Callas never sang the role of Elena again. Rather surprisingly she agreed to produce the opera in Turin in 1973 in collaboration with the tenor Guiseppe di Stefano. This was her only venture as a producer and the result was disappointing. Despite her achievements in the part at the start of her career, Elena in *I Vespri* is not a role generally associated with Maria Callas.

Nor is the role of Euridice in Haydn's *Orfeo ed Euridice* which she also sang at the Florence *Maggio musicale* in June 1951. There are no recorded relics of the two performances though the press received them favourably. Kleiber was once again the conductor for this opera which had never before been performed, not even during Haydn's lifetime. It was an operatic event, but as nothing came of it it was really more of a curiosity. It is probably the least-discussed of all Callas's roles, perhaps because very few people saw it.

Her Violetta on the other hand was the third of her five key roles, along with Tosca and Norma, which she had already sung, and Lucia and Medea which were soon to follow. These were her essential roles, because of the intensity with which she sang and acted them, and the number of times she sang them: *Norma* 89 times, it is reckoned, *Traviata* 63, *Lucia* 45, *Tosca* 33 and *Medea* 31. She worked on the role of Violetta from Florence, early in 1951, to Dallas in 1958, transforming it as her own character and life evolved. Tosca kills because she is driven to it, a victim who kills herself. Norma is a sacrificial victim who gives herself up. Now comes Violetta, a woman who renounces love for love's sake and dies for it like the others. She dies exhausted, sapped, sucked dry of her vitality by all the men who have devoured her as their prey. Often in speaking of Callas and Traviata, of Callas in *Traviata,* the image of a woman drained of her life blood springs to mind. For Callas was *Traviata.* No other role so completely lives up to our idea of Callas as the victim of men and fate. Not Callas the tigress, Tosca the murderess or Medea the jealous, but the real Callas, our Callas. A fragile, trembling woman who knows she is dying of consumption and makes us tremble too. Violetta, torn to pieces by men who wish to possess her. La Traviata, dazzled and in the end killed by money. Three hundred pairs of shoes in the wardrobe and a lonely death in a silk dressing-gown, with only a servant to watch over her.

Callas never acted any other role as fully as Violetta – deliberately singing in a weak, broken voice because Violetta in Act III is weak and broken. She lived the role as she acted it. At least seven complete recordings have survived, showing all the improvements made, all the subtleties introduced from Mexico City in 1951, with Oliviero de Fabritiis conducting, to the Covent Garden performances in 1958, with Callas's favourite conductor at that time, Rescigno. The two highlights are the 1953 Cetra records with Santini, and the 1955 pirate recordings made during Visconti's marvellous La Scala production and reissued commercially by Cetra in 1977, with di Stefano and Giulini, a monumental performance against the background of Visconti's sets.

However in 1951 in Florence, where she sang the role for the first time, and in Mexico City, where a recording was made, she still seems to have been dominated by the passion the character inspires. The recording made in Mexico in July 1951 is not up to her later standard, but is nonetheless already a striking portrayal of Violetta, youthful and fragile, violent yet tender. Her performances in Bergamo with Giulini the same year and in Parma with Fabritiis were triumphs. She sang *Traviata* fifteen times in a year and made it one of her most characteristic roles.

Meanwhile she completed her by now regular tour in Mexico, where as well as *Traviata* she also sang a new *Aida.* She also went further afield in Latin America, visiting Argentina and Brazil that same year, but more will be said later about her misadventures during this trip. During this period she finally signed the contract which opened wide the doors of La Scala to her. She was to make her début there the following season on 7 December, during the annual gala, and to appear thirty times in all in three different roles. A new phase of her life – Callas, queen of Milan – was about to begin.

The Maria Callas who stepped on to the stage of La Scala on 7 December 1951 as Elena in *I Vespri Siciliani,* this singer who was to be feted, adored and envied, was already a highly controversial artist whose sound and style were not liked by some lovers of traditional beautiful voices. She was also a star whose outbursts and rages were already newsworthy. From 1951 Maria Meneghini-Callas became a personality who split public opinion and attracted journalists, a controversial artist and woman who for twenty years was to be in the forefront of the international scene.

The major flaws of her voice have already been mentioned several times: the breaks between registers, the strident upper notes, the almost cavernous sonority of her bottom notes. Those who like singing to be pure and uniformly beautiful at all times may well find Callas a vocal monstrosity. But listening to her is an adventure. Following her as she scales phenomenal cliffs of sound – her crescendos in Nabucco, say – one never knows what lies at the end, though during the early part of her career major disasters were rare. But what is amazing is that when these accidents do occur, Callas's musical sense is such that she manages to retrieve the situation, and turn it to supreme artistic effect. The sudden stridency which sometimes affects her high notes becomes a different kind of musical quality which she can mould at will as if she had invented not only new dramatic accents but also a new voice. A new voice, a new kind of singing, all her own and quite unforgettable: an experience clearly not to everyone's taste.

This explains why during her early years she met with semi-failure and defeat as well as success. Her 1949 *Turandot* at the Colón Theatre, Buenos Aires, was greeted with indifference. So was her first *Aida* at La Scala, when her talents as a tragic actress were discussed but little was said about her voice. Her 1951 performances of *Tosca* in Rio provoked mixed reactions, probably because of the jealousy of a local artist, herself a great singer, who had her own claque of supporters. Her *Trovatore* at the San Carlos, Naples, in 1951, was so badly received that the great tenor Lauri-Volpi – who was singing Manrico with her – wrote a letter to the Neapolitan press complaining about its chauvinism. Listening now to the Cetra records of the 27 January 1951 performance and to the beauty of Callas's timbre it is difficult to see what the Neapolitans were complaining about, though Lauri-Volpi himself was booed after his rather poor performance of the bravura aria '*Di quella pira*'.

So from the beginning Callas was not a universally accepted singer. Given contemporary attitudes to opera singing, we can now see that it would have been surprising if her unorthodox voice, as far removed from the traditional canons of disembodied *bel canto* as from the sob stuff of post-*verismo,* still so much in demand in Italy, had not produced a sense of shock and unease.

But Callas herself, as woman and public figure, did nothing to soften the effect. If she had been all sweetness and light, one of those singers people love to engage because you know where you are with them, our perhaps unhealthy interest in her might have been less. The heroi-comic details of her quarrels with her partners which so appealed to the general public merely aggravated her detractors.

Today, looking through the file of hundreds or even thousands of press cuttings about Maria Callas is a nightmarish experience. Twenty or so background pieces which really tell us something about her – Derek Prouse's articles in the *Sunday Times* in 1961, the *Observer* 'Profile' from the same year, Sylvie de Nussac's interview in *L'Express* in 1970 – about two hundred serious and considered reviews of her voice and performances in Europe or America throughout her career, and all the rest is gossip, slander and scandal-mongering. Starting with the vile leading article from *Time* magazine, supposedly to welcome her New York début in 1956. Then a dreary flow of headlines – 'The tigress strikes again' or 'I meet Maria Callas: she is as gentle as a lamb!' Nor did things improve later. Then it was Onassis, Onassis, Onassis all the time. . .

What attracted public attention during these early years were the first 'incidents', so gloated over later. In Mexico City in 1950 she fell out with Kurt Baum who was singing Radamès, Pollione and Manrico with her in *Aida, Norma* and *Il Trovatore.* The reason was that Callas wished to take a curtain call on her own after the final curtain. This question of curtain calls was to play a decisive part in the behind-the-scenes quarrels which caused so much spite and back-biting. Customs vary from theatre to theatre: in some singers come on alone, in others the whole cast takes its bows at the end of the performance. Individual curtain calls are the norm in Paris and London, but not in New York. So one evening on leaving the stage, Kurt Baum, the overlooked tenor, swore that she would never sing at the New York Metropolitan from which he came. However this did not stop them working together a few years later in London and even in America.

The following year, again in Mexico City, she quarrelled with Mario del Monaco over the E flats in Aida. Del Monaco, with whom Callas often sang, was one of three or four tenors – Giuseppe di Stefano and Franco Corelli were others – who crossed her path throughout her career and with whom she quarrelled quite regularly, to the delight of gossip-writers. With his rousing voice and keen dramatic sense del Monaco was an unfailing heroic tenor who always held his audience, though sometimes displaying lack of finesse or even coarseness. Like Callas and Ponselle, he was one of Tullio Serafin's protégés. Callas and del Monaco's first meeting was an angry affair from the start. On stage at the Palacio de Bellas Artes in Mexico City each tried to stop the other singing the long and difficult top notes and it was said that they almost came to blows back stage. True or false, that was the rumour.

There was another violent altercation with Boris Christoff at the end of a performance of *I Vespri Siciliani*. The gigantic Bulgarian bass threatened to crush Callas, herself no weakling, if she insisted on taking a curtain call alone. The press loved these incidents and later added racier details to their anecdotes.

Finally the quarrel with Tebaldi was already beginning to loom over the two singers' careers. Renata Tebaldi was slightly less than two years older than Callas, an exquisite soprano with an almost flawless voice even in the highest register which she could sustain at length with a sweet, gentle tone. She quickly became one of the most famous singers in the world, superb both in the *verismo* repertoire and Verdi. Her supporters were as fanatical as Callas's. As regards their records, while Callas teamed up with di Stefano for EMI, Renata Tebaldi was the principal soprano in the Decca stable with Mario del Monaco. Finally in 1946 it was Toscanini who chose Tebaldi for the reopening of La Scala, destroyed during the war. Soon she was Callas's only rival of international stature. When they met in Latin America their paths had already crossed several times, in Verona and at La Fenice, Venice, during the winter of 1947. Callas had twice replaced Tebaldi when indisposed – in *Aida* at La Scala in 1950 and in *Traviata* in Bergamo in October 1951. In the spring of 1951 she had refused to help out La Scala by singing *Aida* again instead of Renata Tebaldi, insisting that she would only return to Milan if offered a proper contract, which she was soon to get, and not through the back door. During the short season Callas gave in Brazil during late summer of the same year, the press carried unkind comments which she was alleged to have made about Tebaldi who was alternating with her in the role of Violetta in São Paulo. This brought the first stage of hostilities to a head. A few days later in Rio the two singers had a real argument, exchanging hard words and quarrelling openly. During a concert in which they were performing together Renata Tebaldi, who had been enthusiastically applauded by the audience, without warning gave two encores which the two singers had not agreed on beforehand. Tebaldi seems to have been in the wrong here, but it was Callas who was furious and broke off relations.

The whole of Callas's stay in Rio, at the end of her 1951 South American tour, was punctuated by rows, but it was also marred by her exhaustion. Already in São Paulo, her previous port of call, she had not sung her scheduled performances of *Aida* and had been criticized for this. When she reached Rio she was at the end of her tether. The incident with Tebaldi stretched her to breaking point. On top of everything else, on the evening of 24 September, Barreto Pinto, the director of Rio Opera, perhaps egged on by Callas's enemies, told her that she had sung so badly in her last *Tosca* that she might as well go home. Her contract was ended.

Bitterly Callas demanded to be paid even if she did not sing. She finally forced Pinto to let her sing her two remaining performances of *Traviata*. Too bad about her last *Tosca* – if Pinto did not like her he would have to make do with Tebaldi. Though furious he had to agree. There was a storm in the director's office, where a heavy bronze inkwell stood on the ministerial leather-topped desk. Callas sang her two performances of *Traviata* and was roundly applauded. This was too much for Pinto who had predicted disaster and now lost face; he tried to go back on their agreed financial arrangements. But no one could defy Callas and remain unscathed.

From this came the exaggerated tale of the bronze inkwell from Pinto's desk flying through the air at Pinto's head. True or false, the episode of the bronze inkwell – or the brandy bottle as it became elsewhere in the press – and the opera director became a damaging item in the increasingly public record of Callas's alleged misdemeanours, all of which contributed to the legend of a spiteful, stubborn, grasping woman.

Meanwhile, exhausted, Callas returned to Europe, to play the piano. Brazil was far away and three months later, on the traditional feastday of St Ambrose, came her La Scala opening. A star was born. The beginning of a legend.

As Lucia di Lammermoor, the last of the five great roles which made Callas's reputation (opposite)

'Callas returned to Europe to play the piano'

THE CONQUEST OF LA SCALA
(1951-1954)

When the curtain of La Scala went up on the new production of *I Vespri Siciliani* which was to open the 1951-52 season, the singer facing the most difficult audience in the world for the first time was a consummate artist. For four years all her days off, all her free time between performances, and even the two or three holidays she had taken because of her health had been devoted to work and more work. Nearly every day she spent time on vocal exercises and the piano, which she still played enthusiastically. As a result Callas had made remarkable progress with her voice.

With fierce determination she had set herself two main aims – to correct the imperfections in her voice and to achieve even greater musicianship.

She wanted first to remedy the famous dead notes between her three registers. If one listens carefully to recordings made in 1949 and in 1951 – for example *Nabucco* and the second Mexico City *Aida* – the difference is scarcely perceptible. It was later in her career, when her vocal resources were less, that her incomparable technique allowed her to cope more easily with these danger points. But the excessive vibrato and the stridency of her high notes became more pronounced as Callas began to pay the price for Abigaille and Turandot.

Callas's struggle for mastery of her voice had already begun. Her efforts to correct its imperfections meant a constant striving to bring this exceptional instrument – one has only to think of the Florence Elena or Fiorilla in *Il Turco in Italia* – under the control of her incomparable musicianship.

From the time of her Verona début onwards this was where Callas made the most impressive progress. If one compares her 1950 *Aida* with the 1955 recording under Serafin, or the San Carlo *Trovatore* with the 1953 version under Votto or the 1956 version under Karajan, it is a delight to hear her extraordinary use of colour, harmonics and nuance quite apart from considerations of dramatic effect – though her dramatic sense bordered on genius. If Callas's voice is sometimes irregular, if certain sounds jar as music, as intensity of sound, it is of unsurpassed splendour. Rosa Ponselle perhaps, Caballé in moments of genius, Mirella Freni's *mezza voce* in *Simon Boccanegra*, Sena Jurinac's 'Tu che le vanità' in the Salzburg *Don Carlos* . . . other singers have their great moments too, and this is not one of those fulsome life stories which pretend that no other singers existed before or afterwards. But Callas's art, her talent and her understanding of the voice, involved her voice, technique, heart and brain all together in a way which no other singer ever seems to have matched.

Callas's own account of the different stages of her approach to a score is a good description of her brand of genius – diligent and painstaking, but always inspired. In a number of interviews, and particularly in Derek Prouse's article which appeared in the *Sunday Times* in 1961, she gave a shortened version of the master classes she was later to give in public in the United States and in private in her Paris flat:

'In the first place you see if you like the music and if it means something to you "All right," you may say, "on the whole I enjoy this work, so let's do the opera." Then you start to learn the music. At this stage you don't let yourself be drawn into your beautiful world of creation; you become like a pupil in the Conservatoire again. You learn the music exactly as it is written – you take no liberties, even with the written recitative. Only the rhythm counts at this point – *that* you must respect.'

This is Elvira de Hidalgo's pupil listening to her teacher, the young student from Athens Conservatory devouring scores day after day. She worked in bed at night, poking her heavy glasses back into place as they slipped down her nose. First the music and the music alone. The notes as written in every minute detail.

'Then you come back to the words. What do they say? If I were to speak this recitative how would I say it? And you keep on saying it to yourself, noting the accents, the pauses, the little stresses that create the right balance between the different accents of speech and music. Naturally, this isn't something you find in one day. It comes with rehearsals and grows even with the performances. Sometimes vocal technique stands in your way. Today a phrase might not come off, but tomorrow, to your delight, it does. Then, gradually, familiarity with the music and the character enables you to develop all the tiny nuances which you could only hint at in the beginning. But for me that's only the beginning. After that the trouble starts; or rather, the really rewarding part of the work.'

Here Maria Callas's teaching becomes a lesson which all singers might usefully study:

'After you've learnt the music rhythmically then you say: "Right: now *this* is the tempo of Bellini. Donizetti would have felt it this way, Wagner would have felt it another way." They might all write *allegro* or *adagio*, but each composer has his particular rhythm, and that is too elusive to put on a metronome (I never use a metronome). The essential qualifications at this stage are instinct, experience and good taste. Now, coming back to the words and the music: you start to free yourself, and you apportion what you feel is the correct emphasis to each phrase; you come to an agreement about this with the conductor and the other singers. Together you decide the musical shape of each passage and how it will relate to the whole. It is like analysing a balanced piece of architecture. When you think you've found it, then you have to see how it sounds sung in full voice – where you can spare yourself for a few phrases, where you must give everything in order to lend the opera its maximum impact and meaning. Then the theatre person in you starts to judge, and you say to yourself: "Now wait a minute! If you had it this way, as the composer originally wished it, a modern audience will just die yawning.'' So you have to take necessary liberties, animating it a little more, adding a touch here and there. Finally, after all this, it could take two or three weeks, your mind is so confused and over-charged that you simply have to get away for a day or two. So I just disappear out of circulation. And I stay by myself – that is, I no longer need the accompanist with me; I have it in my head. I could start the opera and go through, reading it as you would read a book. And with the music going on in my head I try speaking the words aloud.'

Callas is now talking about creating a character and about acting, and this is a different, if related story. The story of a young woman of twenty-eight who in three years conquered La Scala and established a world-wide reputation, with her records and her presence, as one of the greatest artists of her time in all respects. It is also the story of a young woman undergoing a personal transformation.

Callas's conquest of La Scala took three years; three years in which she sang ten roles, after a glorious début as Elena in *I Vespri Siciliani;* three years in which she established herself as the uncontested star of Milan's great opera house. From then on she reigned supreme, with the famous 1954-55 season perhaps the greatest in her career.

Constanze in Il Ratto di Seraglio, *the very first production of this Mozart opera at La Scala*

During the first season Maria simply prepared the ground for her rise, with *I Vespri Siciliani, Norma* and *Die Entführung aus dem Serail.* A new production of a recent success, one of her greatest roles and a new part which showed her in an unexpected light. Callas displayed three sides of her talent – dramatic soprano, classic coloratura and Mozartian dramatic soprano – as she marked out her territory.

December 7 was the first night of *I Vespri.* No recording of her interpretation of Elena that evening has survived, but it was probably close to her performance in the Florence *Vespri* a few months before. The cast was much the same, but with two important exceptions – the conductor Victor de Sabata and the American tenor Eugene Conley as Arrigo, Elena's lover.

Callas immediately followed up the seven performances of *I Vespri Siciliani* with eight of *Norma.* In this she scored a tremendous personal success. The critics noticed a few strident notes, but were unanimous about her musicianship, her technical skill, and above all about her dramatic sense. This was the thirtieth time she had sung *Norma* and she was making the character of the druidess betrayed in love her own, a noble, beautiful figure whose development and death we can follow with each recording, each set of photographs, showing Callas in white raising her arm, Callas threatening, Callas about to die.

Finally, in April 1952, she sang Constanze in *Die Entführung aus dem Serail* (or rather *Il Ratto di Seraglio* as the opera was performed in Italian).

Surprisingly, this was also the first performance of *Il Seraglio* at La Scala. The Milan public has never been particularly keen on Mozart and Callas herself never showed much interest in his operas. She had a highly personal view of them and once remarked that, 'His operas are too often performed on tiptoe. They should be sung with the same openness as *Trovatore,* but in the style of Mozart.'

Two surviving extracts from *Il Seraglio,* recorded in 1954 and 1957, do not perhaps quite reflect this view. Maria Callas gives an admirably spirited rendering of the famous and diabolically difficult *'Martern aller Arten'.* Effortlessly she does everything the score says, but in Italian and in a taut, dramatic style with sombre colours which are not quite Mozart. Later when she was asked to sing Mozart again she refused. The most she would do was record individual arias from *Don Giovanni.*

However the Milan performances, with Leonor Fini's superb costumes, were a success. The press admired the agility and sensuality of Callas's voice, moving with such ease in the airy realms where Constanze has to perform all the feats demanded by a Mozart who rarely expected such dexterity from his sopranos. And so this first season ended with all the eulogies Callas could have hoped for.

But at La Scala Callas was still only one star among several. The same year Tebaldi had sung Boito's *Mefistofele* and Verdi's *Falstaff* with comparable success, and the two singers avoided one another in the corridors. Besides Callas and Tebaldi, Rosanna Carteri, Clara Petrella and Margherita Carosio (whose indisposition had allowed Maria to sing her first *Puritani* in Venice) were also important stars. But it was the quarrel between Tebaldi and Callas which aroused such passionate interest, dividing public opinion and causing the ink to flow. Milan soon heard about the incidents in Rio and as early as 1951 the La Scala audience was split into two camps. For several years a relentless battle was fought with bravos, applause, boos and silence, under the dubious arbitration of the leader of the theatre's official claque which did not hesitate to hire out its services at a price to both factions at once.

During the first years the arguments were confined to those in the know and the general public was not really involved. Tebaldi's golden timbre was compared with Callas's music and power of expression and discussions went on late into the night after performances.

During Maria's second season at La Scala, Ghiringhelli, the superintendent, tried to come to some arrangement to calm down tempers which were becoming heated over the two rival sopranos. It would never do if the quarrel moved beyond the drawingrooms and smart parties of Milan. He decided to get Maria Callas to sing during the first half of the season and Renata Tebaldi during the second – just as in China, after the days of Princess Turandot, there was an Empress of the West and an Empress of the East; one of them sometimes ended up at the bottom of the well but that was the law of a different jungle.

Maria Meneghini-Callas was to open the season with Verdi's *Macbeth* followed by *Il Trovatore* and *La Gioconda.* The evening of 7 December 1952 was a foretaste of the great evenings of the 1954 season, Callas's apotheosis.

Lady Macbeth is perhaps the most ambiguous role in the Italian repertory. It demands powerful resources and a voice capable of moments of great beauty. But Verdi himself remarked that the harsher and less pleasing the voice of this deadly woman was, the greater her impact. It is a part one associates with very sombre timbres (Elizabeth Höngen in Germany or Galina Vishnevskaya), or even with mezzos (Grace Bumbry, or Christa Ludwig in the splendid 1970 *Macbeth* with Karl Bohm); however this has never stopped clearer true sopranos like Leonie Rysanek, Anja Silja or Inge Borkh attempting it. It is one of those rare roles in the Italian repertoire in which any excess is allowed: a black-hearted Lady Macbeth unleashing hatred, ambition and cruelty is a feast for the senses, a release for our own dark dreams.

But Lady Macbeth was always an unlucky role for Callas. She never sang it anywhere else after the La Scala season, though not because she did not want to. She had already had the disappointment of the *Macbeth* Toscanini was to have conducted two years before. Later *Macbeth* was twice the cause of disputes which closed the doors of two of the United States' most important opera houses to her. In 1957 she had to cancel an engagement at San Francisco Opera because of fatigue, and the following year at the Met she refused to sing the demanding role of Lady Macbeth turn and turn about with *La Traviata,* with its very different colours and tessitura.

However 7 December 1952 was a great day in Callas's life and career which has survived in a pirate recording reissued by Cetra. She spent a long time preparing her part in this production by Carl Ebert, co-founder of the Glyndebourne Festival, with designs by Nicola Benois who worked on many of the great Callas productions at La Scala. Long in advance the evening was billed as an 'event'. The theatre was decorated with red carnations and an ingenious shirt-maker even gave all season-ticket holders at the first night lengths of material for matching evening shirts. The blaze of publicity and press coverage were already taking possession of Callas.

Verdi's opera is a chaotic, harsh, gloomy world which follows Shakespeare's tragedy closely, though in a rather disjointed manner. The scenes follow one another without real logical connection and act by act the cold fury, terror and uncontrolled violence are intensified. The music demands dark voices. Macbeth is a baritone, Banquo a bass, and the two tenors, Macduff and Malcolm, have only minor parts. Callas, using her voice's extraordinary potential, its extraordinary lucidity to the full, was far more than just a singer. She was a demon haunted by fear, a superhuman soprano capable of monstrous ravings and the utmost gentleness, an apparition uttering harsh cries and a noble lady inviting those whom she wishes to lull into trust to drink with her. Swathed in veils Callas's Lady Macbeth is consumed by hatred and ambition. She was greeted with thunderous applause and received seven or eight curtain calls. The next day the press was beside itself with admiration. Callas seemed to have conquered Milan in a single evening.

But conquering Milan was never that simple. The factions, the back-stage hatreds, Tebaldi and her admirers, were waiting in the wings. Over the years too much emphasis has been placed on the blameless

Lady Macbeth

Tebaldi, a lamb to Callas's ravening wolf. But on the battlefield of La Scala it was Tebaldi's side which cast the first stone.

After *Macbeth* the public expected a dazzling *Gioconda,* and they were disappointed. This was the role in which Callas had made her Verona début and Nicola Benois's fine sets were worthy of later productions specially designed for her. But despite a cast which also included di Stefano, Stignani and Carlo Tagliabue, the press was cool and the audience judged her even more harshly, with boos and catcalls. A triumph must be paid for and the cost can be high. Callas, who had just finished her performances of *Macbeth,* was not in good form, di Stefano even less so. She was not restored to favour until her outstanding *Trovatore* at the end of the season when even her fiercest enemies could hardly have booed her sumptuous Leonora.

The struggle for supremacy at La Scala was by no means over, and during the 1953-54 season the two sides became even more entrenched.

Callas first appeared in Cherubini's *Medea* which she had already sung the first spring before in Florence. As with *I Vespri Siciliani,* she made her début in a role at the *Maggio fiorentino* and consolidated it a few months later at La Scala. Her Medea, first in Florence and then at La Scala, was to become one of her greatest parts. When little was left of her voice, and her music and tragic sense were all she had, Callas still sang *Medea* together with *Tosca* and *Norma.* Her last appearance at La Scala in 1962 was as Medea – a failing Medea, nearing the end. When she wanted a dazzling occasion to renew her links with her native Greece she chose to appear as Medea, a proud majestic figure in the ancient theatre at Epidaurus. Medea, the stranger among the Greeks, the alien devil, threatening the classical edifice of order and logic, love and beauty which Corinth, most hypocritical of cities, tried to impose in spite of this sorceress-princess. A more than human character, forged by Euripides from the blackest of metals, and transformed by Cherubini into a torrent of icy lava.

Medea is classical tragedy at its darkest and most powerful. Deserted by her husband Jason whose life she saved, the sorceress Medea seeks him in Corinth, Creon's kingdom, where he is about to marry Princess Glauce. Medea's despair turns to hatred. She will go to any lengths to get Jason back, but when she fails she gets her revenge by killing Glauce and her own children. She obeys her destiny to the end, brandishing her bloody knife as the temple is destroyed.

First performed in Paris in 1797, Cherubini's *Médée* soon became *Medea* and has usually been sung in the Italian version. It was frequently performed during the nineteenth century, but completely forgotten from 1909 until the Florence revival with Callas.

The role itself is one of the most testing in the entire repertoire. Legend has it that the original singer, Madame Scio, died after singing the part too often. After Callas the opera became popular again, and notable exponents of the role since have included Gerda Lammers in 1958, Rita Gorr in 1962, Leyla Gencer in 1968, Gwynneth Jones in 1969, and Magda Olivero, Anja Silja and Leonie Rysanek in Vienna and the ancient

Medea: 'classical tragedy at its darkest and most powerful'

theatre at Arles. Callas seemed to have sensed something in the air, and others followed in her footsteps.

Medea is one of the five characters, the five women of Italian opera, on whom Callas was to make a lasting mark. This time the victim becomes a she-wolf and kills to save herself or what is left of her love. But she is nonetheless a victim. Jason's betrayal in leaving her for another woman and Corinth's shameful treatment of her turn the sorceress into a murderess. After her humiliation she takes up the knife instead of offering her throat. Once again we are the cause of her fatal rage. *'Atre furie, volate a me!'* ('Black furies, fly to me!') she cries in Act III, her voice suddenly raised in the most terrible resounding threat. Then it wavers, and we wonder what would have happened if Medea had been loved.

Medea is an impossible role, like all the roles Callas now chose, roles which allowed her temperament to express itself in all its boundless energy, which allowed her voice to scale the peaks she had conquered, the furthest limits of classicism and *bel canto*. What Callas made of the role seemed beyond the humanly possible. It was as if some demonic power were responsible for her phenomenal climbs to the blackest of top notes, her impeccable timbre, her never-flagging power.

There are several recordings of Callas in this role in which signs of weakening were never forgiven her, as was apparent at La Scala in 1962. The most impressive is probably the pirate recording made in Dallas in 1958 with Teresa Berganza and Jon Vickers. Here Callas-Medea is suddenly assailed by doubt, as if she had looked in the glass and been appalled by the murderous fiend reflected there. In 1953 at La Scala with Leonard Bernstein, the beginning of a partnership which was to continue over future years, Callas was superb. A torrent, a frenzy of sound. The theatre shook with applause. Though Renata Tebaldi had opened the season in Catalani's *La Wally* – with Toscanini himself, who had called his daughter Wally in honour of the composer, watching from a box – Callas's triumph was of a quite different order from her rival's mere success.

The quarrel now entered its fiercest phase. Each singer kept a close watch on the other and scored points. The rain of red carnations which greeted Callas at the end of *Lucia di Lammermoor* was a sign from heaven – or the gods – to Tebaldi that the other singer, her enemy through others' scheming and gossiping rather than because of any genuine personal animosity, had triumphed.

Callas with Karajan

Lucia was the last of the five great roles on which Callas's reputation was based. She had already sung it in 1952 in Mexico City, in January 1953 in Florence, in Genoa, Catania and Rome. After Florence came Milan of course, and after Bernstein, Karajan. In the space of three weeks two of the world's greatest conductors came to work with Callas, and three months later Carlo Maria Giulini conducted Gluck's *Alceste* for her. Maria's third season was a magnificent prelude, an introductory fanfare, followed by the triumphant allegro of her fourth season.

However this *Lucia di Lammermoor,* both conducted and produced by Karajan, was not really to the Milanese taste. But Callas's voice and stage presence swept away all reservations and carnations showered down on her. Callas was now almost an Italian, almost a Milanese.

There are plenty of recordings and photographs to show us what Callas was like in *Lucia.* Wearing a long white robe over a white nightdress, with immense sleeves opening in a hundred pleats like a flower, a silky train with hundreds more pleats sweeping behind her, Callas steps out of the darkness in the mad scene. Her hair flows behind her, her arms at her sides open slowly in a gesture of resignation and powerlessness, and she offers herself up as a sacrificial victim. Her voice roams among the intricacies which make the role of Lucia Donizetti's most beautiful – the most varied, melancholy and colourful, with all the sweetness of *bel canto,* a graceful, delicate cantilena with those soaring leaps in the sweet, serene music which Callas's voice alone could tinge with the blackest pathos, the black mood of Walter Scott's or Mary Shelley's gloomy Gothic tales.

This time, with *Lucia di Lammermoor,* Callas was not discovering a forgotten opera. Alone perhaps of all Donizetti's works, apart from *Don Pasquale,* Lucia had remained in the repertoire of opera houses all over the world since its creation in Naples in 1835 with Fanny Persiani, for whom Donizetti had composed the piece, and the formidable Duprez, Berlioz's first *Benvenuto Cellini.* The list of Lucias is impressive, from Julia Calvi to the great Lily Pons, the 'French nightingale' of the Met. It is the archetypal romantic coloratura role. The plot, taken from Walter Scott's novel, describes the misfortunes of Lucia who loves Edgardo but is forced by her brother Enrico to marry Arturo – all Italianized versions of Scots names. Lucia goes mad in the most famous mad scene in the history of opera.

73

Lucia, Callas's fifth key role, and after it a great emptiness. This time we have driven Callas, our heroine, over the brink to death. She can only murmur incoherent, fragmented memories, followed by silence. She sings softly, accompanied by the playing of a flute, which prevents her escape. A flute which gradually encircles her in its sound, traps her there and then leaves her a trembling, exhausted girl dreaming of her wedding. '*A me ti dona un Dio*' ('It is a god who gives you to me') and her final cry '*Non mi guardar si fiero . . .*' ('Do not look at me so cruelly'). She is speaking to us and us alone. The last vestiges of her reason falter. All that remains is the dark tomb, the haunted graveyard of the Ravenswoods, Aida's burial chamber, or the large flat with drawn curtains. Silence.

Callas's mad scene in *Lucia* is one of the great moments of *bel canto* in the second half of the twentieth century. And her portrayal of madness – the spasms of human suffering, all the convulsive, pulsating, fluttering emotions of the human heart – was so lucid and brilliant that she later made a record consisting entirely of arias from mad scenes: *Lucia*, *I Puritani*, Ambroise Thomas's *Hamlet*. To these we could add the sleep-walking scene from *Macbeth*, madness in another form.

Callas and Bernstein in December 1953, Callas and Karajan in January 1954 and now, in April 1954, Callas and Giulini with *Alceste*. Inside La Scala Callas now divided the audience, arousing ecstatic enthusiasm, but the most scathing criticism too. In some circles it was beginning to be said openly that her voice was ugly and incapable of even sound and constant quality.

'The most famous mad scene in the history of opera'

But in *Alceste*, the classical story of the queen prepared to die to save the king her husband whom the gods have condemned, Callas, as the recording of the production confirms, showed that she was capable of the most sober, classical singing and the most rigorous enunciation imaginable. And throughout, underlying the music, there is that greater feeling for tragedy – Euripides is behind Gluck at every bar – which was Callas's mainstay even when her voice later let her down. The work, though less popular than *Orfeo ed Euridice*, is probably Gluck's most beautiful and lyrical, his most consistently noble and lofty. With it Gluck revolutionized French opera, boldly sweeping away artificiality and unnaturalness. The production by Margherita Wallman, another of Callas's companions during her early days at La Scala, and the designs by Piero Zuffi were stunningly beautiful. Austere colonnades supporting a frieze copied from antiquity stood out against a beautiful sky washed unevenly with colour. In this setting Callas moved with an ease and naturalness which seemed truly classical, a quality she later achieved only when working with Visconti or the Greek director Minotis. As for her singing, her aria '*Divinités du Styx*' (sung of course in Italian), one of the operatic masterpieces of its time, is a limpid and pure invocation of death – and hope. The queen of Pharae, clad in black, standing against the broken columns which loom above her, facing a crowd of her subjects, is a truly majestic image. Gradually Callas takes her place in the kingdom we have made hers, where her voice and face, her roles and characters, her private and public life become as one. Only an abominably poor recording of these performances has survived, but Maria shines in what might have been one of her most famous roles if *Alceste* had remained in her repertoire.

Alceste: 'Callas moved with an ease and naturalness which seemed truly classical'

She finished this outstanding season with five performances of *Don Carlos* and it was as unchallenged queen that she left La Scala for Verona, England, America and six months of recording and feverish activity.

We know little about this *Don Carlos*. Rumour has it that a recording of it exists, but I have not heard it yet. All we know of Callas in the beautiful role of Elisabeth de Valois from Verdi's opera, with original French text by du Locle, are two arias – '*Non pianger*' in Act II and above all the marvellous '*Tu che la vanità*' in Act V which she recorded on two occasions. Out of context it is difficult to guess what she made of the part. Elisabeth is in any case far from the key role in *Don Carlos*, which is in many respects a man's opera. Far more than in the play by Schiller which inspired Verdi, the confrontation between different shades of political thought – which range from Carlos's left-wing attitudes to the Grand Inquisitor's intransigent, totalitarian conservatism, from the Marquess of Posa's liberalism to Philip II of Spain's absolutism – is considerably more interesting than the sorrows of the unhappy queen whose stepson loves her too much. *Don Carlos* perhaps is among Verdi's two or three finest operas, but Elisabeth really only comes into her own in the first act, the so-called Fontainebleau act, which is almost always cut. If Callas's reception as Elisabeth was less ecstatic than after *Alceste* or more particularly *Lucia,* it was the season as a whole which concerned her. By the end of the season Callas had won. And Renata Tebaldi – so marvellous in *Otello* and *Eugène Onegin,* in the *Wally* Toscanini had travelled to hear, and in her performances of *Tosca* – this singer whom others had tried to turn into Callas's enemy prepared to beat a retreat, leaving the field clear.

During the last stages of their battle Callas would attend her rival's first nights and applaud enthusiatically, but Tebaldi refused to appear when Callas was singing. Callas, it has even been suggested, used to lurk in a box, an impassive rather than an enthusiastic listener, spying on her victim and bringing her bad luck; Callas the sorceress, Medea or Lady Macbeth, weaving spells, and casting the evil eye. Callas laughingly defended herself against these charges, 'Of course, I went to Renata Tebaldi's performances, but it was because I wanted to hear how she sang.' But it was not as simple as that. If Callas did not go to cast spells or take singing lessons, it seems likely that she wanted to make her presence felt at La Scala even when not on stage. It is easy to see how her rival, constantly under the gaze as she thought of a malevolent ill-wisher, could become obsessed by the situation. Tebaldi sang one more season at La Scala, the 1954-55 season during which Callas triumphed as never before; and Tebaldi according even to her less ardent admirers was superb. Then with a coquetry worthy of her rival she quietly closed the door behind her: if the queen of La Scala had been chosen and it was not to be her she would go and sing somewhere else. Renata Tebaldi never sang again in Milan until Callas had left.

To be fair, in talking so much about Callas I have also tried to rediscover Tebaldi. With time she begins to look like nobody's favourite; though she once had her own supporters and her own claque, over the years she has slowly faded away. Who collects her records now? Ponselle is a legend, Callas is a legend, Milanov is almost a legend, but Tebaldi is not. People remember 'the exquisite quality of her voice,' its 'soft, radiant beauty' and pass on. Yet Tebaldi as Desdemona, as Leonora in *La Forza del Destino,* as Mimi or as Verdi's extraordinary *Giovanna d'Arco* which she sang with Bergonzi in Milan in 1951 is a relevation, with a breathtaking and radiant tenderness, quite different from the more declamatory style of Callas. In adoring Callas we should not forget Tebaldi, for she was more than a sweet voice or the last pretty exponent of *verismo.* The gold of Renata Tebaldi's voice was the stuff of which precious jewels are made, but jewels of a different kind from Callas's — sparkling and pure, more tasteful and less baroque.

The modern spectator or journalist should not be unduly amazed by these tantrums and rivalries. Ever since opera began, ever since the first castrato stepped on stage, there have been quarrels and battles in the music world. In 1727 two queens of London, Francesca Cuzzoni and Faustina Bordoni (known simply as the adored or vilified Faustina or as *la* Faustina) pulled each other's hair on stage during a performance of Buononcini's *Astianatte* in which someone had had the unfortunate idea of casting them together. Three years before the same ladies had caused a riot in the audience which came to blows after Handel's *Ottone.*

There were no fights like this over Callas and Tebaldi in the corridors of La Scala. Tebaldi discreetly retired leaving Callas to reign.

As Elisabeth in Don Carlos, *Callas's final role during the 1953-54 season*

It was Elvira de Hidalgo who told Maria that once she conquered Italy the world would be hers. After her conquest of La Scala, after the first victories of the first season even, Callas was firmly established and appearances all over Italy simply confirmed her glory. The Arena in Verona, the Baths of Caracalla, the magnificent theatre of La Fenice in Venice, the San Carlo in Naples, the *Maggio musicale* in Florence and finally Rome Opera where she sang *I Puritani* in May 1952, were almost yearly ports of call to which she always returned with the same degree of success.

Her return to the role of Gioconda in Verona in 1952 was a tremendous personal triumph. Five years after her first appearance there, earning twelve times more than her fee in 1947, she could look back on her career and see that she had reached a peak which had seemed far away when she first met Meneghini and Serafin. There was more discussion than ever about the intrinsic qualities of her voice, some preferring her as Elvira, others as Gioconda, but no one now questioned her place as leading singer on one of the world's greatest opera stages.

Her trip to Mexico City in 1952 was her last. A singer of the stature of Maria (Meneghini) Callas no longer spent four weeks a year at the Palacio de las Bellas Artes, Mexico City. However it was there that she created the role of Lucia for her Mexican audience. And though tired and aware she was taking on too much, she also rather unwillingly gave the two performances of Gilda in *Rigoletto,* stipulated in her contract, the only time she appeared in this opera on stage. The recording made three years later with Serafin shows her in fine voice with a dark brilliance which is a welcome departure from the popular image of Gilda, a part usually mistakenly left to the lightest of sopranos. But according to the local press her two Mexican performances were not very convincing. Under-rehearsed, with Giuseppe di Stefano in shaky form, Callas did not take to the role, despite some fine moments, and she never returned to it.

Curiously enough those of her keenest supporters who know only her commercial recordings regard the records of *Rigoletto* and *Il Barbiere di Siviglia,* two roles which were not great stage successes, as among her most interesting performances.

Callas left Mexico in early July 1952 and never again returned to a city where she had had one of her first great successes. She was no longer interested in Mexico or Brazil. Now London and the United States were waiting for her.

When Maria Callas made her début at Covent Garden with other artists from La Scala in November 1952 she was already a legendary figure. The press had kept the British public on tenterhooks waiting for her arrival with useless snippets of information about her public and private life.

Her arrival at the Savoy, the dozen bouquets of red roses which awaited her and the retinue of husband and secretary who accompanied her provided a foretaste of the Maria Meneghini-Callas the press was so soon to tear to pieces before our eyes, with her triumphant entrances, her majestic appearances and the slamming of the door behind her when she had nothing more to say. But apart from her image there was her voice. These five performances of *Norma* in London, conducted by Vittorio Gui with Ebe Stignani and another singer making her first appearance as Clotilda, Norma's nurse – Joan Sutherland – probably gave Callas's career the international dimension it needed. Before a well-versed audience eager to be won over Maria Callas gave herself whoeheartedly and triumphed. Vittorio Gui was popular in London and Ebe Stignani was known and admired. But the public fell at the feet of the twenty-nine year old Callas, described by the press as a pagan goddess. Year by year London's love for her grew. A few years later Paris in turn greeted her with the wildest display of ostentation and ceremonial, with the President of the Republic and Rothschilds or ministers in every box, but by then the whole world knew about her, perhaps for the wrong reasons. London's affection was less extravagant and more reliable.

During her first visit in 1952 the London audience also rediscovered an opera which had not been sung in England since Rosa Ponselle. 'She is not a Ponselle,' murmured one critical voice. But she was still a sensation. In the crush bar at Covent Garden, where the fastest barmen in the world impassively poured champagne, a new audience went into ecstasies. On the last evening the Queen was there, with her cousin Lord Harewood, one of the founders of the English opera revival and champion of the cause of English singing, to explain the finest points to her. The Italian National Anthem and 'God Save the Queen' mingled and thereafter nothing could shake the London public's admiration for the singer they discovered that night. Back in her suite at the Savoy, the Thames flowing beneath her window and the lights of the newly built Royal Festival Hall across the river, festoons of lights along the Embankment and London at her feet calling for her again and again, Callas could well feel that she had just won a crucial battle.

In the issues of the magazine *Opera* which describe those evenings the words 'fabulous', 'incredible' and 'superhuman' trip from the writer's pen, conveying something of the impact Callas must have made. When she flew to Milan at the end of November she promised to come back. In fact she was to return to London five times in six different roles, and it was there, after her outstanding performances of *Medea* in 1959, that she discovered Aristotle Onassis and changed the course of her life.

She was also due to appear in January 1953 at the Festival Hall, London, in Verdi's *Requiem*. The veteran Beniamino Gigli was to have sung the mellifluous tenor part with her in this sublime and immensely theatrical piece. But an influenza epidemic in Milan and the quarantine requirements prevented the singers appearing. Like the Toscanini-Callas

Macbeth, the Gigli-Callas *Requiem* was never heard, and Callas never had another opportunity of singing the *Requiem* in London or elsewhere though a performance was planned for Paris in 1959. The story of a voice is also the story of missed opportunities.

But that summer, in June 1953, less than six months after her triumphant *Norma,* Callas was back in London. She sang *Aida* and *Trovatore* in rapid succession. Opposite her in *Aida* the mediocre Radamès was none other than the unfortunate Kurt Baum who had so rudely insulted her in Mexico City three years before. Amneris, the jealous Egyptian princess, was sung by the great Giulietta Simoniato, also making her début at Covent Garden, and who appeared again with Callas in *Trovatore.* This time Callas was a real star, and now, it was said, she began to show her temperament, complaining about the threadbare sets and shabby scenery. But that did not stop her scoring an effortless triumph, especially in *Trovatore.* Once again the English public and critics were bowled over by this singer who also looked beautiful on stage.

The United States still remained, and there were old memories of New York and her unsuccessful début in Chicago to be erased. So when the sirens of the Met began to call Callas listened eagerly. The siren turned out to be Rudolph Bing and though Callas listened, it was Meneghini her husband, impresario and business manager, who heard the proposals and he was not satisfied with the conditions Bing and the New York Met were offering. During these years Meneghini's slogan seems to have been, 'Pay up if you want to hear my wife.' Bing was also said to have been responsible for the unkind description of her as the elephant who wanted to sing Butterfly. But it was probably her husband's grasping attitude which the New York press, especially *Time* magazine, could never forgive when Callas finally made her début at the Met in 1956. And so, since New York had a ceiling of $1,000 an evening for any singer, even Callas, she made her United States début in Chicago.

The key figure in this Chicago season was Lawrence Kelly, a young concert organizer who soon became a personal friend of Callas and one of her keenest supporters when times were bad. Kelly and his associate Carol Fox had decided to revive Chicago's famous Opera, which had enjoyed its heyday earlier in the century, forming the Lyric Theatre of Chicago. The Opera had been associated with the names of Mary Garden, its general director for a year, and Galli-Curci, and it was here that Lotte Lehmann made her American début. Mary Garden the first Mélisande, Amelita Galli-Curci, one of the few outstanding Elviras in *I Puritani* before Callas, and Lotte Lehmann, the finest Sieglinde in *Die Walküre* and the most famous Marschallin in *Der Rosenkavalier* – this prestigious list also had to include Callas. Fox and Kelly were willing to pay the price Meneghini demanded. Lawrence Kelly was not yet thirty but he was ready for anything.

The Chicago season had began brilliantly with *Don Giovanni,* with a cast which included Rossi-Lemeni, Eleanor Steber, Bidu Sayão, one of the Met's most exceptional Mimis, and Leopold Simoneau, the finest

Mozart tenor of his generation. The conductor was Nicola Rescigno who was also to be closely associated with Callas. Kelly and Fox followed this highly successful *Don Giovanni* with *Il Barbiere di Siviglia,* with Simionato, Tito Gobbi and Rossi-Lemeni, and *Bohème* with Rosanna Carteri. Now the moment had come for Callas's American début.

On 1 November 1954 she appeared as Norma. Once again it was a triumph, her first American triumph, and the public received her with wild enthusiasm. *Time* magazine remarked that though she was not perhaps the most beautiful voice in the world (a title reserved for Renata Tebaldi in Italy or Zinka Milanov at the Metropolitan Opera), she was certainly the most exciting singer in the world. The musical press was won over and the popular press and evening papers were enchanted. For them Maria was an infant prodigy returned, a little American from Washington Heights, New York, who had come back home. They competed to print the most touching anecdotes, the most heartfelt praise. They fought to get photographs of her and bombarded her with idiotic questions, but Callas simply replied with a smile. This was the idyllic spring time of a relationship between her and the American press which was soon to turn sour. And not only the press showered praise on her. Her colleagures, the conductor Nicola Rescigno, Lawrence Kelly and all the rest were ecstatic and congratulated one another. Even Meneghini, who did not speak good English and felt rather out of things, congratulated himself on the brilliant publicity tactic of first attacking America obliquely, with Chicago. The New Yorkers were intrigued and eager, but they could wait. Coolly Meneghini waited for the price to go up.

Meanwhile on the stage of the Lyric Theatre, Chicago, Maria continued to sing without counting the cost to herself. After the storm of applause which had greeted *Norma, Traviata* was tempestuously received and a tidal wave broke over *Lucia*. At the last performance there were twenty-two curtain calls and still the audience shouted for more. A rain of flowers fell at her feet and as Callas bent down and picked them up with a smile the crowd went mad. Then there were the good write-ups, the rave reviews. Meneghini and Kelly rubbed their hands. Callas had conquered the American press and was now a singer of world stature.

Norma in America: Chicago, 1954

In this account of the prodigious rise of the young Greek-American soprano to the rank of star one factor which played a decisive part has perhaps been rather neglected: her records.

As early as 1951, just when the long-playing record stopped being a mere curiosity and became the sole means of musical reproduction, Maria Callas made her first record. Her first contract with the Italian firm Cetra was for three complete operas, including *La Gioconda,* conducted by Votto, with Gianni Poggi and Fedora Barbieri, and *La Traviata,* conducted by Santini with Francesco Albanese and Ugo Savarese. These two albums, launched on the world market in early 1953 and 1954 respectively by Cetra's American director, Soria, caused an unprecedented stir even among the blasé public of opera lovers. Imagine the impact on a listener, unprepared for the first sound of Callas's voice in *Traviata* and knowing nothing about her, who suddenly discovers this sound. Twenty-five years after this first *Traviata* no other version, not even Giulini's La Scala recording in 1955, can replace it. One may hate it, yet swoon with pleasure at the same time.

There was one more recording to be made under the Cetra contract, but Maria, now associated completely with La Scala, was eager to take advantage of the agreement reached between EMI and Milan Opera. The plan was to produce a series of major recordings covering much of the Italian opera repertoire, and designed to replace earlier versions made hastily and rather indiscriminately by Cetra when long-playing records first appeared.

Another man now appeared in Callas's life: Walter Legge, artistic director of EMI and husband of Elisabeth Schwarzkopf. With a stroke of genius he brought the trio Callas-di Stefano-Gobbi together as the basis of an almost permanent partnership, usually under Serafin, but sometimes with de Sabata or Karajan. They became a team of unprecedented stature in the history of the long-playing record. Like Callas, Giuseppe di Stefano and Tito Gobbi were among the finest singers of their generation, and hearing the three together is one of the greatest experiences any opera lover could hope for.

Di Stefano was two years older than Callas and had made his début a year before her in 1946. At first he sang light roles, but he gradually extended his repertoire to all the great roles for Italian tenor. His Des Grieux in Massenet's *Manon,* on an old pirate recording made in Mexico City before Callas's day, is outstanding. His Alfredo with Callas and Giulini in the 1955 *Traviata* and his Riccardo in *Un Ballo in Maschera* reveal a marvellous singer with a velvety sound and unique musical intelligence.

Tito Gobbi was the most incredible Italian baritone of the fifties and sixties. Whether as Verdi's Falstaff or Simon Boccanegra, Puccini's Scarpia or Gianni Schicchi, his interpretation of each role was always highly personal and beautifully differentiated, displaying a staggering degree of versatility, backed up by acting talent and incomparable musical sense.

Callas, di Stefano and Gobbi together were a team unrivalled in opera and even more so in the field of long-playing records. The Legge-Callas partnership, usually with di Stefano and Tito Gobbi as well, produced Callas's finest records, the marvellous 'Teatro alla Scala' collection.

July 21 1952, the day on which Callas and Meneghini signed up with EMI and Walter Legge, marked the beginning of an important strand of the history of Italian opera. In 1953 came recordings of *Lucia, Tosca, Cavalleria Rusticana* and *I Puritani,* followed in 1954 by *Norma, Pagliacci* and *Il Turco in Italia.* Callas's records broke on the world of opera lovers like a great wave and were received with consternation or admiration. Some people hated them of course, but those who loved them loved them passionately. Twenty-five years later we know that no other recordings ever replaced the first *Tosca* or *Lucia* or the 1953 *Puritani.* So far as records were concerned 1953 represented the high point of Callas's art.

The singer who opened the incomparable 1954-55 season in Milan on 7 December 1954 was thus an artist at the peak of her vocal and musical development; she was also a new woman.

When Callas sang *Tristan* at the Grattacielo Theatre in Genoa in 1948 the sight of four giants – Max Lorenz, Rossi-Lemeni, Elena Nicolai and Callas herself – taking their bows together on such a small stage was apparently quite a comic spectacle. Even in 1952, when Callas made her début at Covent Garden, Ebe Stignani as Adalgisa and Callas as Norma looked like two massive columns of some huge ancient temple on the enormous stage of the Royal Opera House. But quite apart from Callas's voice, the nobility and beauty of her face, and her gestures and attitudes, made people forget she weighed over 14 stone. Then between 1952 and spring 1954 Maria Callas dropped to 10 stone on 12 April 1954 when she made her début in *Don Carlos* at La Scala. This was the famous slimming cure everyone talked about – 'Have you heard? La Callas wanted to lose weight – but she's lost her voice with it.' Backstage rumours, gossip and wry smiles. But then people realized what she had achieved. Backed up by Meneghini, Callas decided one day to lose weight. She knew herself, what she was worth and she knew that inside her there was an impassioned actress as well as a singer. She wanted to look like her image, her own image of herself and the image we have of her if we close our eyes. She *was* beautiful and she wanted to look beautiful. So she embarked on a rigorous diet – it was even said that she swallowed a tapeworm – and month by month she got thinner. She sang *Gioconda* at 14st 7lb, *Medea* at 12st 2lb, *Lucia,* the great Karajan *Lucia,* at 11st 9lb and *Alceste* at 10st 2lb. This change totally transformed her appearance. In a year and a half Callas became one of the world's most beautiful women. But remembering the round face of the twenty-four year old Turandot, with her secret and sublime beauty, it is clear that Callas's beauty existed beneath the surface before 1954. Those who crossed her path and were so readily captivated by her knew it well. And when she came to sing *La Sonnambula* at La Scala early in 1955 Visconti (the director) remarked that she was as slender as any film star – a ballerina captured at a supremely graceful moment.

Visconti's film-star ballerina: Amina in La Sonnambula

Meanwhile all the swellings and the aches and pains which had been caused by her over-weight – during her unlucky 1951 season in Rio for example – disappeared, at least for several years. All her life Callas had thought of herself as delicate but this was largely because of her weight problem – another reason for her bitterness towards the mother whom she accused of overfeeding her. Now, suddenly, the slim and beautiful Callas rediscovered health, and with it a second youth.

Much has been said of how all this affected her voice. The same old chestnuts. Certainly in 1954 Callas's voice was not the same as at the time of her 1948 *Turandot* or, judging by the records, her 1949 *Nabucco* or the first performances of *Aida* in Mexico City. It was lighter and more transparent, as if Elvira de Hidalgo's predictions were coming true and pure *bel canto* was becoming her true repertoire. This did not stop her singing the dramatic or *verismo* roles in which she always excelled through the subtleties of her timbre. But the mighty outbursts of Abigaille or Turandot were now beyond her, on stage at least. At concerts or on records she continued to sing these roles successfully, but in a different way. Infinitely varied colour and shimmering timbre now replaced simple force.

Her weight loss was probably partly, but only partly, responsible for this development. Another factor was the natural fatigue of her voice after the heavy roles she had sung too soon, as well as physical changes in the voice itself as a result of the repertoire on which she had concentrated for two or three years. To say Callas lost her voice with her pounds ignores what in fact happened to her voice. The real crises came much later.

Her weight was not the only aspect of her physical appearance which changed. When Callas returned from Chicago at the end of November 1954 she had her hair dyed a light blonde which suited her well. And she was now elegantly and stylishily dressed, scarcely recognizable as the dowdy lump poor Hidalgo had tried so hard to convert from sack-like dresses to tailored skirts and well-cut bodices.

If we accept that Callas was made and moulded by people close to her, then one woman who played a decisive role was Madame Biki: one of the most famous dress designers first in Milan, then Europe. Callas met her in the middle of 1952. Biki, who was Puccini's grand-daughter, moved in musical and particularly operatic circles. Designer and singer immediately hit if off, and Biki set herself the task of transforming Callas's appearance. First her stage costumes, for *Macbeth* and *Gioconda* during the 1952-53 La Scala season, then her own everyday outfits were designed by Biki, who became another of the Pygmalions to create this Callas-Galatea.

But dark clouds were already gathering over Callas: the slender, blonde, beautiful, goddess-like Callas found herself the victim of one of those conspiracies which played such a baleful part in her life. Once again rumour of the worst kind created an image of her as an ungrateful daughter who had disowned her family and refused to help them.

Her mother was an impossible woman. Georges Callas was certainly no angel, but he was a retiring and modest man. His wife had had no compunction about leaving him, first for family reasons and because of the children, later because she simply could not stand him. During their quarrels Maria had followed her mother to Greece and had almost forgotten about her father. But on her return to America in 1945 she was overjoyed at finding him again and moved in with him. Father and daughter were reunited again on several occasions. Georges Callas was entranced by his daughter's success and Maria had grown to love this tall, pale gentleman with the old-fashioned diplomat's manner.

After that she could hardly avoid taking sides in her mother's and father's quarrels. She could not forget incidents from her early life and Evangelia's determination to deprive her of her childhood. Evangelia had followed Maria to Mexico in 1950, but in 1951 Maria refused to let her share her glory so closely. The possessive, overbearing Evangelia was furious and there was a bitter quarrel. It was no use pointing to Jackie's career and telling Maria it was her duty as daughter and sister to promote it. Maria couldn't care less.

Hence Evangelia's fury. But so far it was just a private quarrel. Evangelia had to swallow her rage the following year when Georges Callas went to Mexico alone with his famous daughter. She wrote letters which were hardly ever answered and matters rested there, until the beginning of summer 1952 when a crisis broke. To even more insistent letters from her mother Callas now replied by refusing to pay her a pension. Evangelia is still young enough to work, Maria is alleged to have said. She also refused to back Jackie's career as a pianist, though her mother claimed Jackie had quite as much talent as Maria. 'Callas the tigress', at this stage still fairly calm, soon became 'Callas the ungrateful daughter', living in the lap of luxury amid diamonds and mink, while her mother barely had enough to live on. Like Medea the monster who murdered her own children Callas was a vengeful fury – with three hundred pairs of shoes in silk-lined cupboards. Soon the press would get hold of this private quarrel and make it public.

Another storm was gathering over Callas's head – the Bagarozy affair. The impresario and co-director of the disastrous United States Opera Company scheme had signed a contract with Callas on the last day of her stay in New York in 1947; this made him her sole agent in return for ten per cent of her fees. Callas had become rich and famous and Bagarozy, who had done nothing for her for seven years, suddenly woke up. Ten per cent of Maria Meneghini-Callas's fees – from the Arena in Verona in 1947 to her performances in Chicago in 1954 – made $300,000, reckoned Bagarozy. He filed a suit against Callas to recover this $300,000. Nicola Rossi-Lemeni, who had signed the same agreement, had managed to reach a settlement and got away with paying just a few thousand dollars. But Rossi-Lemeni was not Callas. Meneghini had no intention of settling or giving up anything and in any case Bagarozy was out for everything he could get. But the niceties of American law meant that for Bagarozy to institute proceedings the summons had to be served personally on Maria on American soil. Otherwise no action could be taken against her. So for the time being Callas and Meneghini on the one hand and Bagarozy and his lawyers on the other contented themselves with manoeuvres. Bagarozy demanded what he called his rights. Callas claimed that her 'impresario' had done nothing to promote her career as the contract stipulated and that their agreement was therefore null and void. But a law suit loomed, and the press was again delighted to pick over the details.

However, Callas left America at the end of November 1954 with high hopes.

Now the legend began to take its final shape. Callas, queen of La Scala, was about to become the leading singer of her time. Now at last Malibran and Callas really could be mentioned in the same breath. Like the legendary Malibran, whose voice had the same dead notes between the upper and lower registers which alarmed her admirers too, Callas now had the most famous voice in the world. And like Malibran Callas was more than a singer. Malibran died in the flower of youth in 1836 when she was twenty-eight, after being thrown from her horse. Callas, too, was to disappear suddenly from the opera scene. Like Malibran in the years 1820-30 when she conquered Paris, London, Milan, Naples and Rome in quick succession after her triumph in New York, Callas was then at her peak and reigned supreme. But already her position was threatened. Though Callas dominated the international opera scene her progress between the end of 1954 and the end of 1958, between the marvellous 1954-55 season at La Scala and the Paris Opéra concert in December 1958, was a perpetual acrobatic tightrope act with a bottomless precipice on either side. Callas became too famous and she paid the price of her fame. Or rather, it was clear that she would soon have to pay, but she herself could not see it. Gracefully, daringly, she walked straight ahead.

Alceste

Visconti embracing
Maria Callas (opposite)

Chapter Four

PRIMA DONNA ASSOLUTA
(1954-1959)

The direction Maria Callas's theatrical career took at the end of 1954 reflected one of the major trends in opera today. In this respect the Callas of the 1954-55 La Scala season can be described as the first 'modern' singer.

The history of opera over the last fifty years falls into three distinct stages. First came the absolute rule of the singer round whom everything revolved. Adelina Patti, the 'new Grisi,' the Bellinian soprano par excellence; operas were staged just for her and on her everything depended. The great Caruso; Geraldine Farrar – so famous as Carmen that when Hollywood made a silent film of *Carmen* she played the part; Emmy Destinn, the first Salome in Berlin, the first Butterfly in London and Puccini's original *Fancuilla del West;* Rosa Ponselle – all were stars. The choice of conductor depended on them, not to mention the producer, since at that time the producer hardly existed in opera. During the second stage the conductor was all-powerful. The soprano or tenor was no longer automatically the star – instead it was Toscanini, Bruno Walter or Furtwängler. People remember Fritz Busch's *Don Giovanni* at Glyndebourne, Solti's or Karajan's *Ring.* Today we have reached the third stage and in most opera houses which regard themselves as 'modern' the producer reigns supreme. Opera is now regarded as lyric drama in which the action – first what the words say, then their underlying meaning – plays an essential part. The old formula *'prima la musica, dopo la parola'* is more or less reversed.

Seen in this light the season which opened at La Scala in 1954 was Visconti's and Zeffirelli's. Or rather Callas's animated and inspired by Visconti and Zeffirelli. These leading directors from the theatre and cinema realized that they were dealing not just with a supremely successful singer but with an outstanding actress, with whom they could let their imagination go and create the total theatre, the perfect fusion of music and drama, of which they had all dreamed. Callas's personality thus played a decisive role in the development of contemporary opera.

Inspired by her presence and by her potential these men of the theatre turned to opera and revolutionized it. The tenor Jon Vickers, Callas's partner in *Medea,* was the first to put it into words: Callas and Wieland Wagner were the individuals who did most to change the course of opera history in the mid-twentieth century. Wagner's grandson revolutionized production at Bayreuth by paring the works down to their essentials, by his sober direction of the actor-singers, by his use of lighting and the spiritual intensity he gave the drama. Callas, with her singing and acting ability, opened up a new vista for singers.

In 1954 when the legendary Scala season opened the producer's day had not yet come. Instead a preliminary stage had been reached – a great singer and exceptional actress inspired a producer to build a lyric drama around her. The starting point was Visconti's passionate interest in Callas. Luchino Visconti was one of the most admired cinema directors of his generation. The superb views of Verona, the leprous walls of Venice in *Senso,* Alida Valli's search for her lost lover – already in this film there was a powerful sense of atmosphere and place, and it opens as the curtain rises on the stage of La Fenice, during a performance of *Il Trovatore* in the early days of Italian independence.

The coming together of Callas and Visconti, a brilliant stroke of fate, played a large part in the creation of the Callas legend. More than anyone else Visconti was able to make her enter into the heart and soul of her characters, to make them flesh and blood in our eyes.

At the time of the Rome performances of *Il Turco in Italia* in 1951 Visconti had observed and admired Maria Callas's intelligence and dedication to her work. During 1953 when the next season at La Scala was being planned, Visconti suggested producing three works with her – Spontini's *La Vestale,* Bellini's *La Sonnambula* and finally his great *Traviata.*

Giulia in La Vestale: *slim, beautiful and blonde*

Leonard Bernstein, who had worked with Callas on *Medea* the previous year, was to conduct the Bellini; and Guilini *La Traviata.* She was also scheduled to sing *Il Turco in Italia* again during the season, this time in a production by Franco Zeffirelli, then a rising star. A revival of an old production of *Trovatore* with Mario del Monaco was also planned, making five different Callas operas, compared with four the year before. The season of the great conductors (Guilini, Bernstein, Karajan) was followed by a producers' festival involving two of the world's greatest producers, with leading conductors as an added bonus and Callas to crown it all.

Visconti described his work with Callas at length. She was, he said jokingly, a little in love with him. Hence her submissiveness, her eagerness, her burning need to give herself body and soul to her work, to achieve more and more. Callas adored Visconti, she was jealous of him and obeyed him blindly. Gradually, stroke by stroke, Visconti redrew our image of her.

'Maria was marvellous,' Visconti said. 'I had already admired her for many years – from the days when she first did Kundry and Norma in Rome. Every night she sang I secured a certain box and shouted like a mad fanatic when she took her bows. I sent her flowers and finally we met. She was fat, but beautiful on stage. I loved her fatness, which made her so commanding. She was already distinctive then. Her gestures thrilled you. Where did she learn them? On her own. But with *La Vestale* we began systematically to perfect them. We selected some from the great French tragediennes, some from Greek drama, for this was the kind of actress she could be – classic. Today, some famous singers try to imitate what Maria did, but they only make fools of themselves. Maria looked a certain way with her long neck, body, arms, fingers. She can never be copied.'

Luchino Visconti died a year before Callas. It was an irreplaceable loss for many who knew that he too had a certain way of showing how things should be done, that he could never be copied. Callas, dressed in a white sweater and long skirt, her blonde hair gathered in a bun at the back of her neck, would listen to Visconti kneeling at her feet, arms flung wide, long fingers outstretched, showing the greatest tragedienne of her time the attitude of an ancient goddess. Moulded by his hands she became a statue, a living statue of ancient Greece.

All that just for Spontini's Roman *Vestale*. With text by Etienne de Jouy originally written for Boieldieu, it is not a very exciting work. After its première in Paris in 1807 it was first performed at La Scala in 1827 and deals with the love of the vestal virgin Giulia and the Roman general Liciano. To be with her lover Giulia lets the flame she is tending go out and she is condemned to death. A shaft of lightning from the sky rekindles the flame, saving her from death. It is *Norma* without the tenderness and without Bellini's glorious melodies. But it was a role ideally suited to Callas and Visconti quickly saw what he could make of it.

The first night took place on the traditional 7 December in 1954. The opera had not been performed at La Scala since 1929, but the audience were eager to see Callas in it and some remembered Ponselle – Ponselle again – in the part. A recording made that evening shows Callas in fine voice, handling a difficult score with incredible ease – a succession of powerful high notes and elaborate *bel canto* embellishments. She dominates the performance. The rest of the cast is good: Votto conducts well, Stignani as the chief priestess who decides Giulia's fate is superb, and Corelli, another imposing stage presence, is warmly applauded. Only the baritone Enzo Sordello is uninteresting. Callas loathed him from the start and there were to be further repercussions. But Maria herself received an unforgettable ovation. At the end of Act II she was showered with red carnations again. Smiling, dressed in the white veils of a Roman virgin, she stepped forward on to the proscenium which Visconti had had extended into the orchestra stalls for authenticity, and picked up a single carnation. This she offered to a white-haired old gentleman sitting in a stage box. The audience erupted. The old gentleman was Arturo Toscanini, fervent supporter of Tebaldi, who had come to 'have a look' at Callas. Completely won over, he joined in the applause.

After *La Vestale* Callas's second new production that season was *La Sonnambula*. The combination this time of a masterpiece, Bellini's opera, and the joint talents of Callas, Bernstein and Visconti. The superb stage designs were by Pierre Tosi with Maria, dressed like a dancer from a ballet choreographed by Petipa, as Amina the sleepwalker.

The tale of the village girl, Amina, in love with a young farmer and in danger of losing him because, the victim of sleepwalking, she has been found in the bedroom of the lord of the castle has more power to move us than a more ponderous *verismo* drama. Amina is touching, her Elvino, the tenor, enchanting.

Callas in La Vestale

La Sonnambula:
Callas and Bernstein

Listening to the recording conducted by Bernstein one is impressed not only by the excellent performance of Callas and a first rate cast including Cesare Valetti, Eugenia Ratti and Giuseppe Modesti, but also by Bellini's music which reaches great heights. It is easy to understand Callas's passionate and lasting attachment to this composer. The EMI recording made two years after the première with the cast of the 1957 revival under Votto is perhaps less moving than the 1955 pirate records. In the earlier recording Callas sings less sweetly and suavely, but reveals at first hand what she could do for Visconti, an unforgettable experience.

In the few notes just before her first '*Come per me sereno*' her voice suddenly lingers briefly, almost imperceptibly on the word *gioia,* communicating to us the tremor of pure joy which runs through her. The whole of the aria which follows (with the superb phrases '*Amor la colorò del mio diletto*') becomes an ecstatic hymn to joy. In the delicate little runs barely hinted at, like the merest sigh or breath, as Amina comes to the end of her radiant dialogue with the chorus, her perfectly controlled voice trembles with emotion, and brings us to the brink of tears. As Amina sleepwalks across the magic bridge watched by those who love her, and dreams of the man who is already standing before her, her singing is like a slow, rippling wave in '*E l'ultima preghiera*'. Her voice dies away gently, with a dreamy lightness unmatched by any other aria in any other opera. Despite its unevenness – Valetti made a few mistakes in an incredibly difficult part originally written for Rubini – the 1955 recording, like *Traviata* and *Lucia* in the same year which have also been preserved, represents one of the high points of Callas's art.

At last we come to Visconti's *Traviata* – the splendid, controversial, criticized, much praised *Traviata* which was the culmination of what had gone before. *La Vestale* was a role, *La Sonnambula* a dazzling vocal and musical display, but *La Traviata* was a portrait of the opera heroine as a lost, bewildered woman. *La Traviata* according to Visconti is a sublime, painful, fragile and noble account of a fall from grace and redemption. Callas in the role, conducted by Carlo Maria Giulini, portrayed a heart, soul and body surrendering totally to suffering and redemption.

Visconti decided to bring his production forward to the 1890s. He asked Lila de Nobili to design the sets and costumes and on the first night when the curtain went up on the salon of the first act, Giulini's heart missed a beat, he was so overwhelmed by the beauty of what stood before him.

What he saw was a long set with a huge round chandelier, heavy, gloomy hangings, Third Republic chairs and armchairs, the most oppressive and tasteless bourgeois luxury, a suffocating hell to live in. Candelabra, a fireplace, a mirror surrounded by a heavy garland of flowers and lamps, and a Chinese vase, a monstrous piece of chinoiserie straight from the sack of the Summer Palace. Finally Callas herself, in a dress of black faille, with a tight waist and a bustle, black lace round her neck, her hair in a bun low on her neck and arms clad in long gloves which left her hands bare.

Violetta in Visconti's Traviata: *'a noble account of a fall from grace and redemption'*

His heart missed a beat on hearing Callas, the wordly courtesan wasted by consumption, suddenly discovering love with Giuseppe di Stefano, whose voice was then at its peak. Hearing her unforgettable '*Sempre libera,*' then her '*Dite alla giovine,*' her whispered reply to the elder Germont who has asked her to give up his son, her renunciation of love, one cannot help feeling the sudden slight contraction of the heart which is the sign of true emotion. Equally moving a few minutes earlier is her dignity as she tells her visitor that he is importuning her in her own house and should behave like a gentleman.

From this moment on all things were possible in this Callas-Visconti *Traviata.* Violetta falters as Alfredo is about to insult her in Act III and her cry, twice repeated and each time more heart-rending, '*Chi figlia? Morir mi sento!*' expresses the deepest despair. With her inflexion on the second '*pietà*' she seems to hesitate before uttering the word, holding her breath, holding back her words so that nothing more can hurt her. The Violetta who declares '*l'amo,*' that she loves another man who is loathsome to her, is a dying woman. Her voice is toneless, all life gone from it.

Fiorilla in Zeffirelli's Turco: 'one of Rossini's crafty and amusing little heroines'

These heights – a sound, an inflexion, a single word – which Callas, Giulini and Visconti reached were not the result of a miracle or a single genius. The three of them worked unceasingly during the weeks leading up to that first night of 28 May 1955. Callas had never put so much into the creation of a role. She often explained that Violetta, la traviata, is weak and broken. In singing the part Callas, in all her glory, made her voice that of a weak, broken woman.

So much has been said about Callas and Visconti during this year that one is in danger of neglecting a masterpiece of a different kind – Callas's revival of the role of Fiorilla in *Il Turco in Italia,* in Zeffirelli's production. Once again this was a surprisingly modern work which Zeffirelli made even more modern by emphasizing the role of the poet who observes the action and composes a poem about what he sees, a poem which turns out to be *Il Turco* itself. The part was played superbly by Mariano Stabile whose '*Là ci darem la mano*' from *Don Giovanni* is a cherished memory.

Zeffirelli was responsible for everything in this *Turco,* production, costumes and scenery. Even more than in the Rome production, he managed to make Callas, Callas the vestal, funny. As he said, it was no easy task, especially as Callas had recently seen William Wyler's film *Roman Holiday* and decided she wanted to look like Audrey Hepburn which meant losing a few more pounds. By inventing a few dodges – using jewels which everyone knew Maria adored, to lure Fiorilla, or moulding a gold lamé shawl to fit her body which delighted and amused her – Zeffirelli was able to turn the classical tragedienne into one of Rossini's crafty and amusing little heroines who gets men just where she wants them, and combines her escapades with her lovers with the most perfect married bliss. The sets seemed to have sprung from the imagination of Gian-Domenico Tiepolo (the younger). On 15 April 1955, when the curtain fell on a cheerful pink Vesuvius framed by the bright housefronts of a dream port, Callas had another success.

The only partial success of the season was an unfortunate revival of Giordano's *Andrea Chénier*. Besides Visconti's and Zeffirelli's four new productions the fifth role planned for Callas that season was to have been Leonora in *Il Trovatore*, due to open on 5 January 1955 with Mario del Monaco as Manrico, the troubador. But Callas was not the only temperamental star. A few days before the first performance del Monaco declared himself indisposed; too tired for such an exhausting role. There was some argument, then del Monaco himself suggested a solution: he would be willing to sing the Giordano opera instead of the Verdi if asked. Callas agreed without more ado.

Del Monaco's reasons were clear. *Il Trovatore* contains a demanding aria, '*Di quella pira,*' which he was afraid of muffing. The La Scala audience who regarded '*Di quella pira*', like '*Va pensiero*' in *Nabucco,* almost as a national anthem would have been merciless if he had faltered. *Chénier* was not only easier but it was also a tenor's opera, calculated to show off the role of the revolutionary poet destroyed by the revolution.

Composed in 1886, Giordano's opera was only remotely connected with the real life of Chénier, author of such poems as '*La Jeune Tarentine*'. It is a splendid and masterly display of *verismo* in which tenor and soprano are once again thwarted in their love by the baritone, in this case Gérard, a servant who has become a leading revolutionary and bears a grudge against Madeleine, the heroine, for rejecting him. The poet and his beloved end up on the scaffold together with an ecstatic love duet, '*La nostra morte è il trionfo dell'amor,*' a mixture of voluptuous sighs and eloquent sobs. The role of Chénier was created surprisingly enough by a Wagnerian tenor, Giuseppe Borgatti, but all the great names of international *verismo* appeared in it, from Zenatello to Gigli, including Lauri-Volpi.

Though a great singer like Claudia Muzio had sung the part of Madeleine de Coigny, the soprano, it is a nondescript role with only one bravura aria usually sung with all the passion of decadent post-*verismo*. For Callas it was a trap; and was at La Scala a role associated with Tebaldi.

The Milan audience is pitiless. After their enthusiastic reception of *La Vestale* and before the tumultuous applause which greeted Amina and *La Sonnambula* they voiced their disapproval of Callas as Chénier's lover during the performance. She played the part as she saw it, an interpretation echoed by the recent recording with Renata Scotto and Placido Domingo, as an intimate and subtle work. Madeleine de Coigny is a timid, well-brought-up girl who grows into a woman and speaks her views quietly. Traditionally she follows her poet to the scaffold bawling her heart out. Callas's '*La mamma morta*', all the world's grief expressed in three words whispered rather than sung, was greeted with boos and catcalls by an audience ill-prepared for such delicacy and by a claque got up to oppose Callas. Besides, stealing one of Tebaldi's roles was a crime of lèse-majesté.

An excellent set of pirate records has preserved all the delicate nuances

Madeleine de Coigny,
a timid
well-brought-up girl

which coloured the intensity of her singing. Callas rarely sang with such vibrancy, even though it was not a role she had chosen. A photograph shows her standing in front of a Louis XVI armchair, dressed in a maidenly white frock, holding a pale bunch of flowers. Her face is turned slightly to one side and she is gazing intently at the man she comes to love as he sings the couplets of *L'Improvviso* in which he declares himself both poet and politician. In the steady gaze of her black eyes as she looks towards the poet, in the break in her voice as she leads up to '*La mamma morta*', there is depth of emotion which is somehow curiously welcome. Callas, as we listen, seems to be turning into the child she never was before. So though *Andrea Chénier* was a semi-failure at the time, it has since become a poignant memory for those of us who remember it.

While Callas, the unchallengeable queen of La Scala, challenged but for the wrong reasons, continued this unique season in Milan, she also sang in Rome, Berlin and above all Chicago. She recorded *Butterfly, Aida* and *Rigoletto*. She continued to be drawn into petty squabbles and disputes. A lukewarm reception at a performance of *Medea* in Rome was due less to her singing than to the fact that she was 'Callas, Tebaldi's enemy'. There was another row with Boris Christoff over curtain calls; and another more serious quarrel with di Stefano who refused to appear in *Traviata* at La Scala after the first night and had to be replaced by

Giacinto Prandelli. On the third evening her *'Sempre libera'* was booed by a hard core of detractors who never gave up. Finally there was Tebaldi's departure from La Scala. Could she sing Lucia one night, then Violetta, La Gioconda or Medea the next? No cried Callas, 'Then and only then will we be rivals. Otherwise it is like comparing champagne with Coca-cola!' The press was outraged. Their hostility showed that even at the height of her career Callas was a controversial figure, whereas Ponselle had been an idol worshipped by all. But listening to Callas and loving her was an adventure, and what mattered was the Callas-Visconti, Callas-Zeffirelli partnership. Or those two evenings in Berlin with the La Scala company, under Karajan, in the finest performance of *Lucia* ever given – and recorded. Di Stefano, Panerai and Zaccaria with Callas and Karajan, a moment of genius from Donizetti.

Callas's last season in Chicago and her return to Milan at the end of 1955 marked an important turning point. For Callas it was a shattering experience. She was still queen, but there were murmurs of discontent and suddenly she had her first serious collision with the press and public opinion.

At first it was a prima donna's dream. The list of singers due to appear that season – di Stefano, Rossi-Lemeni, Astrid Varni, Tito Gobbi, Ebe Stignani, Ettore Bastianini, Jussi Björling and Rosanna Carteri – was all a prima donna or her public could wish for. Di Stefano, Rossi-Lemeni and Gobbi; Astrid Varnay, one of the finest post-war Wagnerian singers, one of the great Bayreuth Brünnhildes; Björling, the Met tenor – Chicago could do no better. To crown it all the programme included both Callas and Tebaldi, the famous rivals in their well-rehearsed number of mutual hatred and strife.

Lawrence Kelly had done well. But as there was only one dressing-room for the leading ladies before, during and after per-formances, they had to share it on alternate nights, wiping away Butterfly's tears or Bohème's smile in the same looking-glass. Everything was arranged so that they never met, so that nothing marred the peaceful atmosphere of these exciting evenings. To prevent Callas being bothered by lawyers or minions from the impossible Bagarozy, Lawrence Kelly and Carol Fox undertook to protect her from harassment of any kind. Callas, Meneghini, her secretary and little dog felt they could expect a glorious ending to their year.

It was indeed an apotheosis, though one with unpleasant reper-cussions. While Tebaldi sang *Aida* and *La Bohème*, Callas sang *I Puritani, Madama Butterfly* and *Il Trovatore*. October 31 to November 15 was a triumph. Her Elvira in *I Puritani* is well-known, her Leonora in *Trovatore* a universal success – a well-loved interpretation, even if she perhaps did not live the part fully. But she achieved great beauties in it. Singing opposite the magnificent Björling, one of the greatest Manricos of his generation (as the RCA recording with Zinka Milanov and Leonard Warren testifies) she displayed the wealth of her musicianship. 'Her voice,' one American critic remarked of her 1955 performances, 'has a pungent quality, all the richness of the clarinet, warmed and softened by her immense femininity. Her voice floats with effortless grace, swells fill the house, then sinks to the merest thread, tracing decorative arabesques with all the sensuality in the world. She hits you in the pit of the stomach.' A knock-out in the first act, and the American public clamoured for more.

Rudolph Bing, General Manager of the Metropolitan Opera, was well aware of it. Pen in one hand, cheque book in the other, he was there in the wings with a contract in his pocket. His famous maxim as manager of the Met that he would never go over $1,000 an evening was forgotten. Meneghini did not need to haggle any longer, nor Callas to play the reluctant diva. Her New York début had waited long enough. The press wanted to know what the Meneghini-Callas duo had settled for – $2,000? More? Rudolph Bing smiled, bowed and kissed his diva's hand in her dressing-room where he had gone to visit her. 'Come, come, our artists work for the love of art! Or sometimes for a few flowers . . . Let's just say that this time she'll be getting a few more flowers.' Bing acted like a gentleman, with the press and public snapping at his heels. That was on 8 November 1955. Callas was to open the New York season on 26 October 1956 with *Norma*.

Carol Fox and Lawrence Kelly were triumphant, Meneghini rubbed his hands, and Callas was jubilant. A kindly angel giving Chicago its finest hours of operatic glory since the war, she had never been nicer to journalists. When Tebaldi sang Callas, as in Milan, was there, though her rival did not bother to appear when she was on stage but stayed prudently in her hotel or with friends. But Maria listened, applauded and made friendly comments. Elsa Maxwell, the worst gossip that America has ever produced, a great friend of Renata Tebaldi and her champion in the divas' quarrel, could not get over it – could it be that Callas was an angel after all? In due course Maxwell became a temptress. She suddenly fell for Callas, and wanted to be her friend, her lost mother, her accomplice whose gossip columns filled with poisonous concern brought out in Callas everything which was to ruin her when the time came.

Meanwhile the idyll with the press continued. The critic Roger Dettmer spoke for the whole of Chicago when he said he adored her and was under her spell; the whole town, he claimed, was just mad about Callas.

However her performances of *Butterfly* were to end in tragi-comedy, or rather knockabout farce. Till 1955 Callas had never sung *Butterfly* on stage. A few months earlier she had recorded it with Karajan and Callas – the pagan goddess, Medea, Tosca, the noble *bel canto* coloratura – had entered into the skin of the little Japanese geisha, seduced and abandoned by her American sailor, with startling simplicity. Listen to Callas as Cio-Cio-San at the beginning of Act I, whispering like a little girl, soon to be plunged into sadness, *'Nessuno si confessa mai nato in povertà'* (Nobody ever admits he was born poor). It sounds like some childish counting-out rhyme or song, spoken rather than sung, harking back to the age-old emotions of childhood. This is Puccini without lyricism, without any thrilling appeals to the senses. Yet the music sends

Cio-Cio-San in Madama Butterfly, *at the Lyric Opera of Chicago in 1955*

a shiver through us – a shiver of inexpressible tenderness for this child-like Callas. One critic described the love duets from these performances of *Butterfly*, sung by di Stefano and a meek Callas, as man's growing passion in the face of woman's silent ecstasy. When 3,600 people burst into wild applause as the curtain fell on the first night, when the baritone Robert Weede (previously Scarpia in Mexico City in 1951), bowed to her and withdrew, Callas stretched out her arms and alone received the frenzied bravos of all Chicago. She was soon to leave after a scene of extraordinary hysteria – on the part of the press. Callas simply lost her temper.

Kelly and Carol Fox had planned only two performances of *Butterfly* on 11 and 14 November. But after the opera's success they asked Callas to sing the role a third time and she agreed. It was greeted with the same excitement and applause, but then the guard round the prima donna was relaxed. The two impresarios had undertaken not to let Bagarozy's emissaries harass the singer, but now that the season was drawing to a close they probably thought the danger was over. The staff of the Chicago Lyric Opera may even have included some disgruntled admirers of Tebaldi, infuriated by Callas's success. As Cio-Cio-San left the flower-strewn stage to return to her dressing-room the farce began.

Suddenly two men materialised from nowhere and burst into the little room. A photographer ensured their dubious immortality and their names are enshrined in grotesque legend: Marshall Stanley Pringle and Deputy Sheriff Dan Smith, dressed in felt hats, loud ties and gaberdine macs, two American bulls in a china shop of precious Japanese memories. But they were the law and summons in hand they forced their way into the diva's privacy, thrusting a crumpled scrap of paper into her kimono when she refused to receive them.

All hell broke loose. Callas shouted, screamed and raged in Italian and English. The lackeys mouthed their legal formulae at her. And a photographer from Associated Press Wirephoto happened to be there to take the picture which the whole world saw – Callas beside herself with fury in her kimono, hurling abuse at cops, journalists and the people of Chicago indiscriminately. In a shriek rising to high C – according to the press, now out to destroy the woman it had adored – Callas reviled everyone and above all Chicago, its public and the opera administrators who had failed to keep their promise and protect her. Callas suddenly turned into a tigress and remained one for ten years. Formerly she had just been 'temperamental', 'difficult' or 'moody'; now she was a harpy or fury. One glimpse of her face, her overmade-up mouth twisted with hatred as she rounded on the two comic cops of the Chicago police force, Dan and Stan in their soft hats, was enough. One burst of temper, one unflattering photograph, and Maria Meneghini-Callas, the fighting kimono, became the prime target of the world's press.

Maria never again returned to Chicago Opera, except to give concerts some time later. The first door slammed shut on her and angrily she left for Italy where the second farce of the year awaited her.

The press was delighted to be able to make fun of Maria Callas. Now the first stone had been cast there was nothing to stop them following it up. On her return to Milan Callas discovered that a firm of pasta manufacturers, the Pastificio Pantanella Co., had launched a press campaign based on the slogan 'Callas lost weight by eating our spaghetti'. A distinguished doctor, claiming to be the singer's brother-in-law, even supplied a medical certificate to support the claim — 'I, Dr Giovanni Cazzaroti, certify that ...' Callas complained, threatened legal action and finally took action; after that it was a free-for-all to see who could raise most laughs. Someone discovered that Prince Marcantonio Pacelli, the head of the pasta factory, the emperor of spaghetti, was Pope Pius XII's cousin. Callas, the idol of those who believed she had changed the whole course of opera, became the heroine of a ludicrous saga.

The court case dragged on until 1959, but after the Chicago affair the Pantanella pasta episode started an irreversible process. For a section of the public who had never heard her sing, Callas was now both a figure of fun and a bad-tempered shrew. It was a goldmine for the press and one they intended to exploit.

But the general public who gloated over the troubles of their favourite singer as reported in the *News of the World* or *France-Dimanche* were simply a low-comedy counterpart of the solemn conclave of gentlemen who gathered round Callas the singer and urged her to sing again; the Serafins and Meneghinis, killed her too, but at least they had first taught her to be Callas for the benefit of the rest of us.

Callas-Violetta, young and sublimely beautiful

Violetta – Dallas, 1958

*Norma, the virgin
vanquished by love*

Year by year until the end of 1958 Callas's career continued as a confirmation of her unprecedented international stature. But it was also a succession of incidents and later scandals which delighted those who could bring themselves to read about her daily life and her life in the theatre. Her supremacy was sometimes challenged, but in the end Callas always triumphed. Meanwhile scandals were lovingly orchestrated by a press which never for a moment stopped to ask whether the legend it was creating was true.

The 1955-56 season at La Scala was not one of Callas's greatest. She appeared almost forty times but only sang four roles, compared with five during the 1954-55 season. Her voice was not at its best and each series of performances was marred by unpleasant incidents. Callas's star shone over the rest of the world, but at home, as Milan had now become, her glory was still questioned.

Old grudges die hard. Tebaldi's friends and those who disliked Callas's overpowering personality were out to get her. She became easy prey for *paparazzi*. Her opponents tried to find a chink in her armour on every possible occasion – *Norma, Fedora, Traviata* and *Il Barbiere di Siviglia*.

The season opened with *Norma*. Once again the house was in festive mood. The President of the Italian Republic was present and there were red carnations everywhere. Pierre Balmain had designed special decorations for the theatre. The audience waited quietly. Then Callas, the virgin vanquished by love, made her appearance; soon the audience had something else besides the music to talk about. Mario del Monaco, a great tenor with a rather heavy voice and sometimes rough intonation, who often relied on sheer brute force to make the gallery ring, was singing Pollione. He and Callas, whose art was always obedient to the subtlest nuance of music or text, had long been at loggerheads. They had not forgotten their first performances of *Aida* in Mexico City and their quarrel there over the high notes. This time it was the old question of curtain calls which soured the atmosphere. Though an agreement had been reached at the beginning of the season forbidding solo bows, they were jealous and suspicious. One January evening there was a commotion: according to the press Callas struck or kicked her partner. 'As I was preparing to leave the stage', the tenor is reported to have said, 'I felt a hefty kick on my calf. I stopped for a moment in surprise to rub my leg and when I could finally walk again Maria had taken all the applause.' Peace was restored, and del Monaco later said that the incidents had been exaggerated, but the atmosphere was poisoned throughout these performances.

Norma

At the beginning of the season Callas sometimes seemed tired, but still her *Norma* at the beginning of the 1955-56 season was one of her most beautiful. Her '*Casta diva*' had never been more inspired and compared with del Monaco's more brutal singing her masterly tenderness was a delight. Once again we have a pirate recording of a performance which was much enhanced by Margherita Wallman's fine production. The critics however began to wonder whether she was not overdoing it.

The second incident was the episode of the radishes. She sang seventeen performances of *Traviata* that season, all successes, but one evening a bunch of radishes landed on stage at the end of a shower of flowers. There are two versions of what happened next. Either Callas scornfully kicked them into the orchestra pit, or, short-sighted as ever, she mistook them for gladioli or carnations (roses she would have recognized) and clutched them gratefully to her bosom. Maria was furious, Meneghini outraged. The newspapers were delighted at this chance to make fun of the diva and the story went the rounds of Milan, New York, Paris and London.

Yet her *Traviata* was sublime. For the Milanese public to hear her 'Addio del passato', her voice hanging as if by a thread from Giulini's baton, and then see her die in Visconti's production seventeen times in a single season was itself one of the miracles of twentieth-century opera.

Her next role was less successful. Public and critics regarded her *Barbiere di Siviglia* which opened on 16 February 1956 as a bitter disappointment, though some of her keenest aficionados claimed her Rosina had a vivacity rarely found elsewhere in Rossini. The first-rate cast – Callas, Tito Gobbi and the young Peruvian singer Luigi Alva, still one of the finest Almavivas of his time – had to struggle along with little direction in a revival of an undistinguished production.

Maria Callas as Rosina, with Tito Gobbi as Figaro

After the splendours of Visconti or Margherita Wallman this was something of a let-down. Giulini, who conducted the performances, had unhappy memories of them: 'Callas never was Rosina,' he declared. Though Rosina was certainly meant to be crafty, successfully fooling her guardian Bartolo to marry the rather sickly Almaviva with the blessing of Figaro, the barber of quality, Callas went beyond Rossini's intentions. Her pert voice murmuring the couplets of 'Contro un cor' during the music lesson produces a curious reaction: Callas seems to be making fun of herself. She overplayed her part, making Rosina a mocking stage Spaniard. For the first time the damning adjective which springs to mind is, unbelievably, 'vulgar'.

In fact Callas probably misjudged the part. Though she sang the role as it was written, for coloratura mezzo, she transposed its lowest phrases and the result was uneven and rather disconcerting. Also, she played Rosina as a shrew. Poor Bartolo certainly gets his come-uppance, but one dreads to think what will become of the hapless Almaviva once he marries this uncontrollable coquette. Everyone, most of all Callas, seemed to have forgotten that the Rosina of *Il Barbiere* grows into the Countess of *Le Nozze* and that the joyful girl who sings Rossini's 'Una voce' with such sparkle is so soon to make us weep with Mozart's 'Porgi Amor' (God of Love). It is difficult to believe in Maria when she sweetly sings 'Io son docile, ubbediente, dolce. . .'

'She made Rosina a kind of Carmen,' concluded Carlo Maria Giulini his unquestioning admiration for Callas somewhat shaken by these performances. He henceforth abandoned opera almost totally to devote himself to orchestral music. Callas however did not notice anything wrong, or did not want to notice. She enthusiastically took a solo bow after each curtain and even made fun of her fellow artists who – Rossi-Lemeni as Basilio for example – were she thought getting more applause than they deserved. Which meant more applause than she got. In fact Rossi-Lemeni, Gobbi and Alva were perfect, while Callas, apparently taking herself off in this undistinguished *Barbiere,* is rather irritating, uncomfortably close to the image people tried to project of her. Even so the recording of the Giulini performances is vivid proof of her skill as a tightrope artiste. A year later, under Alceo Galliera who did not have Giulini's finesse, she recorded a commercial version. In better voice, less aggressive, less ironic, sweeter-sounding, she is more appealing but perhaps less interesting. With the passage of time the *Barbiere* of Giulini and Callas seems an amusing episode and the audience's cool reception of her performance in 1956 is easily forgotten. In any case the première of *Il Barbiere* in 1816 was itself one of the most scandalous flops in opera history, as Stendhal reported. Rather than Rossini's fertile invention, the Roman public preferred the limp prettiness of Paisiello who had also written an opera based on Beaumarchais' play which had been performed all over Europe for a quarter of a century.

'She made Rosina a kind of Carmen'

The Princess Fedora Romanov

The season ended with *Fedora*. Giordano's opera is no masterpiece, but like *Tosca* it provides scope for a splendid dramatic display. Both *Fedora* and *Tosca* are based on plays by Victorien Sardou and both were performed in the theatre by Sarah Bernhardt. It is a sombre tale of Russian exiles, international spies and beautiful adventuresses, with love thrown in, in a cosmopolitan *fin-de siècle* setting. At the end of the work Princess Fedora Romanov takes poison for bringing misfortune on the man she loves and the tenor, a role created by Caruso, mourns bitterly. In the 1920s New York staged *Fedora* for the blonde and beautiful Maria Jeritza and more recently the exquisite Magda Olivero has given moving performances of it.

The six performances in May and June 1956 were really only a *succès d'estime*. Nicola Benois' outrageous stage designs – elaborate, hot-house, spun-sugar confections topped with swirls and arabesques of whipped cream, fit for the great-nieces of a tsar – emphasized the libretto's melodrama. Fedora's death, with Callas lying on a flight of steps murmuring her improbable last lines, was a unique, supremely theatrical moment. Above all a number of critics noticed that her voice, while perhaps losing some of its power, had freed itself of those jarringly strident tones in her upper register which had so often been criticized. Her voice seemed to be undergoing a transformation, gaining in quality what it lost in power; yet this did not stop the whistles and catcalls of some spectators in the gallery. They may have been right, for *Fedora* like *Il Barbiere* was the wrong opera for Callas. So far as Callas and La Scala were concerned the season now drawing to its close represented a marked decline on the previous one, despite her many appearances on stage. Giordano and Rosina were a far cry from Callas's superb achievements in *La Sonnambula, La Vestale* and *Traviata* as seen through Visconti's eyes.

A few months after the end of the La Scala season New York finally opened its doors to Callas.

Her début at the Metropolitan marked the beginning of a new era in her life. Not that a curtain went up on a new world of singing and acting as it had when the scarlet velvet of La Scala parted to reveal the splendid *Vestale* of 1954. Nor did a curtain fall to mark the end of an epoch in her career, like the painted curtains of the Paris Opéra at the end of 1958 which declared her queen, but queen without a kingdom, a goddess spurned by each of her children in turn. Callas's arrival at the Metropolitan was a beginning of a different kind. Till then, in the hands of Meneghini, whom she could now manipulate at will, Callas had been a singer living in the world of song, her friends singers or musicians. Visconti and Serafin were gods or demi-gods in their way. This was because so far Callas had escaped New York. The eager but calculating kiss which Rudolph Bing in Chicago planted on the fingertips of the prima donna he had just bought for the following autumn was poisoned. It was an entrance ticket – and the only way out was resignation, a headlong drop into the oubliette – to the artificial paradise of jet-set café society, where another race of quarter-gods reigned. Purveyors of scandal, collectors of ships and beautiful women, old masters nailed to the bulkheads of every ship: this was the world Maria Callas was to enter when she arrived in New York at the beginning of autumn 1956, a world suited to those who wish to mix with people whose only concern is success.

Real music plays little part in this world. But as Callas was above all a musician she recorded three more operas for EMI before her arrival. *La Bohème,* which she never sang on stage and in which she is a fragile, touching Mimi, *Il Trovatore* with Karajan and *Un Ballo in Maschera* with Votto. This season Serafin did not appear in the EMI/Callas programme; he was being punished for his treachery, for recording *Traviata* with dreary Antonietta Stella. It was true that under the terms of her old contract with Cetra Callas could not re-record *Traviata,* but that was no excuse.

After this Callas sang *Lucia di Lammermoor* with Karajan in Vienna. It was a triumph, like the year before in Berlin, and she promised to return – although she quarrelled once again with Giuseppe di Stefano, and was angry with Karajan for allowing an encore just before her mad scene so that she had to do double the amount of work before her bravura piece.

The last recording of a Verdi opera that Maria Callas made was as Amelia in Un Ballo in Maschera, *on stage at La Scala in September 1956*

Now she landed in New York. In welcome she found herself on the cover of *Time* magazine; there was also an article several pages long which pretended to give the background on her but was in fact a rehash of all the old rumours with some new ones thrown in. In this unsavoury hotchpotch the fact that Callas might also be the greatest singer in the world was completely lost. The New York public was given to understand that she was a bad-tempered monster who bullied her friends and neglected her mother shamelessly.

This time the charge of ungrateful daughter was launched as a vigorous attack. Reporters from the magazine sought out Evangelia and wheedled her into telling them everything they hoped to hear – the older sister's neglected career, the poor old mother forced to go out to work while her daughter lived a life of caviar washed down with pink champagne, while she glittered with diamonds.

However on 13 October 1956 Maria had only just arrived. Her spectacular entrance with fanfares and full supporting cast was so much in keeping with her legend that one could almost say she brought the outburst of bad taste which followed on herself. At the airport a delegation led by Bing met her with her retinue of two young and exquisitely beautiful secretaries, husband and little dog, and she smiled at photographers and looked more and more like her photographs. After this build-up, and despite Callas's reputation as a singer, it was in Callas the star that people were most interested.

Between 29 October and 19 December Callas sang *Norma* five times, *Tosca* twice and *Lucia* four times in New York. She also sang *Norma* once in Philadelphia and gave a televised concert in New York and a recital at the Italian Embassy in Washington. On each occasion her fellow artists were struck by her professionalism, her painstaking

preparation and her critical and lucid approach to everything – including the shabby sets and appalling stage designs of the United States' leading theatre, which also claimed to be the greatest opera house in the world.

With the conductors Fausto Cleva and Dimitri Mitropoulos she discussed the characters of her heroines bar by bar, the colour of their singing and the tempi she wanted. Mitropoulos admired her discipline. She knew where she was going, what she wanted and why she wanted it, but ultimately everything was designed to enhance the beauty of the drama and the music. The critics were slightly cool about her first performances but melted when she reached *Tosca* and declared *Lucia* a miracle. There were always some provisos and reservations: perhaps Maria Meneghini-Callas did not have the most beautiful voice in the world – New York was after all part of the kingdom of Zinka Milanov (who received more applause as she took her seat on the first night than the prima donna herself) – but she was certainly the most interesting singer of the moment. Her musicianship and technique sent them into raptures.

However, despite this, Callas's stay in America did not have much to do with music. It was a circus, the greatest cocktail party of the season under the greatest big top in the world. At $35 for a seat in the stalls and with a thriving black market in tickets, Callas's appearances attracted all the limelight and a crowd of potential admirers queued day and night round the Met. If the public were enchanted, they were also surprised: del Monaco, with whom Callas had sworn never to appear again, they thought, was to sing Pollione in *Norma* and Callas seemed to accept it as a matter of course. Similarly Kurt Baum, who had once declared in Mexico City that Callas would never set foot in the Met, replaced del Monaco on 22 November. Even the baritone Enzo Sordello with whom she had quarrelled in Milan was there as Lucia's wicked brother.

After the final curtain on the first night of *Norma,* Callas picked up two roses from the armfuls lying at her feet on the stage and, repeating her gesture after *La Sonnambula* in Milan, offered one to Mario del Monaco, the other to Cesare Siepi, the great Mozart and Verdi baritone. Drum rolls and salvos of applause, Marlene Dietrich duly photographed kissing Maria in her dressing-room, and then to dinner at the Ambassador Hotel. Everyone from the Metropolitan was there, and the first representatives of the jet set, eager to make the diva one of them.

From then on Callas's misadventures in America began, a story which could almost be told in newspaper headlines alone.

First the Tebaldi quarrel was resurrected. For the *Time* magazine article the muck-rakers had unearthed a comment about Tebaldi attributed to Callas, 'She has no backbone'. Tebaldi decided to hit back for the first time, with a letter published in the same magazine. Angrily and rather foolishly she explained her attitude to Callas. She claimed to have left La Scala of her own accord because life there had become unbearable and she implied that the real Callas was every bit as bad as her legend. It was not that Tebaldi had no backbone – Callas had no heart. This was fuel to the fire.

Elsa Maxwell, the dreaded columnist, then took up the cudgels for her 'friend' Renata and published a few venomous lines about Maria, ridiculing her voice for a start.

Callas was attacked on all fronts. George London, the leading American baritone on the international scene who had sung Scarpia with her, was brought into the witness box where he was prodded towards saying that Callas had ill-treated him on stage like a real-life Tosca getting her revenge on the chief of police who had played with her life. Instead he chivalrously defended her against all accusations.

It was the Enzo Sordello incident above all which ignited the powder keg. Sordello was the ambitious young baritone who had sung with Callas before in *La Vestale* at La Scala in 1954, and was now singing Enrico in *Lucia di Lammermoor* – Lucia's brother who forces her to marry a man she does not love. In Act II Enrico has a brilliant duet with Lucia, a superb piece of Donizetti, ending in a heroic G. Quite unexpectedly, apparently in defiance of the instructions he had received from the conductor Fausto Cleva, Sordello decided to show off on stage at the Metropolitan and held his high note for as long as his powerful lungs allowed. Callas could not keep up and the orchestra was left floundering. Contented and out of breath Sordello fell silent. He did not sing at the Metropolitan again that season.

The press made a scandal of it. According to them Callas, jealous of her partner's power, demanded his immediate departure – 'him or me'. In bed in her room, they said, Callas refused to leave her hotel until she heard Sordello had been replaced. The next morning Sordello received an urgent note from Rudolph Bing telling him that the Met no longer needed him. Sordello was furious. He was twenty-nine, his career ahead of him. He cursed Maria. But he had to leave.

Callas was not the only one annoyed with Enzo Sordello. Fausto Cleva had expressed dissatisfaction with him as well and the two had exchanged words; officially it was Cleva who insisted on Sordello's departure. But the press would never believe that and so far as they were concerned Callas the tigress had struck again. When leaving New York to return to Italy she met Sordello in the waiting lounge at the airport and in full view of all the accompanying journalists refused to shake hands with him.

In a few days Maria Callas the prima donna became a comic-strip heroine in New York. She had only to appear in her mink hat in an entrance hall, a hotel lounge or a department store and the journalists were there, microphones and cameras at the ready. Maria had to smile and answer politely otherwise she would immediately be accused of the most heinous crimes.

The press were not the only jackals circling round Callas seeking to devour her. Bagarozy had not given up. To avoid an incident like the one which had occurred in Chicago, Callas's lawyers persuaded her to receive the summons from her former impresario officially; she agreed to meet her opponent's legal advisers at her hotel for a few minutes. Now her life was soured by writs, hearings and lawyers' meetings.

The prima donna in her mink hat

But Maria was not yet aware of the diabolical game she was being drawn into. She got some rough treatment and she defended herself, but she did not really mind all that much. She and Meneghini were one of the most famous couples in the world and they reckoned that sometimes they had to pay for their fame. Meanwhile Elsa Maxwell now decided that it was her turn to take a leading role in the drama of Callas's life.

Elsa Maxwell was like a torrent sweeping everything before her. She lived in a fantasy world in which millionaires were mistaken for princes and princes for mummies or demi-gods, where money sanctified everything and the kiss of the gorgon Maxwell choked anyone she trapped.

Even the setting for their meeting was something out of a fairy tale of New York – the Waldorf Astoria where people in evening dress danced till dawn after dining with the President or Salvador Dali. The scene of charity balls and gala buffets, the haunt of affluent matrons. Intoxicated and overwhelmed by New York, Maria meeting Maxwell for the first time surrendered to her. As Maxwell was thrust towards her, smiling, Maria humbled herself: 'I esteem you as a lady of honesty who is devoted to telling the truth.'

For three years Maria and Elsa were great friends, 'best' friends in fact. Super-exclusive charity galas, Princess Grace, emeralds, yachts and mink: this was life as Elsa Maxwell saw it in her magic columns. All Callas had to do was go on singing – the others would do the rest.

At that time Callas, even when tired, still had only to utter a few words from *Tosca* – '*Vissi d'arte, vissi d'amore*' – to carry her admirers beyond the frontiers of love and art. When she left New York to spend Christmas in Italy she was unchallenged queen of the world's greatest opera house, and if people laughed at this empress's new clothes it was because they were angry that could find nothing better to mock.

With Simionato

Callas as Amelia in 1957 superb in ermine and lace

Callas's absolute rule was to last another two years. The horrifying brevity of her career must now be apparent to anyone who knows anything about a singer's life-span. Milan had just declared her the greatest dramatic and coloratura soprano of her day, New York had just acclaimed her for the first time, and already we are talking about the end of an era.

Distressing as it sounds, this was indeed the case. Callas had pressed on regardless while her voice was young, living at fever pitch, and she wore herself out. Her resources ceased to be those of the 1949 Abigaille, or even of the 1957 *Anna Bolena* and the 1958 *Il Pirata,* her last great lyric creations before the final *Poliuto. Anna Bolena* was her greatest triumph in Milan, *Il Pirata* her swan song there. Her return in 1964 was another story – another woman, another voice, but the same artist.

After the excitements of New York, 1957 began well for Callas and Meneghini. At home in Milan, in via Buonarroti, Maria cooked Titta's favourite dishes and the future looked bright. Callas had not opened the Milan season because she was busy elsewhere, but she had engagements planned all over the world – *Anna Bolena* and Gluck's *Ifigenia in Tauris* at La Scala, performances in London, Vienna, Switzerland, Germany and at the Edinburgh Festival and, the ultimate accolade for the return of a prodigal daughter, a concert in Athens in the Theatre of Herod Atticus. She also planned to return to the United States, this time to San Francisco, where she had agreed to appear in September and October. However, two of the trips planned would never take place and another would end in disaster.

In the New Year Callas threw herself whole-heartedly into the new life she had glimpsed during her weeks in New York. It was a triumphant progress. Dressed in scarlet, she gave a concert in Chicago before a select audience who had paid extravagantly for seats as a mark of their solidarity after the Soviet intervention in Hungary. Her programme included arias from *Lucia, La Sonnambula, Il Trovatore* and *Norma.* She also sang the taxing 'In questa reggia' from *Turandot* only a few moments after the airy, transparencies of Dinorah's 'Shadow Song', as if eager to show once again that she was capable of anything.

Though Callas had sworn never to return to Chicago, she had come back: she never hated a tenor, a baritone or a town for more than a year. Her concert there on 15 January 1957 was one of the great moments in the story of her voice – one of the great musical moments. Three days earlier she had danced at the Waldorf Astoria, dressed as an Egyptian princess, where she met Elsa Maxwell, smiled and let herself be photographed at a ball in aid of Hospitalized Veterans. Three days after her concert she flew to Milan for the first night of the *Dialogues des Carmélites* and appeared at La Scala on 26 January wearing a chinchilla coat and diamond-encrusted spectacles: all in honour of François Poulenc. She was photographed more than ever, photographs and rumours all helping to create a new image of Callas. These were her unmusical moments.

Maria, dressed as Hatshepsut (Egypt's first empress) for the Imperial Ball at the Waldorf Astoria in January 1957. She was said to have worn emeralds worth three million dollars

Then came London and there, in spite of the fuss surrounding her arrival, music was what mattered. She was to give two performances of *Norma* at Covent Garden on 2 and 6 February. Before the box office opened 'sold out' signs went up. Compared with the audience of two thousand at each of her performances, the whole of England seemed to be waiting for her. Jacques Bourgeois, a French critic, described how a passport official, hearing he was staying just two days in London to hear Callas sing, enthusiastically declared, 'She's fantastic.' The *Daily Mail* devoted three columns to the suspense of waiting and her arrival. Again there was the rose-filled suite at the Savoy, the eager staff, the horde of journalists and eager photographers. But Callas was already on stage in the theatre where she was to appear a few days later, discussing with the conductor, John Pritchard, the *fioriture* for her arias. Adalgisa was again sung by Ebe Stignani and Clotilda, the nurse, by Marie Collier who later sang *Tosca* after Callas in Zeffirelli's production, wearing the same deep red dress.

Maria gave two performances in London on 2 and 6 February 1957. On the first night a few listeners expressed reservations: was her upper register perhaps a little pinched at times? Had 'Casta diva' ended rather abruptly? Was the whole aria spoiled by excessive vibrato? Her performance was weighed up carefully, but by the second interval the mood in the crush bar was one of unmixed pleasure at rediscovering this opera in its purest form. Callas had perhaps never sung her duets with Stignani, herself outstanding, as beautifully as on these two evenings. Her performances of *Norma* in New York had been uneven, those in Milan the year before beautiful but predictable – as if genius had become routine to her – but in London she was miraculous.

There are no records or secret tapes of these evenings. All we have is hearsay – and the general critical acclaim. According to *The Times*, Callas displayed that art which conceals art. For the first time in almost thirty years Covent Garden had an encore. Stignani and Callas were wildly applauded for their superb duet in Act II, and as they came forward the audience fell silent at last; John Pritchard's baton rose and they repeated their duet. Bellini swept all before him and Callas repeated the triumph of her first London appearance in 1952.

Now the whole world belonged to her. For the time being people seemed to have forgotten about her supposed misdemeanours and rediscovered their love for her.

First came the revival of *La Sonnambula* on 2 March at La Scala. Callas was again marvellous as Amina, a diaphanous dancer like a pale flower tossed this way and that by a hurricane of voices. The part of Teresa, her foster-mother, was sung by a near-beginner – the outstanding mezzo, Fiorenza Cossotto, who was to appear again with her eight years later in Paris and would then take no pity on her failing powers. But in March 1957 Cossotto was still unsure of herself, while Callas was radiant and fully in command. *'Come per me sereno. . .'* On the word *'sereno'* there is a barely perceptible tremor as Amina tries to make herself believe in her happiness. She is a tender-hearted country girl discovering the world; she will be deceived and hurt, though she does not yet know it. Young and trusting she simply expresses the love – fluttering, quivering, ecstatic – welling up within her. A pirate recording of the first night of the revival has preserved it all. Even more than at her previous performances, the La Scala audience and critics found in her all the qualities of the most exquisite coloraturas of the past, and once again, as with her performances of *Norma* in London, Callas showed she belonged to the finest *bel canto* tradition.

The first six months of 1957 were a time of untroubled achievement in Callas's life. After the triumphs of the 1953-54 season when she was expected to perform miraculous tricks at each performance and did so, after the amazing feats of the 1954-55 season when Callas, given new life by Visconti, established herself as an actress whose like had never been known in opera before – after these two seasons there had been a kind of slowing down. There was no sudden crisis, but her vocal fatigue, the price to be paid for her earlier exertions, and the effects of her famous slimming cure were beginning to make themselves felt. Her high notes no longer had the vigour, her low notes the disturbing depth, of the *'Suicidio'* in the 1951 *Gioconda*. Above all a certain unsureness had been apparent throughout her New York season: her *Lucia* was acclaimed, but it came after performances of *Norma* and even *Traviata* which her keenest admirers had frankly to admit were a little disappointing.

All this was forgotten during the early part of 1957. Her voice showed signs of its misuse at the start of her career, but she had regained her equilibrium. Her excessive vibrato had settled down and the famous strident notes in her upper register seemed to be improving. Callas was perfectly in control of the changes her voice was undergoing and she had corrected its most pronounced flaws. The results, which were to be heard in the forthcoming *Anna Bolena,* were the outcome of constant practice combined with incredible professional dedication.

The result was her superb *Anna Bolena* which she sang for the first time on 14 April 1957 when it was recorded. The opera, one of Donizetti's finest, is one of the 'English' operas in which the composer of *Lucia de Lammermoor* gives his own account of Stuart fortunes. Compared with *Elisabetta al Castello di Kenilworth,* a minor rather clumsy work which seems to be based on a topsy-turvy reading of Walter Scott, or with *Roberto Devereux,* another hybrid in which arias and ensembles are strung together without real passion, *Maria Stuarda* and above all *Anna Bolena* are supreme examples of Donizetti's art – the art of using the female voice and all the trills, intricacies and ornaments of *bel canto* to express genuine emotion compared with which other composers like Rossini, even at his dramatic best, seem superficial.

Anna Bolena

113

Once again Visconti and Callas created the opera together. It had not been performed in Milan since 1877, so was new to everyone. It was a revelation. Visconti, helped again by Nicola Benois' designs, gave an interpretation of the unhappy queen, destroyed by her faithless and unscrupulous husband, which goes far beyond the conventions of grand opera. Through the magic of the Callas-Visconti partnership *Anna Bolena* becomes an intensely searching and painful exploration of a woman's suffering. Callas first remembers her former happiness and as a moment from the past transfigures the present her voice quivers with calm, sweet emotion. Then, as she is brought sharply back to the present – '*Son calde ancor le ceneri del mio primo amor*' ('The ashes of my first love are still warm') – she achieves a fleeting lyrical intensity as if possessed by everything she has just dreamed about and must forget. The end of the opera, the scene in which the condemned queen losing her sanity forgets about her execution, about the executioner, the block and the axe which await her, is one of the supreme moments of Callas's art. She uses her full range, moving from one register to another, elaborating the gentle, barely whispered notes until her final unbearable outburst '*Coppa iniqua*' at the unjust and bitter fate she must endure.

For those who saw her then Callas was never more beautiful than as the sorrowful Anna Bolena at La Scala in April 1957. She was even more beautiful than as Violetta in 1955, that other pinnacle of her art.

Callas and Rossi-Lemeni as Anna Bolena and Enrico VIII in Donizetti's opera

Iphigénie en Tauride (Ifigenia in Tauris) which followed immediately after did not arouse the same enthusiasm if only because Gluck's music, however fine, does not have the emotional force of Donizetti at his best. Callas felt this herself and was initially reluctant to take the part, until Visconti persuaded her.

There had been several revivals of this opera in previous years, including one at La Scala in 1937 with Maria Caniglia, Beniamino Gigli's usual partner, and another in Berlin in 1941 with the outstanding Maria Müller (recently rediscovered thanks to the reissue of Furtwängler's *Meistersinger*). More recently in 1952 there had been a production at Aix-en-Provence.

Gluck composed the opera in 1779 for Paris Opéra, five years after *Iphigénie en Aulide,* which described Iphigenia's early misfortunes, following Euripides's tragedy closely. In *Iphigénie en Tauride* Iphigenia achieves glory and discovers Pylade's love: it is a noble but rather dull part. Callas, still in excellent form, declaimed Gluck's music with a certain coldness well suited to the style of the work but which failed to arouse an emotional response in the audience.

Ifigenia

Visconti had decided to transpose the action of Euripides' tragedy to an eighteenth-century 'classical' Greece. The huge set was based on designs and ideas of the Bibienas, the greatest stage-designers of their day. Callas was a memorable, imposing figure, in a handsome, low-necked dress adorned with pearl necklaces. A cloak twenty yards long which flowed behind her, blowing gently in a wind from the wings, a diadem with baroque pearl pendants surmounted by a crescent on her head, her hair tied tightly back, completed her appearance – that of a princess from a fresco in some Venetian villa. Giambattista Tiepolo had shown Iphigenia on the walls of the Villa Valmarana near Vicenza wearing a white sacrificial robe, but Callas's and Visconti's Iphigenia is the girl, now a queen, who greets Antony on the banks of the Nile on the walls of the Palazzo Labia in Venice.

Ifigenia in Tauris was a slight disappointment for those who had been expecting a sequel to *Anna Bolena,* though the overall effect, with Callas's noble protrayal of her role and her astounding beauty, saved it from being boring (unlike the recording made on the evening of 1 June when neither the conductor, Nino Sanzogno, nor Francesco Albanese's Pylade, brought much fire to the performance). Her reputation at La Scala at its peak, she was applauded by an audience which welcomed this heroine from a world quite different from that of Bellini or Donizetti. Three weeks later she was awarded the honorary title of 'Commendatore' of the Italian Republic by the President.

When the curtain fell at the end of Gluck's opera it marked the end of another stage in her career. It was the last time that she worked with Visconti; he refused to direct *Poliuto,* Callas's great venture in 1960, because the Italian government had censored a play he wanted to produce as well as his film *Rocco and his Brothers.* Callas turned down other suggestions he made. Visconti would have liked her to sing *Carmen, Der Rosenkavalier* or *Salome,* but she refused each time. She told him she was not a gypsy, that she did not feel sufficiently Viennese or that she could not see herself dancing half-naked. . . .

In fact Callas only had one more season at La Scala ahead of her, though she would have laughed if anyone had told her this. She had recorded Puccini's *Turandot* and *Manon Lescaut* in the opera house under Tullio Serafin with whom she was now reconciled. In some respects this 1957 *Turandot* was the greatest achievement of Callas's collaboration with Walter Legge, Columbia's artistic director, to whom she was under contract. Opposite Callas as the awe-inspiring princess who is afraid of love and kills for it, Prince Calaf's slave, the touching little Liù, was sung by Elisabeth Schwarzkopf, Walter Legge's wife. This unique recording – with Callas no longer the astonishingly powerful *Turandot* she had been in 1947 or 1948, but capable of dazzling subtlety and versatility in an incomparable '*In questa reggia*' – brought together the greatest Latin soprano and the greatest Germanic soprano of the day. On the one hand a tragic, awe-inspiring goddess, a woman who may be a victim but who also knows how to kill; on the other a woman who is also a mother, a comforting child and a light-hearted forgiving slave. Schwarzkopf was perhaps too regal a singer for the part, a little too much of a sophisticate even. But as faithful Liù she gave a performance of Viennese subtlety, all sighs, veiled tears and gentle restrained sweetness, which sets off Callas's rich and noble interpretation.

Callas's *Manon Lescaut* leaves us with only one cause for regret – that she never sang it on stage, since she would have been superb as Puccini's weak, bewildered heroine.

A few weeks later she also recorded *Medea* at La Scala, the last of her great recordings for the fine EMI-La Scala collection.

Callas had promised to return to Austria; after her fine performance of *Lucia* under Karajan in 1956, she was to have sung *Traviata,* again under Karajan. But Meneghini was watching over her interests and his old motto, 'Pay up if you want to hear my wife', was more than ever his watchword where his wife's engagements were concerned. Rather late in the day discussion of money matters took a disastrous turn: Meneghini announced that Maria's fee had doubled and Vienna refused to pay more than $1,600 per performance. Karajan lost his temper, Callas herself remembered the unfortunate encore of the year before and Meneghini broke off negotiations. Callas never again sang in Vienna.

Elsa Maxwell did not help by coming to Callas's resuce. The day after the première of *Anna Bolena,* for which she had flown over from New York amid a flurry of over-eulogistic news reports, she had annoyed people with a blind attack on all Maria's enemies, acccusing them of plotting against her dear friend. After Vienna she returned to the attack, as clumsy as she was ineffectually well-meaning. She and her over-keen colleagues described a Karajan beside himself with rage, swearing never to see Callas again and tearing up a non-existent contract in front of ten photographers. The curtain had scarcely fallen on *Ifigenia* when Elsa Maxwell struck again, indiscriminately insulting anyone who did not happen to like Callas's voice. This did Callas's reputation no good.

In April Callas returned to Athens for the first time since 1945. The atmosphere there was already thick with scandal and on this occasion her private affairs became political questions. Could a poor country like Greece, the local press wondered, afford to pay so much for an ungrateful daughter who could only be lured back to her homeland by hard cash? Questions were put to the Karamanlis government in Parliament. Callas had become a public institution, a budgetary item discussed by MPs.

But she was coming anyway and her fee was settled, however much political demagogues might rant. The public waited, hoping for a miraculous visitation when Maria Callas appeared in the theatre of Herod Atticus. On the evening all seats were filled beneath a clear August sky – and Callas failed to appear. Because of nervous exhaustion she had cancelled the performance an hour before it was due to start. The next day the newspapers burned with righteous indignation – they had foretold the worst and it had happened. Maria said nothing and it was Meneghini who had to defend her. She herself was bitterly disappointed since she knew she should have appeared, but had just not been up to it.

The cancellation, the result not of temperament but of exhaustion, was a serious moment in Callas's musical life. After the marvellous first six months of 1957, and her magical London and La Scala performances, this was the first sign of stress. Though a few days later on 5 August she had an easy triumph with arias from *Il Trovatore, Lucia, La Forza del Destino* and a breathtaking *Liebestod;* though the whole amphitheatre rose to give her a wild ovation where thirteen years before almost to the day she had had her first triumph in *Fidelio;* though the sordid quarrels, public and private, stirred up by the Greek press, were forgotten – despite all this, the cancellation of the concert was the first sign of her decline.

Maria Callas's health was the only real worry for her true admirers. In Milan her doctor found she was suffering from total exhaustion, and very low blood pressure. She had lost too much weight and her entire physical system seemed to have suffered. She would have to put on some weight and stop travelling so much. He advised her not to go to Edinburgh, where she had promised to appear with the La Scala company in four performances of *La Sonnambula* during the last fortnight of August, but to stay at home in Italy instead. However Meneghini and she decided that a cancellation would look too bad; when the La Scala management were consulted they would not even consider it. Edinburgh was expecting Callas – and La Scala was not La Scala without her – so Edinburgh would get her. Maria did not press the point. There was also a ball in Venice at the end of August which she did not want to miss. She decided to go on singing and travelling. She spent a week resting in via Buonarroti, then set off for Scotland.

The Edinburgh Festival, together with Glyndebourne, is the only British festival of international importance. Opera has always played a large part in it and by 1957 it was already one of the major events of the international opera year. Now Callas was to appear at it in her first *Sonnambula* outside Italy.

Callas was already unwell when she reached Edinburgh. The weather was wet and overcast and she had a sore throat. She made the best of the situation and visited the King's Theatre where she was to appear and which, with its tiny stage and orchestra encroaching on the stalls through lack of space, is far below the standard of the opera house in Glasgow, one of the finest in the world. However Callas expressed satisfaction with everything.

By chance Ghiringhelli, the superintendent of La Scala, had engaged Renata Scotto – a young beginner, just starting to make her name – to join the rest of the company: Nicola Monti, Nicola Zaccaria, Fiorenza Cossotto and the conductor Votto. On 18 August, the day before the first night, Maria felt tired enough to ask to see a doctor and asked Luigi Oldani, the tour organizer, whether Renata Scotto could not sing Amina instead of her. No one would hear of it. Callas had to sing. The audience had paid to hear her and now it was her turn to pay, whatever the price might be.

On the first evening she was obviously not in good voice. Her throat was still troubling her and she was extremely tired. *La Sonnambula* is a very different role from Bellini's other heroines. It depends for effect not on passion or strength but on subtle half-tints, a role which has to be dreamed on stage rather than sung. By some miracle Callas got through it, since she was absolute mistress of her means and technique. But so far as Oldani was concerned she was not at her best on 19 August so she would just have to do better next time. Her doctor insisted she should cancel her remaining performances and Meneghini again suggested to Oldani that Renata Scotto should be brought in, but it was all in vain. So Callas sang and a recording of the performance of 21 August shows she was very good. She then went on to give the remaining two performances agreed in her contract. On 26 August she sang indifferently, but three nights later she was superb, greeted with wild enthusiasm and the public asking for more. Without consulting Maria, Oldani promised a fifth performance on 3 September.

This was the last straw and Callas refused. She had had to summon up all her energy to give the four performances agreed, she was exhausted, the Scottish climate did not suit her and she only had one desire – to get back home to Italy. She had also promised Elsa Maxwell to be at the ball she was giving in Venice. Oldani was furious and talked about Callas's loyalty to La Scala, but it was no use.

More scandal followed – stories about the impossible star who would rather go dancing in Venice than sing in Edinburgh, the fickle prima donna and so on. That her doctors had told her not to sing, that she had not even been sure she could complete the engagements from the start or that the fifth *Sonnambula* was not in her contract was not mentioned. The press were only interested in what corresponded to their image of Callas.

Elsa Maxwell too had the knack of putting her foot in it. The day after the ball, held on 3 September with – as she had promised – the cream of international society there, she told the world that Callas had been there

Maria Callas with Elsa Maxwell at the ball given in Venice

and had refused to sing in Edinburgh in order to be her guest. It is difficult to imagine more damaging publicity than that.

The ball itself was a success. Maria sang the blues, Elsa Maxwell played the piano, the aristocracy of Venice was there and planeloads of Americans. There was also a Greek called Onassis whose boat was anchored nearby. The party lasted eight days, moving between Venetian drawing-rooms, the alcoves of the Café Florian, Harry's Bar with its white cloths, the gaudy awnings of the Lido and Aristotle Onassis's yacht. Maria, who had recovered her health and good humour, was delighted by it all. Aristotle Onassis, biding his time, smiled behind his thick spectacles. He would send over his motor boat with two sailors dressed in white and everyone would go off for a picnic on the Lido or a meal in a fish restaurant on Burano. People sensed that Onassis had chosen Maria, but he knew he had to play a cautious game. Meanwhile Meneghini was blissfully unaware. 'Poor Maria never knew how to pick her men', one of her friends would remark later.

Once again the press had a field day. They pooh-poohed the suggestion that Maria had refused to sing in Scotland because she was ill – she had never looked better, according to them. But despite her smiles Callas had still not recovered from the exhaustion which had floored her during the summer. Edinburgh and San Francisco – the thought filled her with dread. The superintendent of La Scala would not listen to her, he refused to accept her defence that she had fulfilled all her contractual obligations.

Finally Callas made up her mind. As she was not well she decided to send a telegram to Kurt Herbert Adler, the general manager of San Francisco Opera, telling him she would be unable to sing her scheduled performances of *Lucia* and *Macbeth* in the autumn. In fact she only asked for the cancellation of her first appearances in September, and was willing to do *Macbeth* in October as planned. But since Callas, all in the space of a few months, had failed to appear in Vienna, in Athens one evening, in Edinburgh another, then sent a telegram from Venice to the other side of the world asking for changes in an agreed programme, Kurt Herbert Adler interreted Maria's message as a prima donna's whim. In a rage he cancelled everything – both *Lucia* and *Macbeth*. Leyla Gencer, an outstanding Turkish soprano, little known outside Italy where she has made her career, was brought over from Milan in record time to sing *Lucia*. Rysanek, a favourite *Frau ohne schatten* and the most moving Sieglinde since Lotte Lehmann, was to be Lady Macbeth. Callas's case was referred to the AGMA, the American Guild of Musical Artists, for its judgement on her sincerity – a kind of trial.

Opera directors all suddenly seemed to have decided that Callas was a black sheep. They admired her talent and her voice, though they reckoned that her tiredness, her lack of stamina and generally poor form were undesirable features in a soprano of international stature, but they felt they could treat her with the same lack of regard which they believed she showed towards others. Moreover, Callas though claiming to be 'exhausted', had just made a new recording of *Medea,* under Serafin, with Renata Scotto (who had replaced her at short notice in the fifth *Sonnambula* in Edinburgh), in the part of Glauce. Surely if she really was ill she would have stayed at home?

Maria shrugged it all off. If she had refused to do this recording, far from her best, she would have been even more severely criticized. She put the Adler affair out of her mind. San Francisco Opera was closed to her, before she had even been there, but there was still Rome, La Scala, New York and plenty of other theatres. She decided to rest quietly in Milan with her husband and dogs; she played the piano and did some cautious singing practice. She made only one trip abroad, for a concert in Dallas where Lawrence Kelly, the agent and impresario, from Chicago, had decided to settle. Then she returned to Milan for more rest and to prepare for the 1957-58 La Scala season which was to open with a triumph.

La Scala announced that the season would open on 7 December 1957 with Verdi's *Un Ballo in Maschera,* a production by Margherita Wallmann with stage designs by Nicola Benois. The rehearsals were fraught. Ghiringhelli, the superintendent of La Scala, had cold-shouldered Callas ever since her return from Edinburgh and all the La Scala staff treated her with hostility, as if she had deliberately dishonoured the famous theatre in a foreign capital. Then there was di Stefano: over the years the splendid Callas-di Stefano partnership was constantly disrupted by violent upheavals followed by passionate declarations of friendship. Sometimes the tenor accused Callas of spoiling his performance and stealing all the applause, sometimes he was her staunchest defender against her detractors. Between recordings and performances they were always together, the best of friends, but during December 1957 they were at loggerheads. Rumour had it that Callas, tired of waiting for di Stefano who was late for the last rehearsal before the dress rehearsal, had stormed out of the theatre. The next problem was that people suddenly declared that Callas had lost too much weight and that the wonderful costumes created for her would not fit. Her doctor began to wonder whether she could stand the strain of these rehearsals and performances. But when the time came the curtain went up on a great La Scala occasion. It was a miracle.

Un Ballo in Maschera,
with Ettore Bastianini
as Renato, Antonio
Cassinelli as Samuel
and Marco Stefanoni
as Tom

121

Once again Callas looks superb in her photographs, wearing a long dark cloak edged with ermine, an ermine muff and collar spotted with black and a wide-brimmed hat decorated with a long white feather. The opera is set in seventeenth-century Boston where Verdi had to place the action instead of in Sweden as he had originally intended. Callas sang Amelia, wife of Renato, private secretary and friend of Riccardo, governor of Boston against whom conspirators are plotting. Originally Scribe's libretto dealt with the assassination of Gustavus III, King of Sweden, but in Italy before the Risorgimento the murder of a king, even on stage, was unforgivable. Anckarström, the murderer, became Renato and Gustavus Riccardo, but the plot remains the same. Riccardo loves his friend's wife and learns that she loves him too, but resolves to give her up. At this moment Renato, who has learned the truth, decides to join the conspirators and kill the governor. Riccardo dies, pardoning the conspirators, during the masked ball which gives the opera its name.

Callas had already recorded *Un Ballo* in 1956 for EMI under Votto, but the La Scala performances, conducted by Gavazzeni and recorded on a pirate tape, are much more inspired. Di Stefano is at his best and his duet with Callas in Act II is a superbly elegant and lyrical performance. Ettore Bastianini sings the deceived husband, a proud, despairing figure ('*Eri tu*') with admirable melancholy, though his performance is not quite up to the noble sorrow expressed by Tito Gobbi on the EMI recording, or the incredible musicianship and the misplaced but sublime, almost Schubertian, emotion of Fischer-Dieskau when he sang the role under Fritz Busch. Callas's entrance in Act II has terrifying force. Beneath the gallows where she has gone to gather the herbs which will make her forget her love she sings '*Ecco l'orrido campo ove s'accoppia. . .*' expressing both fear and hope that her love will last. In the long love duet which follows, one of Verdi's greatest, comparable with the duet in Act I of *Otello,* she and di Stefano achieve a powerful intensity of emotion. Callas's voice, now light and airy, now displaying its full range and unexpectedly dark in colour, makes her Amelia a woman passionate yet tender. Unlike many of the heroines Callas played, Amelia does not die – but her love brings death and Riccardo is murdered because of her. In her powerful outburst of passion one feels that she bears death within her – another's death – like a wound.

Though *Un Ballo in Maschera* is one of Verdi's masterpieces, and Callas as Amelia a Verdian heroine comparable with Violetta, she sang the role only five times, between 7 and 22 December 1957. The year which began so well and continued so chaotically ended in triumph.

The next year, 1958, was the year in which Callas the supreme soprano suddenly found herself alone – or almost alone.

On 2 January 1958 Maria Callas was due to appear in *Norma* in the gloomy hangar that is Rome's opera house. Gabriele Santini was to conduct, Miriam Pirazzini and Franco Corelli were to be Adalgisa and Pollione. Everything went well at the first rehearsals, with Callas apparently in excellent form, but on 29 December she woke up with a severe sore throat. Meneghini warned the theatre management who expressed pious hopes – there were still four days to go before the first night. Maria stayed in her hotel room, at the Quirinale near the Opera, and felt better the next day. On the evening of 31 December Italian television had arranged to televise a studio concert. Callas, in good form but no more, sang '*Casta diva*'. Then she saw the New Year in, and late that night was seen at a fashionable private club drinking champagne and enjoying herself with Meneghini and his friends. When she woke up the next morning she had lost her voice.

She immediately decided she could not sing the next day. Meneghini told Latini, the Opera superintendent, but like the organizer of the La Scala tour in Edinburgh he would not hear of cancellation. The 2 January performance had been organized long before and President Gronchi would be in the audience; there was no question of Callas not singing.

Maria waited anxiously in her hotel room with Elsa Maxwell, and Meneghini fretted nervously. On the morning of 2 January Callas felt considerably better and resolved to sing as planned.

That evening the curtain went up on one of the greatest scandals in opera history. The audience in evening dress and furs waited for Callas, ready to applaud or to be in at the kill. They had heard she was not at her best and wondered what surprises she had in store. Silence fell as Santini stepped on to the rostrum.

As soon as Callas appeared the audience realized that she was not well. There is a recording of these first scenes which shows the blank indifference of Callas's voracious public, her admirers, impresarios and theatre directors who made her sing even when she was weak and faltering. Her voice was worse than uneven. It was muffled and unbearably strident in the upper register. The audience understood and was silent. There was no expression of hostility, just silence. At the end of the act there was a little applause and a few protests, but both were half-hearted. The audience waited.

Backstage there was commotion. In her dressing-room Maria, in a state of collapse, decided that she could not go on with the performance. The director Latini and his underlings fussed round her, trying to persuade her to continue — President Gronchi was out there getting impatient and even in Italy one does not keep a president waiting. But Maria could not go on. Elsa Maxwell stroked her hands and face, told her she was right and that everyone else was a monster. Meneghini did not know where to turn. The interval went on and on. The audience in their seats and boxes began to get restless, but Gronchi was still in the presidential box, a sign that Callas would return.

In Callas's dressing-room someone had an idea which took the prize for stupidity — why didn't Callas go back on stage and recite the part of *Norma* without singing? Latini tore his hair. No understudy was available. In spite of all the warnings given over the last few days — Callas's temperature and her sore throat — no one had thought of providing a replacement.

Suddenly the audience in the auditorium realized that President Gronchi, tired of waiting, had left. (His chauffeur lost his job over this episode for instead of waiting in his car he had worked out when the performance was likely to end and gone off to the cinema.) Finally the curtain parted and the usual embarrassed official made his announcement to boos from the audience: Maria Meneghini-Callas was unwell and could not continue the performance. The audience, requested to leave, burst into a storm of angry shouts. How could *Norma* end after one act? No one thought of blaming Rome Opera for their lack of foresight in not providing an understudy. Callas, up to her tricks again, was their target. Refusing to sing in the middle of an opera was just another whim; it was also an insult to the President of the Republic.

A furious crowd laid siege to the wings and the stage door out in the street, shouting abuse. Fortunately Maria and her retinue had already returned to their hotel by an underground passage which linked the Opera directly with the Hotel Quirinale. Anxiously they awaited the next morning's papers. 'This second-rate Greek artist,' commented *Il Giorno* the next day, probably summing up fairly accurately the audience's mood, 'Italian by her marriage, Milanese because of the unfounded admiration of certain segments of the La Scala audience, international because of her dangerous friendship with Elsa Maxwell, has for several years followed a path of melodramatic debauchery. This episode shows that Maria Meneghini-Callas is also a disagreeable performer who lacks the most elementary sense of discipline and propriety.' The public — becoming increasingly xenophobe — were after her blood.

The press coverage was vile. The article from *Il Giorno* set the tone. 'No talent, no glory can justify such behaviour,' declared *Il Messagero*, while Maria, now quite ill, stayed in her room. She wrote to President Gronchi who sent her a friendly reply, but tempers continued to rise between Meneghini and the Opera's representatives Latini and Sanpaoli. Both sides demanded compensation — the directors because Callas had not sung on 2 January, Meneghini because he realized that even if his wife recovered her voice she would not be allowed to sing the rest of her performances. A lawyer, Ercole Graziadei, took up the case. On 4

January an over-excited audience heard Anita Cerquetti sing *Norma* with the partner planned for Callas. Like Leyla Gencer who sang instead of Maria in San Francisco, Anita Cerquetti was little known outside Italy where she made her short career, and she made few records. A superb dramatic soprano, a great Abigaille, a dazzling Amelia, she only sang for seven seasons and then retired because of serious illness at the end of 1958, the year she began by standing in for Callas in Rome. It was as if those who took Callas's place, like Marie Collier in the last performances of *Tosca* in 1965, were singled out by destiny and could never escape. But Cerquetti's unforgettable performances in *Un Ballo in Maschera* or Rossini's *Guillaume Tell* are something to be grateful for, and the fact that she replaced Callas cannot be held against her.

Meanwhile the affair had been blown up into far more than a quarrel among opera-lovers and over-zealous officials, and its repercussions reached beyond Rome and Italy. Elsa Maxwell had to be sent packing because her eager defence of her dear friend against 'the barbarians' in the American press was goading the Roman public into noisy demonstrations beneath Callas's window. The superintendent of Rome Opera even asked the local administration to ban Callas from the Opera. If Callas had been too tired to sing on Monday then she shouldn't sing on Tuesday or Wednesday either, it was decided. The performances planned for 9 and 11 January would take place without her. Anita Cerquetti would continue to replace her. Eventually Maria won her action against Rome Opera, but for the time being she had to beat a retreat, in a state of furious indignation. Humiliated and embittered she left Rome.

She was almost as unwelcome in Milan as in Rome. The press was no kinder to her and Ghiringhelli, still in charge of La Scala, did not even bother to go and see her when she got home to via Buonarroti.

She had not yet been heard in Paris, but had promised to sing there at a gala at the end of the year. Amid all this confusion, as the legend turned into a farce in which music played little part, the account of a brief stopover she made in Paris has a hollow ring to it. On 18 January 1958 *France-Soir* described her programme in detail – her arrival at Orly airport at 16.15 hours with orchids to greet her, a short rest at the Hotel Crillon, then dinner at Maxim's, the whirl of departure and take off from Orly at 22.55 hours after a twenty-five minute delay to find lost luggage. Vanity, all is vanity – this is the picture given of Maria Callas. But during her short time in Paris she had time to realize that this was the town she really loved. Her Parisian friends, offering her friendship, fanaticism and warmth, might have the same short-lived enthusiasms as New York and Milan, but they were blind and often deaf and their love would last, come what might. Callas quickly fixed up her December concert at the Opéra and met some of the people who were to play an essential part in her life in later years, including Michel Glotz, French director of EMI. Paris loved Callas at first sight, as much as Callas loved Paris.

But Maria, now recovered from her exhaustion, had already left for the United States for a concert in Chicago. There would also be a hearing before the American Guild of Musical Artists to find out whether she had broken her contract in failing to appear in San Francisco, and another season at the Metropolitan.

Everything went well in Chicago. Callas, finally drawn to Mozart, sang 'Non mi dir' from *Don Giovanni*, and arias from *Macbeth, Nabucco*, Boito's *Mefistofele* and *Il Barbiere di Siviglia*. None of the masterpieces of *bel canto* with which she had made her name, but she was in good voice and the audience was well disposed towards her, clapping for ten minutes before she even began.

Her dispute with San Francisco Opera turned out as well as could be hoped. It was a serious matter, for if found guilty of unprofessional behaviour she would be forbidden to make her planned appearance eight days later at the Met. The AGMA listened to her for over two hours. She had copious medical evidence to support her claims, but Kurt Herbert Adler pursued her vindictively. She explained that her health had made it impossible for her to travel to California at the end of September 1957; that she had wanted to appear for the second series of performances in San Francisco but that Kurt Herbert Adler, like Latini and company in Rome, had issued an ultimatum – all or nothing. Finally the twenty members of the board who made up the jury reached their decision. As Callas had not sung elsewhere while under contract to San Francisco she received a simple reprimand, and she could appear at the Metropolitan on 6 February.

Callas's month in New York was once again something of a tight-rope act, for public and press were even more prepared than for her first visit and were not going to let her get away with anything. They were on the lookout for weaknesses, wrong notes or wobble so that they could reassure themselves that Milanov and their dear Tebaldi (who had had to cut short her previous season because of a bereavement – a reasonable excuse, unlike a sore throat) were the greatest singers in the world. Callas was just a star.

Radio and television joined in with their leading interviewers. Callas was grilled by Ed Murrow and Hy Gardner: who was she? Why was she so temperamental? Where did her voice which came and went come from? What about her mother? Madame Evangelia Callas had continued her campaign against her daughter – what truth was there in these rumours? Callas avoided tricky questions as best she could. She came across as straightforward, easy and well-meaning, as a good wife and above all as what she was – a singer of iron discipline, an indefatigable worker constantly striving for perfection. This was enough for some people, but others were still not satisfied.

On stage however it was a different matter. Her previous season, when her reputation had gone before her, had been disappointing overall; but at the beginning of 1958 when she was regarded as a sour and temperamental monster the public suddenly discovered that she really *was* the greatest singer of her time. This month at the Metropolitan was one of the highlights of Callas's career.

She opened her season with the first of the eleven performances of *Traviata* which she gave during 1958, her last appearances in this role, one of those on which her reputation was founded. After the upheavals of previous months, in early 1958 Callas was in full possession of her means, but her voice had changed perceptibly since as recently as 1954. Surprisingly over the years her timbre was becoming lighter. At the same time, as was apparent at the five La Scala performances of *Un Ballo in Maschera,* the intrinsic beauty of her voice was greater than ever before and through hard work she had eradicated some of her earlier imperfections. Her art allowed her to make the most both of the text and of her own vocal resources, to explore her characters in depth, bringing out the subtlest shades of meaning, depending to some extent on her own mood at the time. Five months later Harold Rosenthal, editor of *Opera* magazine, published a serious and enlightening study of her London performances of *Traviata.* On different evenings her Violetta was more fragile or more determined, more distressed at the end or filled with a desperate eagerness to live. Callas never saw a character as limited to a single interpretation. When *Traviata* opened in New York on 6 February 1958 it was the first of a series of outstanding evenings on which Violetta with all her emotions was revealed as the most human, perhaps the warmest of all characters in Italian opera. Though her 1955 *Traviata* conducted at La Scala by Giulini was an unequalled masterpiece, her New York performances under Fausto Cleva and those in London under Rescigno show Callas at the height of her powers as a dramatic singer. Her *'Dite alla giovine'* is breathtaking: Violetta-Callas gives up happiness and we know only too well that Callas-Violetta will die for it.

Once again the Metropolitan production was old-fashioned and the sets shabby, even though the Met is the only opera in the States to have a proper season, all the rest making do with a few months or even few weeks a year. This production of *Traviata* had been intended for Tebaldi and Callas soon realized that she had not been allowed enough rehearsal time. The baritone who sang Germont père was a musician but nothing more, and Daniele Barioni, the tenor, was frankly second-rate. But from the start Callas sensed that she was embarking on one of the greatest public successes of her career. The audience applauded her entrance and applauded each great moment of Act I, a succession of bravura pieces sung with full voice by the woman who is soon to be broken. As she dreams alone, *'Ah fors'è lui che l'anima'* (For him, perhaps, my longing soul'), the music sinks to a thread of a sigh. New York groaned with pleasure. Then comes her mood of forced joy, the joy that a Violetta Valery, courtesan and party-giver, must show to all comers – *'Sempre libera'* ('Ever free shall I still hasten madly on from pleasure to pleasure'). At the end of Act I New York shouted with delight. By the last act as her voice broke on *'Addio del passato',* New York could only weep.

When the curtain fell there were thirty minutes of curtain calls as Callas returned again and again. This time there was no arguing about whether she should take her bows alone or with her fellow artists, and no question of kicks on the shin to prevent a partner sharing the applause.

Traviata continued with equal success until 5 March. Rudolph Bing and Callas were enjoying a honeymoon period, though Callas did remark that she would have preferred one Alfredo for all her performances. Instead Barioni was succeeded by Campora, Campora by Bergonzi – the great and much-loved Carlo Bergonzi, still the finest exponent of a splendid pre-*verista* tradition of singing – and Bergonzi by Eugenio Fernando. Callas also let her views about the Met's productions be known. After Visconti's *Sonnambula* or *Anna Bolena* New York's old painted back-cloths were hardly appealing but she did not press the point. Bing began to discuss plans with her for the 1959 season which was to include *Traviata* and a new *Macbeth*. They had only to agree on the timetable.

After *Traviata* Callas sang *Tosca* and *Lucia di Lammermoor*. There is little to say about *Lucia*. The performances were not quite up to the standard of her Violetta, though Bergonzi made a fine Edgardo. On the first night Maria had some problems with her high notes, she muffed an E flat and did not do too well in the mad scene. True, these were only minor incidents, but her days as Lucia were clearly drawing to an end.

However the two performances of *Tosca* conducted by Dimitri Mitropoulos bring us nearer to the image of Callas as she was during the last seven years of her career. She will always be associated with Floria Tosca which was one of her first roles, her very first professional role, and the last role she sang on stage, on 5 July 1965 in London. She also recorded it twice for EMI. However, as we know, whenever she got the chance she would say that she did not particularly like *Tosca*. Between 1953 and 1957, when her voice was at its most splendid, she only sang it seven times. From 1958 she returned to *Tosca,* but she brought to it a radically different vocal interpretation: from her New York performances onwards one can say that Callas sang Tosca as a tragic actress, not just as a singer. One has only to listen to her outbursts against Scarpia in Georges Prêtre's 1964 recording – her proud cries, her frail voice pleading, her terrifyingly harsh curses – and compare them with her sublime singing under De Sabata in 1953. These are not two different Floria Toscas, since Callas is still the same Puccini heroine, but two totally different ways of singing the same role. Mitropoulos was too inspired a conductor, too much a man of the theatre – as his recordings of *Elektra* and *Salome* show – not to sense what he could make of Callas's *Tosca*. Callas and Mitropoulos had an almost total triumph, even with a Cavaradossi past his prime in Richard Tucker (only forty-four at the time, though his voice wore out early) and George London as a fine Scarpia, but not as great an actor as Gobbi or Bastianini. When the New York performances finished on 5 March 1958 Bing had made up his mind to repeat the experience the following year, though discussions about the programme dragged on, with Bing suggesting too full a timetable and two quite different roles with too little time between them. Maria hesitated before committing herself.

After every performance, and on the evenings when she was not singing, Maria flung herself wholeheartedly into the life Elsa Maxwell and Co had revealed to her: luxury restaurants and parties, diamonds and smoked salmon. She was seen in stores on Fifth Avenue, in penthouses high above. There had been no tickets for sale at the Metropolitan for weeks, but they were available on the black market at three or four times face value. Elsa Maxwell's columns fed the legend – Callas was a diva and must behave like a diva.

It was a painful sight and Meneghini, whose English was getting worse and worse, sometimes found it difficult to understand what was happening. He loved luxury too, and happily bought rings and necklaces at Tiffany's as he had at Van Cleef or Cartier in Paris or London, but suddenly Callas's career amidst all these men ten or twenty times richer than he, the 'rich industrialist from Verona', seemed to be moving on without him. He still guided her career, but nothing more. Maria smiled at him distantly, but seemed completely taken up with the people around her.

After this taste of fashionable cosmopolitanism it was for the first time hard to return to Italy. This was Callas's seventh consecutive season at La Scala but the atmosphere was embittered. It seemed a long time since the superintendent of La Scala had welcomed the diva into his own box to listen to other singers. Maria had not apologized to the Edinburgh Festival organizers since the *La Sonnambula* fiasco in 1956 and Meneghini and Callas resented Ghiringhelli's insistence that they should. At the time of *Un Ballo in Maschera* in 1956 both sides had kept up a front of strained politeness, but Ghiringhelli could no longer hide his exasperation at what he regarded as mere whims on the part of his former leading singer. Callas herself had finally decided that she could no longer sing in Milan under these conditions – she would not appear in another season there so long as Ghiringhelli was at La Scala. The press was prompt to announce the news.

Maria bore the vexation well. First she sang five performances of *Anna Bolena* in the same production and with the same partners as before, with considerable success. People thought she was even better than before. But no one was at all friendly to her at La Scala any more and anonymous daubers scrawled obscene graffiti on her front door. To escape this hatred and stupidity Callas and Meneghini took refuge in a house they had bought at Sirmione, on the shores of Lake Garda. There she prepared for her last performances at La Scala – *Il Pirata* which she was to sing in May.

This was one of the last moments of peace Meneghini and Callas shared together. They had been together for eleven years, but apart from the sentimental gossip of the press we can have little idea of what their everyday life and happiness were like. A year later they had separated. Maria knew what she owed Meneghini and she respected him. Apparently she took great care of him and he repaid her lavishly – ruby bracelets in return for ravioli. During these last peaceful weeks which brought them together again, Maria and Meneghini had a chance to get their breath back: New York had gone to Callas's head and she saw herself as the queen of a kingdom which we know was never hers. But New York had hurt Meneghini deeply, for he felt Callas slipping away from him. At Sirmione they found each other again. Maria played the piano as in the past, learned the difficult role of Imogene in *Il Pirata* and then played the piano again. She was only thirty-five, but in a year her voice – her real voice – would only be a memory.

Il Pirata is certainly not Bellini's masterpiece. First performed in 1827 with the great Rubini as the pirate, it was always regarded as a tenor's opera. Surprisingly when the opera was first performed in Paris in 1832 at Rubini's side singing Imogene was Wilhelmine Schröder-Devrient – the famous German soprano whose Agathe in *Freischutz* and Leonora in *Fidelio* played such a decisive part in the history of German opera and so impressed young Wagner. She created Senta in *The Flying Dutchman* and Venus in *Tannhäuser,* but her name also survives thanks to her memoirs, probably apocryphal, which are a masterpiece of nineteenth-century pornography! The opera's libretto – the story of Imogene, married against her will to a cruel husband Ernesto who is killed by her lover Gualtiero the pirate who then dies himself on the scaffold – is no better or worse than any other. With no tenor to sing the part of the pirate the opera was almost forgotten for over a century. The only noteworthy revival before 1958 was in Rome in 1935 when Beniamino Gigli sang Gualtiero. As Callas systematically explored Bellini's operas she could not fail to be drawn to *Il Pirata,* the antithesis of the Rossinian style current at the time and thus in some respects Bellini's first really modern work and the first modern opera of the great Italian school of the early nineteenth century.

Callas knew that her five performances of Imogene would be her last appearance at La Scala for some time at least. *Il Pirata* was to be her farewell to a public which had adored and reviled her and she wanted it to be a great moment in her life as a singer. Unfortunately neither the stage designs by Piero Zuffi nor the production by Franco Enriquez (with whom she had worked during her early days at La Scala) were particularly inspired. On the other hand Corelli as Gualtiero and Bastianini as Ernesto were ideal singers for the parts.

The result was slightly disappointing. Callas does not seem to have entered into the character of Imogene as she did so magnificently into other great Bellini soprano roles. Votto's conducting, though he was used to working with Callas, did not receive special praise either. But gradually the magic of her voice took effect – her pure singing brought to life by a dramatic portrayal less highly developed than usual, but still vibrant and tormented. Nothing has survived of the Milan performances, but there is a recording of a concert performance of *Il Pirata* which she gave on 27 January 1959 at the Carnegie Hall. Not in good voice at first, Callas soon rises to the heights of pure *bel canto.* Her mad scene at the end of the opera when she dreams of her lover mounting the steps of the scaffold – *il palco funeste* – is full of haunting power. *Il Pirata* was her last incursion into that other world of opera, the realm of romantic madness where she had lived as Lucia or Lady Macbeth or as heroines, such as Ambroise Thomas's Ophelia, known only from recitals and on records.

The first night on 19 May was another immense success for Callas.

Imogene in Il Pirata

130

Her public, her real public which went on loving her though it was too late, knew they were losing her and called her back again and again. Ghiringhelli who was driving her away sat impassively in his box. At subsequent performances, Callas, inspired, sang even better, though she never reached the dramatic intensity and richness to which she had accustomed us, and the last night, 31 May, was a triumph. During the last scene, as she sang of the scaffold and her lover's death, Callas turned towards Ghiringhelli's box (in Italian *palco* means 'box' as well as 'scaffold') and hurled a cry of vengeance at the *'palco funesto'* in the darkness – the fated scaffold, the box where the superintendent was sitting. The audience understood and went wild. They rose to their feet and shouted for her until they were hoarse. Then Ghiringhelli coldly had the safety curtain lowered.

Security staff quickly cleared the over-enthusiastic audience from the theatre. Callas's time at La Scala was over – she would return only as a bird of passage – but it ended with a great personal success, a Pyrrhic victory perhaps, but still a victory. 'Prima donnas pass on, La Scala remains,' remarked Ghiringhelli. But Ghiringhelli himself passed on and has disappeared from living memory. At La Scala Callas remains.

That midsummer she was always tired and needed another period of rest and reflection. But first she had a third visit to London for a gala, a television show and five performances of *Traviata*. Covent Garden celebrated its centenary on 10 June. With Joan Sutherland, Margot Fonteyn and other stars Callas appeared in front of the Queen and the whole of fashionable London. It all went very well. So did the television show when she appeared with other stars again and sang Rosina's aria from *Il Barbiere di Siviglia* and *'Vissi d'arte'*. Then came her performances of *Traviata*.

At this time Callas was becoming more renowned than any other singer this century. The whole world had heard of her, not just a handful of established opera lovers and admirers of dead singers. But her health was breaking down and her voice sometimes failed her, so that she had to say no or keep silent. Callas was adored, but she was watched closely for the least sign of weakness. This was the woman who was now in London for her last five performances of *Traviata* in England. As in New York she again reached a peak of musical and dramatic emotion. Violetta dying of love has a quality of voice never heard in any other singer. Sick with love, her voice seems drained of blood. After listening to her – there is a tape of the 28 June performance – we can only close the door quietly.

The critics failed to understand what these performances were about. They were expecting a tigress, a fierce Tosca, and instead they and the audience saw a touching *Dame aux camélias* conscious of all the subtleties of her role. Many people thought she was in poor voice when she was really displaying the finest achievements of her art. But the press – even the London press which is less vitriolic and does not regard artistic character assassination as a fine art – was not ready for what Callas's voice had become.

A curtain call: Il Pirata *was Maria's farewell to a public which had both adored and reviled her*

Callas knew it. It was not that people were no longer kind to her – they never had been – but they were keener than ever to spot signs of weakness. For the second time that year she retired to Sirmione. While the gossip continued (people were beginning to talk about the book her mother was going to write which would finally tell the truth, the whole truth and nothing but the truth about her daughter), while Meneghini sent cables all over the world setting out Maria's terms for her return to work, Maria herself played Chopin and Brahms, looking out over one of the most peaceful and civilized landscapes in the world.

In September Callas made two more records for Walter Legge and EMI, but without La Scala with whom she was at loggerheads: *Verdi Heroines (Macbeth, Nabucco)* and *Mad Scenes (Il Pirata, Hamlet, Anna Bolena)*, perhaps two of her finest recorded recitals. The rest had done her good and she was now full of plans.

Three weeks later she left for the United States where she was to finalize the details for her 1959 season at the Met and do a tour round the country, ending with a short season in Dallas where her friend Lawrence Kelly now was.

Callas/Violetta in rehearsal in London

On 7 October 1958 Maria and her suite were in New York. Problems immediately arose with Rudolph Bing and the Met. Everyone agreed in principle on a series of performances in February 1959, but that was as far as it went. Bing promised a new production of *Macbeth* and Callas, who had not sung Verdi's tragedy since her great performances in 1952, was delighted with the prospect. She was also nervous as Lady Macbeth was one of the most taxing roles in her repertoire, one she had long abandoned though she always dreamed of reviving it. Singing a single aria from *Macbeth* at a concert was one thing, singing the whole work on stage was another. It would be a formidable test for a voice which had lost some of its agility and the dark tones which had been its former glory. But *Macbeth* had been one of Callas's most outstanding successes, one of her great dramatic achievements which she longed to repeat on stage at the Metropolitan.

Bing wanted Callas to sing two operas and after hesitating between *Tosca, Lucia* and *Traviata,* they decided on *Traviata.* But no agreement could be reached on dates. Bing wanted her to sing Verdi's two operas alternately, with very little time between. In 1958 Callas was not what she had been in 1949 when she could sing *Die Walkure* one night, *I Puritani* the next. With all her work on the part of Violetta, her *Traviata* had become a masterpiece of economy and art in which the voice was rarely used pure and free for its own sake. *Traviata* is a role which demands a quality of voice the exact opposite of that required by Lady Macbeth. For the moment Callas refused to commit herself on the terms Bing was proposing. She was no longer able to sing with two different voices on evenings so close together, and she felt he should suggest something else. Bing was unwilling and complained that the Met was a massive organization which could not be changed so easily. At best he could substitute *Lucia* for *Traviata,* but that was not much help.

Without reaching any agreement Callas left for her American tour which was to take her first to Birmingham, Atlanta, Montreal and Toronto for concerts, to Dallas where she was to sing *Medea* and *Traviata,* and then on for further concerts in Cleveland, Detroit, Washington, San Francisco and Los Angeles. Throughout the tour, organized by the impresario Sol Hurok, until her arrival in Dallas, she received messages and telegrams from Rudolph Bing asking whether she had reached a decision. Maria could not make up her mind – bullied and hectored, she became nervous and refused to commit herself, putting off the moment when she would have to give a definite reply. From Atlanta to Toronto she sang '*Vieni t'affretta!*' from *Macbeth* as part of a concert programme which surprisingly also included Musetta's waltz from *La Bohème,* but the Metropolitan *Macbeth* was still only a proposal.

It was in Dallas that the situation turned irretrievably sour. The Civic Opera Company's programme was dazzling. They had Callas's performances and Teresa Berganza, who had just begun her splendid career as an international mezzo at Aix, La Scala and Glyndebourne, and whose Dorabella and Cherubino will always be remembered as great Mozartian experiences; she was to sing Rossini's *L'Italiana in Algeri,* a

133

companion piece to *Il Turco in Italia*. Callas was to sing in a new Zeffirelli production of *Traviata*, and her partners in *Medea* were to be Jon Vickers, the greatest Tristan and the finest Otello of the time, and Berganza again. The production (by Alexis Minotis, the great Greek producer and husband of Katina Paxinou who had revolutionized classical tragedy) was intended as an authentic recreation of the world of the doomed sorceress and the court of Corinth. On the evening of the first night, 31 October, she received a congratulatory telegram from Bing, ending in a question – 'But why in Dallas?' Why bother with Dallas when the Met was waiting and Tebaldi had just opened the season there with del Monaco in a restrained *Tosca*?

What followed was sad, as all great opportunities missed are sad. Callas never again sang *Macbeth* at the Met or elsewhere. First she received an ultimatum from Bing, demanding that she accept his dates and conditions. Then on 6 November another telegram arrived: Bing had cancelled Callas's contract since according to him she had broken it, and he immediately issued a press release couched in abusive terms which deserve pride of place in any anthology of bureaucratic warfare. 'I do not propose to enter into a public feud with Madame Callas,' he began, 'since I am well aware that she has considerably greater competence and experience at that kind of thing than I have.' Soon came the inevitable insult: 'Although Madame Callas's artistic qualifications are a matter of violent controversy between her friends and foes, her reputation for projecting her undisputed histrionic talents into her business affairs is a matter of common knowledge.'

Bing showered Callas with sarcasm and sent her packing. This was quite intolerable so far as Callas was concerned and her rage knew no bounds – justifiably, it seemed. All she had asked Bing to do was change the date of two or three performances. 'My voice is not an elevator which goes up and down,' she remarked bitterly. Meneghini was furious too and threatened legal proceedings, but legally Bing was in the right. Callas tried to convince herself that she didn't want to sing any more 'lousy' Traviatas with awful sets anyway, Elsa Maxwell rushed to her side to assure her noisily that the Met wasn't the end of the world and that the rest of the world was waiting for her, but the press as a whole was hard on Callas.

Would she never return to New York? 'Never is a big word which may outlive us all,' remarked Frances Robinson, Rudolph Bing's assistant. 'For the moment,' added Bing, 'so far as the Met and I are concerned, the matter is closed.' Maria had refused to respect the terms of an $18,000 contract and that was that. Too bad, concluded Callas during a party held that evening, after she had learned of her defeat, 'We are on earth to offer art to the public and that is why they love us. Mr Bing was hardly very co-operative.'

But enough of New York. Callas's stay in Dallas which had begun euphorically ended in musical ecstacy. Zeffirelli's *Traviata* was beautiful and the performances on 31 October and 2 November were Callas's last. She never sang the part again. No record or tape seems to have survived

As Medea in Dallas

of Violetta's last death on 2 November 1958 in Dallas.

The Dallas *Medea* has survived however. The recording made on 6 November, the day Bing sacked her, is perhaps her finest version. The cast also included Vickers and Berganza, an impressive Jason and noble Neris, Medea's nurse, and Maria herself was at her best. I personally do not find *Medea* a very moving work, though it fired Callas whenever she sang the part – Cherubini's music is too glacial, too theatrical. But on this occasion her terrible pity, as she gazes at the children she is about to kill, arouses great tenderness. Callas the vengeful sorceress is suddenly touching – fate has picked her out and she cannot escape.

After the last performance on 8 November Maria left Dallas. The rest of her tour had an air of Barnum's Circus about it. In each town people fought to see her and bought tickets at vastly inflated prices, but for all the wrong reasons. Callas had called Rudolph Bing a 'Prussian corporal', so the plutocracy of Cleveland or Detroit, where cars were still doing very nicely thank you, had to see for themselves what this virago was like. Weighed down with diamonds their husbands had bought them, these wives of bankers and motor manufacturers clapped till they tore their silk gloves. What a pretty voice! Everyone knew the aria from *Il Barbiere di Siviglia,* so that was the favourite in the concert which Callas gave in town after town without changing a note. It was very rewarding to sing six operatic arias in the richest cities in the world, as Meneghini well knew – he had agreed fabulous terms with Sol Hurok. When the Met has just slammed the door in your face, $10,000 an evening is a welcome addition to the housekeeping, even if the taxman is merciless.

Cleveland on 15 November, Detroit on the 18th, Washington on the 22nd, San Francisco on the 26th. We can picture Callas appearing in each Public Music House, Masonic Hall, Constitution Hall or Civic Auditorium with a kind of cold methodical rage. She was charming to the press, journalists and guests, to everyone eager to make up for all their earlier insults. A hotel in Miami Beach offered her $5,000 just to sing one or two arias to the old folk wintering in Florida.

Callas could look back to Chicago, Vienna, Rome, San Francisco, La Scala and the Met, all now closed to her. On 26 November she sang in San Francisco – but in the Civic Auditorium, on 29 November in Los Angeles – in the Shrine Auditorium. The dollars were pouring in and Callas was at the height of her career, but London and Paris were really all that was left for her.

On 19 November 1958 Maria Meneghini-Callas sang in Paris for the first time. Paris only knew her by hearsay and was ready to welcome and adore her. 'Only the French have tried to understand me,' ran a headline in *Le Figaro* of 17 December. The French were only too eager to understand her. If America had reviled her and Italy driven her away Paris would adopt her. A flood of articles, newspaper reports and interviews, accounts of Callas's day, what she wore, what she said, what she felt, a blaze of flash bulbs, prepared the Parisian public for the occasion.

On the evening itself there were fanfares and republican guards for

Callas's gala evening, given in aid of the Legion of Honour and attended by the President of the Republic. The occasion was also sponsored by the magazine *Marie-Claire* and indirectly by Luchino Visconti who stopped off between two flights to give detailed instructions about the evening's arrangements, but was too busy to stop for the concert itself. Fashionable young women were to sell programmes weighing over two pounds (with a record inserted into each) and Callas herself donated her fee to the cause. The audience was very select – at the price the tickets were going for, one would hope so – and all seats were sold within forty-eight hours to an exotic mixture of people ranging from Brigitte Bardot to Elisabeth Schwarzkopf, Emile de Rothschild to Charlie Chaplin. The concert was to be followed by a magnificent supper for 450 people.

There could be no question of putting on a complete opera on such an extraordinary occasion before such an audience, though all the ladies would have swooned if *Norma, Lucia* or *Tosca* had been suggested. These would have to be left till next year. This time Callas was simply asked to sing her usual '*Casta diva*', Rosina's aria (which gave the press a chance to remark that 'The dreaded Medea became a smiling Rosina for the Parisians'), two arias from *Traviata* and the whole of Act II of *Tosca* with Albert Lance and Titto Gobbi.

Callas was superb, though a few critics expressed some reservations. But the audience which was ready to applaud anything it heard – *Norma, Lucia* or *Les Cloches de Corneville* (Parisians have improved since then in this respect) – gave Callas a deliriously enthusiastic reception, abandoning themselves to her utterly. Though some of the world's most famous theatres were now closed to her, in a single performance Maria had conquered Paris and Paris had conquered her.

After a year of vicissitudes during which she had known many musical triumphs, but many personal defeats as well, Callas returned home with this tremendous victory behind her. Paris had treated her like a queen, and she was a queen. No singer in the world had ever attained such notoriety. People did not argue about her voice any more – they simply knew it and could recognize it with its subtleties, its accents and its limitations among thousands. Callas the actress defied description. 19 December 1958 was the final recognition of her supremacy. Callas was now the world's greatest wonder.

Paolina: Callas's last new role (opposite)

Chapter Five

THE QUEEN WITHOUT A KINGDOM 1959-1963

In 1959 the Callas machine stopped and her voice fell silent. The queen had no kingdom. At the age of thirty-six the career of Maria Meneghini-Callas, shortly to become plain Maria Callas again, ground to a halt. Then in 1964-65 came her final swan-song, followed by silence. This time there was no going back.

The figures speak for themselves. Counting only complete operas sung on stage, in 1958 Callas sang seven different works twenty-eight times in six different places, including two concert performances of *Il Pirata*. In 1960 she sang only two works seven times in two places. In 1961 she sang *Medea* five times at Epidaurus and La Scala (to which she returned, as we shall see) and nothing else. In 1962 she sang *Medea* twice at La Scala. Finally in 1963 she sang nothing at all. In 1959 she gave fourteen concerts in a year, something she had never done before, but she gave none in 1960, none in 1961, only five in 1962 and six in 1963. Between 1959 and 1963 we witness the almost total extinction of a voice. Callas's real career lasted thirteen years, from 1947 to 1959. Her 'second wind' allowed her a further thirty stage appearances in 1964-65 when she sang *Norma* twelve times and *Tosca* eighteen times – two roles she could have sung equally well standing on her head, alone on the stage.

This gives us a measure of the drama of Callas's career. Birgit Nilsson, the great Wagnerian soprano of the third quarter of this century and her near contemporary, made her début in Stockholm in *Freischutz* in 1946, a year before Callas's début in Verona. She is still singing now, in 1978, thirty-two years later. Monserrat Caballé who was to succeed Callas as the leading soprano of the Italian repertoire has been singing for twenty-two years. Leonie Rysanek, the superb Sieglinde in *Die Walküre* and an outstanding Empress in *Die Frau ohne Schatten* has been singing since 1949. During the last century Adelina Patti sang twenty-five consecutive seasons at Covent Garden. Malibran's career ended after only eleven years, but this was because she died after a riding accident. It is true that Rosa Ponselle, so often compared with Callas, retired after a career of only seventeen years, but in 1935, when she decided to leave the stage, she was still at the height of her powers.

Callas only sang for thirteen trouble-free years; fifteen if one includes her early performances of *Tosca* and *Fidelio* in Athens. Or nineteen if one counts her difficult last years. Yet she was never so famous as when she was only heard intermittently, when she no longer had an opera house to sing in.

Certainly she had and would continue to have problems with her voice, this voice which trembled, soared and broke in turn. Then there was her health – her tiredness, her increasingly severe sinus trouble and her low blood pressure. But it is impossible not to see a connection between the sudden drop in Callas's activities, the decline of her vocal powers from 1959 and the shape her private life took from 1959. The Callas who became an international social figure from August 1959 was not the woman we have watched for twelve years, following in Meneghini's doubtful wake. This was significant. It was as if Callas the star, buffeted by all the emotions, sufferings and stresses of the world, could not also be the uniquely gifted singer who had everything in her favour – voice, stature, music, acting ability, elegance, beauty, and voice again.

From 1959 Callas was no longer the same woman as before. We must follow the new Callas into her private life to understand her better since from now on her life both illuminates her voice and undermines it.

On 21 April 1959 Maria Meneghini-Callas made her entrance at Maxim's in Paris. She was wearing a short, close-fitting evening dress of matt satin, with a black velvet belt, a square low-cut neck and narrow straps. She had a stole of the same material round her shoulders and was wrapped in a chinchilla coat while her only jewellery was a pair of pear-shaped diamond earrings.

On her arm was Giovanni Battista Meneghini: they had come to celebrate their tenth wedding anniversary. Callas smiled and rested her hand on her husband's. For the moment Meneghini and she were still together.

All through dinner she was handed letters, telegrams, bouquets, baskets of red roses. They ate caviar, saddle of lamb 'à la Callas', asparagus tips and an almond birthday cake. At the end of the evening violins played 'Happy Birthday to You' and everyone around clapped. It was the day before – or the day after – that she said of Meneghini, 'I am the voice, he is the soul.'

Once, two or three years after their marriage, Callas had said, 'If he asked me to, I would stop singing.' It is hard to imagine Meneghini in his Veronese accent telling Callas, 'You are not to sing any more!' Harder still to imagine a Callas who had stopped singing in 1951 or 1952 after her triumph, which revived a whole new repertoire, as Elvira in *I Puritani*.

For ten or twelve years they had a solid mutual understanding. They were two divergent forces which converged, their energies fused. Meneghini was always there; he discussed her roles, signed the contracts, cashed the cheques and invested the money.

For twelve years, just as she had previously given in to her mother and Elvira de Hidalgo, Callas let herself be guided by her husband. On 21 April 1959 they blew out the candles on their cake together at Maxim's. On 17 June after the first night of a stupendous *Medea* at Covent Garden they attended a reception at the Dorchester and met Onassis again.

Onassis's life is like a rousing adventure story or cloak and dagger intrigue. A few images and clichés give an idea of the man – his 'meteoric rise', his 'dazzling career,' his marriages, his dark glasses. A man of overweening ambition and colossal fortune, with the shadow of his rival, Niarchos, always looming over him. A string of wives, mistresses and boats. Oil. Old masters, and houses and flats, all over the world. In the gallery of characters from grand opera, Onassis, a rugged, sombre, black and white figure, is more like a tyrannical king, a grasping banker or a stern father than a passionate lover. But when one has everything – pictures and women, yachts and white villas – why not treat oneself to a beautiful prima donna too?

Maria was Greek and she was the greatest singer in the world. Onassis was Greek and he was one of the richest men in the world. Nothing seemed more natural than that he should give a party to celebrate his distinguished fellow-countrywoman's success. They hardly knew each other and had met only by chance, notably in Venice at the time of the famous Maxwell ball, and after the gala evening at Paris Opéra. But when an Onassis honours a diva he invites no fewer than five thousand guests and he hires one of London's three greatest hotels and decorates it entirely with red roses.

Callas, accustomed to the homely luxury of her homely husband, was bowled over. That this man with the muscles of a retired wrestler, this symbol of wealth and the dubious international society to which she had been introduced; that this man, Aristotle Onassis (Ari to his friends) should suddenly be there waiting to receive her as father, probable lover, possible friend and certain protector all in the person of a single seducer with greying temples – all this was like something out of a dream, a scene from opera. Women danced attendance on Onassis, ready to surrender before he even noticed them, ready to give everything for one glance or even more for a single night on his legendary yacht, and Callas the bourgeois wife of a provincial millionaire fell straight into the trap. She fell in love like a little girl.

Onassis was probably flattered to be recognized as what he was, or thought himself to be – the greatest – by almost the most famous woman in the world. He accepted her choice as a tribute, but it unsettled him and he would leave the singer for the former first lady without a shade of remorse. As Callas was suddenly there asking to be taken he would take her – he, the little Greek from Smyrna, who had worked his way up through the backrooms of Buenos Aires, amazed and impressed by his luck.

Did Meneghini realize what was happening straightaway? He trailed along behind his wife. He was her husband and he was there. But when he saw all this luxury, the crowds of people, the minks and chinchillas finer than any he had ever been able to give Maria, he felt curiously afraid. He clung on tight. At the end of the evening Onassis was to be seen hugging Callas and Meneghini, both of whom had strained smiles on their faces. An even more incongruous picture was Callas in her furs as she entered the Dorchester, intertwined with both Meneghini and Onassis. The Italian's hand clasped round the Greek's and Onassis's bowed head seemed to be resting on Callas's breast. The two men and Maria clung together for a few weeks until the strange threesome fell apart and

Aristotle Onassis

Maria, without Meneghini, was left to live up to her new image.

At three o'clock in the morning on 18 June 1959 as they were leaving the Meneghinis were invited by both the Onassises (Onassis was married and his wife Tina was almost as famous as he) to go on a Mediterranean cruise. Maria accepted with alacrity, but Meneghini needed persuading. Tina insisted: they would be couples together and they would call at the Greek islands; Callas and Meneghini mustn't say no; it would be so delightful. . . Maria left dreamily.

Back in their villa at Sirmione in early July the Meneghinis did not get on too well. Titta seemed to have sensed something. How could he fail to? Maria was over-insistent – poor Titta was tired, he needed a nice rest at sea. And guess who else was going on this dream holiday – Winston Churchill and his wife, no less. In the end, Titta let himself be persuaded, since it seemed to matter so much to Maria.

The cruise of the *Christina* has been described a hundred times. A voyage of the damned that no film maker would dare to invent – two couples intent on destroying one another beneath the placid gaze of Churchill, quietly relishing the calm, the sea and the blue sky. They were even joined at one stage by Greta Garbo. The setting was the *Christina,* at 1744 tons a private luxury hotel complete with swimming pool and old masters, El Greco, Impressionists, china, glass and cellar to match. The crew might have been recruited from Ben Hur's gladiators but the chef had learned his craft in the world's finest kitchens. The location was Greece and the islands, and the journey would last for seventeen days.

Maria told any one who cared to listen that she was planning to rest and study a new role, Bellini's *La Straniera.*

Onassis offered and gave freely. He showed off, overwhelming his guests, flaunting his luxury, his money and his pictures with the mock simplicity of the eternal nouveau riche who cannot get over his luck. Maria was fascinated by Ari's smile; accustomed as she was to luxury, she took what was given. Poor Meneghini realized that it was all over. Everyone around him talked French and English and he had to answer as best he could, and he was seasick.

We are not told whether Winston Churchill in his straw hat did any of his usual oil paintings. One evening he asked Callas to sing for him, but she refused, saying she was on holiday and had no accompanist. Churchill let the matter rest. Later Meneghini explained that he had apologized for his wife and that Churchill, a man of the world, had understood perfectly.

The cruise went on. Somewhere off the Pelopennese the film producer Carl Foreman joined them out at sea, and he suddenly had the bright idea of putting Callas in a film. *The Guns of Navarone* was to be made in Greece and England – he offered Maria a part in it opposite Gregory Peck. Onassis thought it an excellent idea and encouraged her. Meneghini pointed out that Callas was in fact a singer. He could only wait for the inevitable, the explosion he knew was bound to come, hiding in his cabin while Onassis did Maria the honours of their country which she scarcely knew – island beaches and deserted coves, bathes in the open sea and walks in white sun-kissed villages. Maria showed off outfits designed for her in Milan and Paris and photographers were there for rendezvous to which they had not been invited.

At Mount Athos, holy place of the Orthodox Church, where dazzling rock drops sheer into the sea, they were welcomed by the patriarch of Constantinople who was overcome by the occasion. His words were almost a blessing, linking 'the greatest singer in the world' and 'the new Ulysses'. Onassis glowed. There was no place for Meneghini now.

Meanwhile the press played the part of the Greek chorus, a chorus which had not yet grasped what was going on, giving a day by day account of the cruise. Until the moment, at anchor off Istanbul in scorching summer weather, when Callas finally joined her husband in his cabin. Onassis waited with his other guests who all behaved as if nothing were going on. Meanwhile in the cabin prayers and entreaties fell on deaf ears and finally Maria emerged. It was all over. It was 8 August and their cruise was at an end.

The next day Maria returned to Milan with Meneghini. Neither of them had anything to say to each other or to the press. Journalists who met them at the airport enquired why the cruise had continued without them after Istanbul. Maria clutched her Bellini score. She had done little work and she had nothing else to declare. Though she could not explain it, she knew that she now loved another man.

In Sirmione where they took refuge, exhausted, for a few days Callas and Meneghini still scarcely spoke to one another. Giovanni Battista was a broken man. He had reached the stage where nothing more could happen. On 17 August when Onassis arrived – unexpectedly? – beside Lake Garda Battista hardly bothered to argue or explain. Onassis had power, money, glory and Callas too. An hour later Meneghini was alone in his great empty house, staring at the lake. Callas and Onassis had left by car for Milan and no one yet knew what was happening.

Callas had to go on working in this psychological state. She began preparing for a new recording of *Gioconda* with Serafin, her other father figure, but she told him nothing. Her fellow-artists, Fiorenza Cossotto and Pier Miranda Ferraro guessed nothing, though Cossotto was on the look-out for chinks in her armour. (She was still in a supporting role and her triumph came six years later in Paris.) On 2 September everyone attended a tough rehearsal at La Scala and on 3 September, the whole of Milan, Italy and the world learned the shattering news which fell like a thunderbolt from the sky. Callas and Onassis had gone to the Rendez-vous, one of Milan's fashionable clubs, together. There they had danced cheek to cheek and at three in the morning they had returned to the hotel Principe e Savoia together. The news was reported as soon as it occurred.

Meanwhile the machine had been set in motion to turn what was basically a banal escapade into an historical event to bring tears to the prying eyes of *News of the World* and *Samedi-Soir* readers for three weeks – and ultimately for several years in all – along with the shady dealings of a tin king and a royal princess's broken engagement. There were day-by-day accounts of all the husband's, wife's and lover's movements. The husband waited in his villa at Sirmione and travelled to Milan and back. The wife somehow made the recording that was expected of her. The lover signed cheques and flitted between Milan, Venice, his yacht and Greece. So far as the papers were concerned it was marvellous entertainment for a hundred million people taking their late summer holidays at the seaside. Meneghini told them, 'I have nothing more to hope for.' Callas claimed, 'Onassis is just a friend.' In Harry's Bar Onassis ambiguously boasted, 'Maria is a very great singer. Of course I would be flattered if a woman with the class of Maria Callas fell in love with someone like me. Who wouldn't?' The journalists pressed for further details. Finally on 8 September Maria issued a press statement. 'I confirm that my separation from my husband is complete and final. It has been in the air for some time, and the fact that it has actually happened during the cruise on the *Christina* is purely coincidental. . . I am now my own manager. . . Only a profound friendship that dates back for some time exists between me and Mr Onassis. I also have business connections with him; I have received offers from the Monte Carlo Opera and there is also a prospect for a film.'

Monte Carlo Opera or a box-office film when she had been the star of La Scala for seven seasons! She had scarcely looked at the Bellini score she took on board the *Christina* with her, and only four months before she had been blowing out the candles on her cake at Maxim's. While the speculation continued Maria rejoined Onassis on his yacht. On 17 September she honoured a long-standing engagement at Bilbao, but only after almost missing her plane. She had overslept, after getting to bed late. 'Out on the town', commented the Spanish, bitterly offended that *La divina,* whom they had never heard before, should breeze in between two flights, give an indifferent performance of four arias for them, and then rush off. There were twenty-five plainclothes policemen on duty in the auditorium of the Coliseo Albia in case of trouble.

In London too she cancelled a television broadcast (though to be fair her favourite conductor Rescigno was ill) and in Berlin she only sang one of the two concerts originally planned, though there was a rare chance to hear her singing the aria '*Non mi dir*' from *Don Giovanni* again. Finally in Kansas City, to the indignation of the locals, she failed to appear at a reception held in her honour. There was even a bomb scare at the Midland Theatre where she appeared, a hoax but symbolic of the general mood. At New York's La Guardia airport she flew into one of those splendid rages for which she had once been so famous, after getting her feet tangled in the wires of the microphones which she refused to speak into. She was beginning to look uncomfortably like the legend people had made of her. She was even off-hand with journalists, the worst crime so far as American journalists are concerned.

Her 'friends' began to keep their distance. Elsa Maxwell, her 'faithful' companion and also Tina Onassis's 'friend', took the side of the wronged wife. Callas was singing less than before and Tina was Niarchos's sister-in-law. If anyone asked her what she thought of Callas, Maxwell determined not to compromise herself in any way, would simply reply that she was a great singer. Once Elsa had dropped Callas the rest of the press set about raking up anything they could. It is no longer clear whether Callas really did miss that reception in Kansas City or not.

She still had to make the final break with Meneghini who after an initial burst of bitterness had become outrageously, almost theatrically, noble and generous. Wiping away a tear he would reminisce: 'I remember at our anniversary dinner at Maxim's last spring a reporter asked Maria whether it was true that she was expecting a baby. I remember her reply so well. She said, "I wish it were true. But alas it is not". After that we kissed. . . Yes, our marriage was marvellous. We were happy right up till the end.' But when the court hearing to settle their financial affairs was fixed Meneghini made the first move. 'Together' they had amassed a large fortune of over a million dollars and Meneghini had kept careful account of it. But, declared the wronged husband, his feet firmly on the ground, 'I do not intend to reward her for what she did for me.'

An agreement was finally reached on 14 November. The hearing was held at Brescia and the hundreds of curious onlookers gathered to catch a glimpse of the diva jostled her as she forced a way through the crowd, causing a slight bruise on one leg. Maria kept the house in Milan and most of her jewellery, while Meneghini was to keep Sirmione and their other properties; they divided their works of art, furniture and other belongings between them. Even as the injured party, Meneghini did pretty well, though he later went back on the agreement which did not satisfy him. Meanwhile Maria left for Dallas where she opened a new season with two performances of *Medea*. Then she rejoined Onassis, his yacht and her new life.

Onassis sorted out his matrimonial affairs too. Everything turned out for the best after an uncomfortable moment when scandal loomed. Onassis caused quite a stir by offering his wife the famous 'Hope' diamond which allegedly brought bad luck. It was also rumoured in circles close to Ari that he was planning to expose his wife's liaison with a twenty-eight-year-old Venezuelan known simply as the 'emerald king'. But Onassis kept a gentlemanly silence and Tina cited another woman as co-respondent instead of Callas; finally their dirty linen was washed in private. Now each was free to go his or her own way. The question was, would they or would they not get married?

Callas in holiday mood. Taken in Holland, this was one of her favourite snapshots.

In this whirl of court hearings and meetings, balls, parties and time lost in cruises to the end of futility Maria Callas's voice could hardly have been other than it was. From 1959, when she had a fresh triumph in London in *Medea,* until 1963 when she did not sing once on stage, she was engaged in a series of heart-breaking struggles with her declining health and with the voice which at times failed her, making her produce unpleasant sounds which she masked as best she could with her wealth of talent. She did not always deceive her audience but she usually beguiled and always delighted them.

At first everything still seemed possible. In January 1959 Callas was back in New York on business – the Bagarozy affair again – and to give a concert performance of *Il Pirata.* A recording has survived. Her fellow-artists were Pier Miranda Ferraro who took the part Corelli had sung at La Scala, and the baritone Constantino Ego as Imogene's husband; neither of them are very exciting on the recording which survives, but Callas herself, in perfect voice and looking superb dressed in white in the darkness of Carnegie Hall, had a tremendous personal success. Twenty years later her entrance *'Lo sognai ferito'* – 'I dreamed he was wounded', is a model of Bellinian singing and perfect musicianship, light yet gradually swelling to fill the immense auditorium. Though she was rather tired by the end of the evening, her mad scene is far richer and more dramatic than the commercial recording of the aria which she had made a few months earlier.

On 27 January 1959 Callas was still the queen who had conquered Paris, one of poor President Coty's finest memories, and she stayed on form throughout the spring. She had plenty of time to spare as the weeks she had put aside for her Metropolitan performances were now free, so she visited London earlier than planned; here she met Joan Sutherland who after her early Clotilda in the 1952 *Norma* was following the trail Callas had blazed with performances of Bellini and Donizetti. Callas admired the new production of *Lucia* which Zeffirelli had conceived for Sutherland and then went on to make her own second recording of *Lucia.*

A comparison between the 1953 and 1959 recording of *Lucia di Lammermoor* shows the changes in Callas's voice far more clearly than the two *Tosca* recordings. In *Lucia* she drew less on her extraordinary dramatic potential, and as a result the two interpretations are comparable in style. However one can hear the marked deterioration in her means at the same time as her supreme mastery of her effects and her infinitely subtle colouring of the most delicate nuances of Donizetti's music: Unfortunately neither Ferruccio Tagliavini, replacing di Stefano (and well past his prime despite his superb technique), nor his fellow-artists under Serafin in 1959 can be compared with the original cast which had made one of the supreme masterpieces of lyric recording six years before.

Callas continued to make plans, still full of confidence about her voice. She was to sing *Medea* in Paris in mid-December, and Dallas and Covent Garden were planning an exchange of operas for her. Zeffirelli's London *Lucia,* originally designed for Sutherland, was to be performed in Dallas and Dallas's Greek *Medea* in London.

Her London success in *Medea* bolstered her self-confidence. At the end of her performance of 17 June she received a magnificent ovation from a house which had been sold out since the day the box office opened. She remained in exceptionally good vocal form for all her five performances, spread over thirteen days – certainly better than in 1958, declared those purists who had not really appreciated her *Traviata* that year. London, which had not heard *Medea* since 1870, was expecting a tour de force and it was a revelation. Callas successfully combined her vocal mastery with her talents as a tragic actress – too much so, some critics claimed. A private recording of the London *Medea* on 30 June is harder and less moving than the Dallas version, but just a masterly. Jon Vickers, Joan Carlyle and Fiorenza Cossotto were also in excellent form, but Maria was what mattered. Never again would her voice be so perfectly assured. The 1959 London performances of *Medea* marked a turning-point in her career, as after this she had to depend on other, quite different, resources.

It was after the performance of *Medea* on 17 June that she encountered Onassis at the Dorchester reception after which nothing was ever the same again. Her second *Gioconda* was recorded the following September in Milan when she was in the throes of leaving her husband. In those three months Callas had changed her allegiances and this affected her voice. Now that she was no longer guided by Meneghini her career entered a critical period. 'Maria needs a man', Meneghini remarked later, and Onassis was certainly that, but though he had chosen the greatest singer in the world for himself he did not really care what she sang or how. 'She always chose the wrong man', as one of her friends pointed out. But she loved Onassis and could not help herself.

Her 1959 *Gioconda* is far from dull, but it was recorded in disastrous conditions psychologically speaking and shows Callas in far more limited voice than previously, apparently reluctant to let herself go in those outbursts of passion and anger which she formerly displayed in the role. During the remainder of 1959 she gave only concerts and four stage performances in Dallas. Her concerts were still near perfect, particularly the 23 September concert in London's Festival Hall when she sang 'O don fatale' from Don Carlos and extracts from *Macbeth, Il Pirata* and *Hamlet,* again an impressive display of her most sombre vocal colours and her tragic sense. It was the same with her Berlin and Kansas City performances. But each concert seemed to be fitted in between flights, each performance meant time stolen from an increasingly absorbing private life. The cost of her happiness, if happiness it was, was high.

Swept away by Onassis, Callas went on singing, but her singing and her powerful stage presence, formerly her *raison d'être,* now seemed routine, something which happened between two court hearings, two cruises or two balls.

On 6 November she sang her first Dallas *Lucia.* Once again Lawrence Kelly had arranged what promised to be a memorable season – the Covent Garden production of *Lucia,* a revival of *Medea,* and *Il Barbiere di Siviglia* with Teresa Berganza – but he soon had to change his plans as Berganza was pregnant and could not sing. Callas bravely agreed to replace her as Rosina though her first performances of the part had not been a great success. The Dallas season depended on her, but her strength and voice were failing. She was in rock-bottom form for her first *Lucia di Lammermoor,* muffing her high notes through nervousness and almost breaking down in the mad scene, though she sang much better at the second performance on 8 November. She had to cancel *Il Barbiere* at short notice (Eugenia Ratti of La Scala replaced her) and travel to Brescia. Five days later she returned to Dallas and sang *Medea* twice in Minotis's beautiful and 'authentic' production.

Then for six months Callas was silent.

Maria Callas and Joan Sutherland, who did sing in Les Huguenots, *though the plan that they should both appear in this opera in London never came to fruition*

What were the reasons for this silence? It later emerged that from the end of 1959 until the middle of 1960 Callas underwent the first of the vocal crises which on several occasions during the coming years were to reduce her to silence. Quite apart from the upheavals of the previous months, her nervous exhaustion, her separation from Meneghini and the endless excitements of the life Onassis led her, there were more serious reasons. First her health in general was failing; for some years she had assumed that by slimming she could forget all about the physical, basically glandular, problems which had affected her during her youth. She had lost weight, but after a period of calm when her health returned she was not really any better. She suffered increasingly from low blood pressure which made her generally very weak, and she again began to suffer from sinus trouble which caused her severe pain when she sang or produced certain sounds. Later when she returned for a series of performances at La Scala she even had to have her sinuses cleared each evening.

These were the reasons for her six-month retreat. In a blaze of publicity Callas stopped singing.

Slowly a new image of her emerged to replace the picture so often given before. She was shown calm, smiling and relaxed. Though she lived in a whirl of travel, parties and meetings, she seemed kind and understanding – the little sister, the submissive mistress.

'Callas says, "I don't want to sing any more. . . I would like a child"', ran a *France-Soir* headline. Callas explained, 'It is only too easy for accusations of all kinds to be made against me. . . Even the joy of singing has been taken away from me. I have been singing for twenty-three years, but for the last few years it has been an ordeal. People wait for my high C and I am not allowed to have a cold or sing a hoarse note. I should like to sing, but for my own pleasure. The public is a monster and that is why I am not eager to return to the stage.' To those of her admirers who had followed her since her New York and Athens days this sounded desperately unhappy.

Callas waited. There was talk of *Macbeth* at Covent Garden but she fought shy. How could she sing the uncontrolled fury of Lady Macbeth when she was no longer even giving those concerts of four or five arias which had kept her active the year before?

'I do not want to sing any more. I want to live, live just like an ordinary woman.' How could Callas ever be an ordinary woman?

Callas looked back on her past with bitterness. 'Nowadays I would like to be an ordinary woman, with children, a home, a dog. When I met Meneghini in Verona I married him. I believed in love. But he wasn't a husband, he was an impresario who wanted to take advantage of my glory. That is why we are no longer together. Believe me, I long to have a real life, a private life.'

Life with Onassis was far from peaceful. The eyes of the world were always on her – journalists and photographers who recorded every moment for posterity, every visit to a night spot or restaurant, every brush with her friends or enemies whether casual acquaintances, stars, dress-designers or royalty. No details were spared: 'Wild parties on Onassis's yacht. . .' 'Callas fills Monte Carlo harbour with the din of her parties on board the *Christina* which she has turned into a floating palace. She arrives by helicopter deafening the town. At night Monte Carlo belongs to her. Until dawn she is its true princess. . .'

But her life was not always this paradise of furs and gold. The question of marriage came up again. Onassis had got his divorce. Callas had married Meneghini in Italy and could not get a divorce there, but was free to divorce him anywhere else as she had never surrendered her

Maria Callas with spectacles. Onassis is reported to have said that they made her look plain

American passport. 'Yes, I shall marry Onassis,' declared Callas on 12 August 1960, but six days later Onassis claimed, 'Maria and I are just good friends.' An article in *France-Dimanche* described Callas's new image, that of a meek and mild young woman in love: 'She does everything he wants, talks if he wants to talk, keeps quiet if he does, smiles when he is in a good mood. . .She has given him the ultimate proof of submission by virtually abandoning her career for him. Since her legal separation she has not sung once in Europe or America. . . . In Meneghini's day she bought up the great Parisian couturiers each year. Now she goes to Biki, an Italian designer famous for the sobriety of her models. She told her, "I do not want to be like Tina who spent a fortune on clothes each month. Onassis likes me simple". She has always worn spectacles, but one day Onassis said they made her look plain. Since then, without a murmur, Callas has forced herself to wear contact lenses. . .

'In Milan where each of her exploits was more newsworthy than her appearances at La Scala, I was told, "You would not recognize Callas; she is as meek as a kitten. It is Onassis who has performed this miracle."'

So, choking back any resentment, she had to keep up appearances. Onassis accepted all this as his due. Later she commented with a smile, 'Our life then was hell, but with the amount of money we had. . .'

Callas was eager to sing again. Her voice seemed to be recovering, her life had not ruined it totally and Greece was clamouring to hear her (with the blessing of Onassis who regarded a performance at Epidaurus as a sacred event). She stepped into the arena once again at the end of August 1960.

Before that, encouraged by EMI, she had attempted a recording come-back with a session in England in July to record several arias – from Rossini's *Semiramide*, 'D'amore al dolce impero' from his *Armida* and 'Arrigo, ah parli a un cor' from *I Vespri Siciliani*. The recording, conducted by Antonio Tonini with whom she was not used to working, took a long time to make and Callas was not satisfied. She also planned to give a concert in Ostend but called it off at the last moment. All this augured badly for her performance of *Norma* at Epidaurus.

Compared with the scandal surrounding Maria's last appearance in Athens – when a government had almost fallen because of her – things were different in 1960. The diva who had almost stopped singing was not the fiery temperamental performer of earlier years. By sharing Onassis's life she had, once the Maxwells, Rainiers and Graces got over their surprise, acquired a kind of respectability. In Greece as a ship-owner's mistress she was for better or worse an official person. Callas could face the world again, head held high. On the first night there was a downpour just before the performance was due to begin, and it had to be cancelled. This time no one in Epidaurus complained, whereas two years before she would have been accused of conjuring up the storm with magic spells. Two days later, on 24 August, and again on the 28th her performance was a triumph.

As soon as Callas appeared she was greated by a tremendous ovation. Greece rose to its feet – twenty thousand people at each performance – and acknowledged its child. Surrounded by a cast of young Greek singers including Kiki Morfoniou and Emilie Koussi, she was the symbol of a rediscovered tradition – the noble tradition of ancient Greek tragedy. She was also in good form vocally and the critics hailed her as a miracle – but they were also welcoming the return of the prodigal daughter. No recordings have survived by which we can judge her performance. After the first performance to thunderous applause, a crown of laurel leaves was placed on her head. On 28 August she suddenly developed a high temperature and was so exhausted that her doctor advised her to stay in bed, but she insisted on honouring her contract and singing again in the amphitheatre at Epidaurus.

There was one man in the crowd nobody recognized – Callas's father. The family was reunited. Aristotle Onassis was very pleased with himself – his lost singer had been found. And as Meneghini was not there Callas was able to donate her $10,000 fee to establish the Callas Scholarship for young singers.

Maria had now recovered her confidence. After a few days' rest she left for Milan to record her second *Norma,* again for EMI. This time Adalgisa was sung by Christa Ludwig, one of the world's finest mezzos, but oddly miscast, perhaps too warm-voiced for the part. Franco Corelli again sang Pollione, with Tullio Serafin at the rostrum. Callas's voice had evolved strangely since the 1953 recording and her 1960 *Norma* shows her age. The interpretation displays superb maturity and renewed musicianship. There are certainly signs of fatigue, but a depth of emotion and a dense, rich vocal colour too which make her druidess a pitiable as well as a noble figure. She accepts the destiny which makes Roman soldiers prefer young girls to the mothers of their children. Less dazzling than her earlier interpretation, this second version of *Norma* was nonetheless a great commercial success. Callas seemed to have regained her lost position on the international opera scene and one by one theatres opened their doors to her again.

The first was La Scala. She returned on 7 December 1960, St. Ambrose's Day, the traditional first night of the season, as if nothing had changed, to appear in Donizetti's *Poliuto*. No longer the glamorous singer who regularly opened every season, no longer the glorious tragedienne whom Visconti and Zeffirelli had vied to direct, she was simply a distinguished establishment figure – a multi-millionaire's concubine, a figure clad in black or white who already belonged to the past. Soon she was to be reconciled with Tebaldi when the two women fell into one another's arms in New York, a photograph seen all over the world. Soon Joan Sutherland, Montserrat Caballé and Mirella Freni were to become the outstanding sopranos of their generation – yet at this time Callas was only thirty-seven. Those who are only too ready to relegate her to the past should listen to the two records of *Poliuto* which have survived, and look through the photographs of Callas as Paolina, with Ettore Bastianini as Severo and Franco Corelli as Poliuto.

Visconti was to have been in charge of the production, designed by Nicola Benois who had previously worked with Callas on several occasions including *Fedora* and *Anna Bolena*. However for personal and

Callas as Paolina, Franco Corelli as Poliuto

'. . . there is a tenderness, a gentleness, a loving resignation in her portrayal of Paolina. . .'

political reasons Visconti withdrew some time before the first performance. Since the government had censored his film *Rocco and his Brothers* and a play *Arialda* which it considered obscene he refused to work for any official institutions, including La Scala. Herbert Graf replaced him at short notice. But it did not really matter who the producer, designer or conductor (Votto in fact) were since the audience and critics were only interested in Maria Callas.

The opera itself is not one of Donizetti's most interesting and Cammarano's libretto is almost incomprehensible, retaining little of Corneille's tragedy *Polyeucte*. It is better known in the French version, *Les Martyrs,* which had its most famous performance in Paris in 1840 when Duprez, Berlioz's first Benvenuto Cellini, created the role of Polyeucte (a role originally written for an even more famous tenor, Nourrit, who was to have sung it in Naples, until the censor banned the work on grounds of sacrilege). This hybrid *Poliuto* had been forgotten since 1848, but the part of Paolina had the advantage, so far as Callas at this stage of her career was concerned, of posing few vocal problems. She had chosen it with care, because it contained little ornate *bel canto,* no tricky *fioriture* and no excessively long or high notes. Callas's performance was disturbing. Disturbing because the reasons she had chosen to sing Paolina were clear and because her limitations and possible weaknesses were only too apparent. The deterioration in her voice's technical qualities became more and more noticeable as the action progressed – an increasingly disagreeable tremolo in her lower register during the last act and some unsuccessful high notes. Yet despite all this there is a tenderness, a gentleness, a loving resignation in her portrayal of Paolina the martyr, so unlike the Medea and Norma of her last years. She is once again the innocent, fragile girl lost from view since *La Sonnambula.*

Though the critics had reservations and felt in general that she was not in good voice, the audience made the occasion a triumph – for Callas, for Nicola Benois's superb, sepia, *trompe-l'oeil* sets, for Bastianini, for Corelli and for Votto – but above all for Callas. They never suspected that this was to be her last new role, whether or not they were aware of the care she was taking of her voice, of the extreme caution she exercised to such beautiful effect. The society columns of the world's press next day showed the impact of the occasion. Elsa Maxwell, one of those who had come over from America for the performance, described it as something out of the Arabian Nights with garlands of red carnations, sixteen thousand of them, donated by Balmain, hanging from the six tiers of the house. As the overture began Onassis slipped into his box behind a column. Near him, but at a respectful distance no doubt, were Grace and Rainier of Monaco who gave a supper party after the performance, while the Italian police protected the diva from journalists and photographers.

A few days later, with Birgit Nilsson, still marvellously young, and Hans Hotter, still in full possession of his means, La Scala saw the second new production of the season – an excellent *Fidelio.* But only the music critics were there. The gossip-hungry columnists had departed for pastures new.

Callas had departed too. She rested and went on trying to live in Paris and Monte Carlo. Her return to La Scala had proved to the world, above all to herself, that she was once again an admired singer, not just Aristotle Onassis's mistress. But she was paying the price – laryngitis, sinusitis and growing fatigue. She knew what it cost her to sing and she knew her limitations. She now decided that henceforth she would only sing on stage the two roles she had mastered most fully: *Norma* and *Medea*. Three years later she added *Tosca*. Above all she was determined not to embark on any risky undertakings.

But she still longed to be Callas.

Triumphant curtain call – for Callas above all

Callas now settled in Monte Carlo and Paris. Early in 1960 she and Onassis went house hunting for somewhere worthy of her new status, and there was even talk of the Trianon Palace. In May a visit to the Château du Jonchet in the Eure-et-Loir department of France, restored by the architect Pouillon, was the occasion of one of her splendid rages – faithfully reported by the press. 'As soon as she got out of her car the singer bore down on a photographer, shaking her fist. "Go away", she shouted. "Go to hell. We don't need publicity, we're not comedians."' Onassis, one imagines, looked on speechless – to have Maria Callas as your bodyguard was quite an achievement. Next day Onassis flew off to Caracas on business, and Callas on consideration decided not to buy the château.

She began to work more in Paris, encouraged by her friendship with the conductor Georges Prêtre, the presence of Michel Glotz whom she had met in 1958 and by journalists, critics and fans. She was preparing a record of French arias and the press suddenly discovered a new Callas. She lived like a champion before a match – eschewing night clubs, sticking to a régime of early nights and light, simple meals – looked after by her maid Bruna. Full of good humour she worked with dedication at the recording sessions.

The result was a beautiful, slightly stilted record on which Callas, perhaps a little defensively, sang arias outside her normal repertoire: '*Amour, viens aider ma faiblesse*' from *Samson et Dalila*, '*Depuis le jour où je me suis donnée*' from Gustave Charpentier's *Louise,* arias from *Le Cid, Mignon* and *Romeo et Juliette* and others by Gluck and Bizet. Once again she displayed her extraordinary versatility and adaptability as well as a sometimes surprising intensity. Whereas previously on stage or on record she had lived each role to the full, down to the last insignificant word of some obscure recitative suddenly made vital and unforgettable by some characteristic inflexion of her voice, now she was tackling unknown heroines whom she would never portray on stage. Yet she managed to make six of them credible and alive on this one record, each one becoming a character with her own subtle, individual personality. Miraculously, in a single aria, some interior sense brings an unknown heroine into sharp relief as a complete person.

The critics greeted the record with dutiful respect and Callas again disappeared from sight. She was now leading a curious existence, for having become an institution to both press and public her outbursts were regarded as a kind of formality. People respected the life of semi-retirement she had chosen and whenever she emerged she was treated with all the pomp a goddess surrounded by an aura of immortality deserved. And yet she was only thirty-eight. She moved between Paris and Monte Carlo, went on cruises, did business deals and Onassis invested her money for her.

In May she gave a concert in St James's Palace, London, in aid of the Edwina Mountbatten Trust (a charity). Sir Malcolm Sargent accompanied her at the piano. Ladies in evening dress with lily-white shoulders applauded her 'classic' *'Casta diva'*. This was followed by three short arias which could not possibly tire either singer or audience: *'Tu che la vanità'* from *Don Carlos*, and arias from Massenet's *Le Cid* and Boito's *Mefistofele*. After one last photograph in which she is very beautiful, standing bare-armed beside Sir Malcolm Sargent at the piano, she left for another cruise.

Come the summer she was back at Epidaurus, true to Greece, her new-found origins and Aristotle Onassis's sense of public relations. After *Norma* in 1960, she sang *Medea* with Jon Vickers and several young Athenian singers.

The opera was produced by Minotis, husband of the great actress Paxinou, and conducted once again by the old maestro Serafin. Minotis has described how Maria by some marvellous sixth sense, and without being told, recaptured the gestures of ancient goddesses used by great Athenian actresses in the tragedies of Euripides and Sophocles, gestures which he had previously studied with his wife. At Epidaurus Maria symbolized the return of living theatre to the most ancient of all theatres. Kneeling, she begged for pity from those on whom she would later take her terrible revenge. On stage she moved like a dancer, humbling herself so that her final triumph should be more complete. Her rage is noble, her face reflecting all shades of anger and hope. As an archaic world cast its spell in defiance of the refinements of Corinth in this ancient theatre, the magic of opera worked its spell too – a miracle in which Cherubini himself perhaps played only a small part.

Medea at Epidaurus

Medea was an even greater triumph than *Norma* the year before. This time, after a sudden shower which made everyone fear the worst, the weather stayed fine and Callas revealed the full beauty of her voice again. The audience applauded more enthusiastically than ever. The Mayor of Athens bestowed the freedom of the city on her and on 28 August, the last evening, her father, mother and sister Jackie were all in the audience. She was reconciled not only with Athens but with her whole family as well.

Four months later she appeared in Minotis's production of *Medea* at La Scala, and in fact during 1961 and 1962 that was all she sang there, with varying degrees of success. Her 1961 performances were still passable. The cast was superb: Jon Vickers again; Nicolai Ghiaurov (the young Bulgarian bass, then a relative newcomer, later a formidable Philip II and a great Boris) as Creon; Giulietta Simionato as the nurse, Neris. Another comparative beginner, Thomas Schippers, conducted. The performance on 11 December 1961 which was recorded is famous in opera history for one of Callas's splendid, legendary gestures, on a par with the *'palco funeste'* which she once addressed to Ghiringhelli's box.

With Jon Vickers as Jason in Medea

As she pleaded with Jason a few hostile cries came from the gallery. Callas was not in exceptionally good voice, but she was passable, as the recording shows: that was not good enough for her detractors in the top rows. Carried away by passion, Medea addresses Jason as *'crudel'* (cruel man), a cry she is meant to repeat a second time. Instead there was a silence – perhaps one of the most beautiful silences in the history of opera. The music stopped. Everyone waited. Callas stared out at the audience – those in the stalls who had paid so much to see her rending her voice (shortly afterwards she had another operation for sinusitis), the gallery who had booed her. When it came, her second *'crudel'* was addressed to her audience. *'Ho dato tutto a te'* – 'I gave you everything.' She shook her fist at the audience and at the world.

From then on there were only bravos and shouts of enthusiasm. Callas sang *Medea* twice more at La Scala, then hurried back to Monte Carlo in excruciating pain from her throat and sinuses. In 1961 she only broke her silence to appear on stage in front of an audience five times.

The question was whether she would continue singing or not. There was talk of a production of Meyerbeer's *Les Huguenots* in London with Joan Sutherland, revivals of large-scale French grand opera being back in fashion. A little later Massenet's turn came; now the plan was to see these two great performers together as Marguerite de Valois and Valentine, two splendid roles in *Les Huguenots*. We can imagine Callas as Valentine, the broken heroine.

The following year, 1962, and to some extent 1963, saw Callas vocally in worse shape than ever before.

Her private life still made newspapers but there were fewer press stories about her. Onassis was still there but he travelled more and more, giving rise to rumours about the stability of their relationship, and there was no more talk of marriage. Meneghini had now decided to play the part of the wronged husband seeking revenge. The newspapers sarcastically explained how after agreeing to a separation based on mutual consent he had changed his mind and now wanted to attack his ex-wife. 'Callas's ex-husband makes her miss the royal wedding,' read a *Paris-Jour* headline in May, followed by a story explaining how Meneghini had spitefully arranged for Maria to appear at a court hearing in Milan on the wedding day of Sophia of Greece and Juan of Spain, an important social event at which Callas would have liked to appear. A few weeks later there was a squalid episode involving some photographs, when Meneghini tried to use pictures of Maria and Onassis to prove her infidelity. Maria replied that she was not alone with Onassis in the photos and that the rank of the other people present was sufficient guarantee of the respectability of her relationship with Ari. It was all very sordid and depressing.

Her family affairs – which had seemed to settle down after the historic reunion with her father, mother and sister at Epidaurus, engineered by art, nature and publicity – also deteriorated dramatically. The American press carried reports of Evangelia's attempted suicide. Madame Callas, aged sixty-two, was allegedly working as a dressmaker to support herself and living in lodgings in a crowded part of New York. Callas, ever the ungrateful daughter, had driven her mother to this desperate act.

These trials and tribulations and Onassis's absences did nothing to improve her health, and her voice continued to be affected by her psychological and physical state. On 27 February she gave a recital at the Festival Hall, London. For the first time the London press, usually so well-disposed towards her, was severe. The *Sunday Telegraph* reported that:

It has been clear for some time that her voice has been sinking in pitch a little – or perhaps more accurately, that it is finding itself anew, in a slightly lower range than that of dramatic soprano. Everything about the recital programme, from choice of music to platform demeanour, seemed designed to offset the old tiger-cat image of Mme. Callas and substitute a gentle, girlish creature, vulnerable and affectingly graceful.

A new artist is cracking the chrysalis of the old, and whatever character emerges we may be sure that it will not be dull or superficial.

The Times was scarcely kinder: its critic, while paying tribute to Callas's abilities as an actress and musical interpreter, noted that her voice was now quite ugly, and even out of tune; while the setting of a concert hall concentrated the audience's attention on these shortcomings. On stage, even in an operatic recording, she would have been able to use her other gifts to mask any failings in the quality of her voice; he conceded that certain moments in her performance did give a glimpse of her true powers, notably the final rondo from Rossini's *La Cenerentola* and 'Pleurez, pleurez, mes yeux' from Massenet's *Le Cid*. *The Times* also found that the atmosphere was more suggestive of pop-singing and night clubs than great artistry and the art of music: 'this was unworthy of Mme. Callas'.

Her poor performance in excerpts from *Anna Bolena* and *Oberon* reinforced their criticisms. Add to this the over-long programme, Georges Prêtre's conducting and the use of 'pop' lighting, and nearly everyone agreed that a performance – or exhibition – of this kind was unworthy of the great Callas.

However the timbre of her voice, it was noticed, had undergone a surprising development. True she was not much good in Donizetti, in which she had formerly excelled, but in Princess Eboli's aria from *Don Carlos*, 'O don fatale!' and in the rondo from *La Cenerentola*, 'Nacqui all'affanno' she was sublime. But these two arias belong to the classic mezzo-soprano repertoire. Was Callas, as *The Times* wondered, becoming a mezzo?

If Callas had continued singing this might have been a logical development. By dint of hard work over the years the breaks between her three registers had certainly improved, but until the end of her career Callas continued to sing with three 'voices'. If her upper register sometimes played her unkind tricks, particularly when singing at full power, if her lower register sometimes sounded rough and hollow, her middle register (often previously described as weak) had become much smoother and more musicianly with time. At this juncture it would not have been inconceivable for her gradually to abandon her upper register with conscious effort and practice. Imagine what a superb Carmen or Dido, what a formidable Amneris, what a terrifying Eboli Callas might then have become on stage. But perhaps it was already too late: trapped forever in her legend Callas could henceforth only be Medea, Norma and Tosca – and those only for a short time. The mezzo arias she recorded in April 1962 – Eboli and *La Cenerentola* – were never even issued.

The four concerts she gave in Germany between 12 and 23 March contained one surprise for her admirers – the dazzling discovery of what a fine Carmen she might make. Conducted again by Georges Prêtre, now a close friend, she introduced the conference hall of the Deutches Museum, Munich (followed by Hamburg, Essen and Bonn) to the impudent laughter of a *Habanera* and *Séguedille* sung as no one could remember them ever being sung before – full of mockery, defiance and cruel irony. It was a triumph of art, each sound carefully doctored, but her art and her irony were sublime. She also sang these two arias from *Carmen* to a wildly enthusiastic audience on 19 May in Madison Square Garden, New York, to celebrate President Kennedy's forty-fourth birthday.

After this discovery of *Carmen,* which she recorded two years later to tantalize all those who were uncertain where her talents lay, Callas had no further need to tempt providence. As for singing *Les Huguenots* with Sutherland, then at the peak of her vocal form, even David Webster of Covent Garden who had been chasing her up all over the world, could see that it would be a suicidal and pointless venture. She gave up the idea.

But now we come to those dreadful performances of *Medea* on 29 May and 3 June 1962 at La Scala. Physically her voice had never been worse. A severe case of sinusitis which needed urgent treatment made high or long notes cause her intense suffering – a lacerating pain from the back of her throat up to the bridge of her nose, across her brow and forehead. She appeared with the same cast of friends as in 1961 – Schippers, Simionato, Vickers and Ghiaurov – in Alexis Minotis' monumental production with the same sets by Vannis Tsachouris. Two tiers of columns with unadorned capitals and in front of them a proscenium on which Callas-Medea stood, her arm raised in a gesture which was never anyone's but hers, trying in vain to stop time slipping through her fingers, to stop love dying, to stop relentless fate. She stood there proudly, pleading and vulnerable, dominating and awe-inspiring in turn, like some remote, archaic statue from a long time past which has strayed by chance into our dreams of a distant world.

She prepared to say the words everyone feared. Who was this mysterious stranger, cloaked in black, defying Corinth and those who knew her? *'Io? Medea!'* 'I am Medea!' and suddenly her voice cracked. Unbearably sad to watch, her voice on the point of giving out, she somehow struggled through the part but her voice was failing and would not obey her. The French critic Jacques Bourgeois was more or less alone

Medea: *'a mysterious stranger, cloaked in black'*

in his opinion of her performance. 'Callas was more astonishing than ever. Even her timbre had recovered a velvety quality free of the stridency for which she is sometimes criticized. . . . Three or four dangerously unstable notes were the only flaws in an interpretation which is probably one of the most outstanding achievements ever in the field of operatic performance.'

An outstanding achievement – this is what we remember when we listen to any of Callas's recordings of *Medea*. It needed Callas to rescue Cherubini's music from the century and a half of pompous dreariness into which it had sunk. Since then, certainly, Rysanek has given some startling performances as Medea in Vienna and Arles, but she is a Medea of a different kind. But in Milan in 1962, it seems, (since there are no recordings of the two performances) only the ghost of a voice survived.

After 3 June 1962, a date to be remembered, Callas never again appeared on stage at La Scala nor, her voice and strength failing, did she return to Epidaurus that year. No more performances either at La Scala or in Greece – the second period of her career was at an end. She rested for six months and only sang once more in public in 1962 for a televised gala at Covent Garden on 4 November. She sang three arias: the *Habanera* and *Séguedille* from *Carmen* again and *'Tu che la vanità'* from *Don Carlos*. She was undergoing the second of her great vocal crises and apart from this appearance she stopped singing for a whole year, from 3 June 1962 until 3 May 1963 when she began recording again in Paris.

For a whole year her professional life consisted of abortive plans. A Visconti production of *Trovatore* at Covent Garden and a Paris *Traviata* which never came off. Later there was even talk of the entire La Scala company taking *Traviata* to Moscow, but again nothing came of it. More ideas were put forward: Monteverdi's *Poppea,* the countess in *Le Nozze di Figaro,* Gluck's *Orfeo* in Dallas with Lawrence Kelly. Or more sensible proposals for *Medea* in New York and *Traviata* or *Anna Bolena* at Covent Garden. Sometimes there were brief discussions, sometimes protracted negotiations, but each time Callas called off. And she never sang the great *Tristan* she had seriously been considering for the winter of 1962, as if still eager to remind the world that though exhausted (in late 1962 she even had an operation for hernia) she had been Isolde in 1947, a role of which nothing remains.

She had the support of a few friends who helped her all they could and protected her from herself, among them Michel Glotz of EMI and Georges Prêtre. 'Though many people (including Maria) may think it sounds funny,' said Georges Prêtre, who became her favourite conductor in Paris, 'I know that when she is about to appear on stage in front of thousands of people who have come to hear her voice, she looks more like a little girl about to take an exam than the best-paid singer in the world. . . . When she arrives in a town where she is to sing, she immediately goes to her hotel, shuts herself in her room, only emerging for important occasions. Inside she rests, sleeps, works and above all keeps herself to herself. She likes to stay well away from noise and people. She knows that if she so much as lifts a finger people will talk about it for days. And yet. . . .'

Onassis appeared in public far more, alone or with other women. Princess Radziwill crossed his path and once again there were headlines in the gutter press and a whiff of scandal. But Princess Radziwill passed on, Onassis remained and Maria appeared little in public.

The press as a whole – the French press since Callas was now living in Paris – adopted a false pitying tone towards her. Opening at random *Ici-Paris* of 2 December 1963, we find 'Callas is back on spaghetti. She wants to put on a few pounds and explains, "Yes, it is true, beautiful voices like fat." ' The papers discussed her health at length. Everyone now knew that it was delicate, and it was a long time since people had called her temperamental when she cancelled a concert. ' "It is not the pounds that matter," she says, "It is the amount I eat. The fact is that I am always starving. I am ravenous and it wears me out." '

As Ifigenia in June 1957, six years before she recorded show-pieces from this opera in a collection of arias from French operas

Maria's every step was watched, like those of an invalid. If she didn't want to buy Fernand Pouillon's château, how about retiring to Luis Mariano's villa in Le Vésinet which she visited? There were sentimental stories about her family life, though she had previously been accused of the most monstrous behaviour, ingratitude and even matricide. July 1963: 'A few days ago the diva made a newsworthy appearance at Monte Carlo Casino on the arm of a slender gentleman in a white dinner jacket, wearing amazing round glasses. This was thought to be a rival to Onassis, but it turned out to be her papa. . .' Or again: 'Evangelia Callas Kalogeropoulos has closed her dress shop in New York and is to join her daughter in France for a holiday. She will stop off in Paris, perhaps to choose presents for Maria. A room has already been booked for her at the hotel Prince de Galles.'

In May 1963, once again with the faithful Prêtre, Maria made a record of arias from French operas – *La Damnation de Faust, Faust, Les Pêcheurs de perles, Werther, Manon* and *Iphigénie en Tauride*. It is another record one listens to with respect rather than passion, affection rather than real joy. On it Callas sounds beautiful but strained, as if anticipating difficulties she will have to surmount skilfully. However Georges Prêtre had reason to feel pleased: thanks to him Callas was confident enough to undertake a series of concerts organized for her in May and June, in Germany, London, Paris and Copenhagen, her only public appearances that year. The programme was unusual – *Semiramide, Norma, Nabucco, Bohème* and *Butterfly*. In London she added 'O mio babbino caro' from Puccini's *Gianni Schicchi*.

For her concert in Paris on 5 June she made a few changes. *La Cenerentola* replaced *Norma* and she sang two extra pieces, the *Air des lettres* from *Werther* and 'Adieu, notre petite table' from *Manon*. By now Paris was something more than just another booking. Her friendship with Georges Prêtre was certainly largely responsible for the special treatment Paris received during the course of an otherwise undis-tinguished tour. It was Prêtre who accompanied Maria on her European travels and he and Michel Glotz who persuaded her to sing *Norma* at the Paris Opéra the following year. Needless to say some newspapers speculated about their friendship, drawing attention to the ridiculously low fees Callas was to get from Paris Opéra compared with what she usually asked for her performance. This again was thanks to Prêtre's intervention.

Five days before the concert on 5 June there was a festive atmosphere. There was also panic; the gala was being held in aid of the Knights of Malta, and they had bought up almost all the seats. As a result there was no room for journalists, friends or *le Tout-Paris*. Callas, who had moved from her flat in Avenue Foch to an hotel in the Champs Elysées where she had greater freedom of movement, issued an ultimatum. Either seats were made available for other people besides the godly Knights or she would not sing. Then she flew to London.

In the end everything turned out well. *Le Tout-Paris*, in festive splendour, got their seats – the Begum Aga Khan and Princess Guy de Polignac in a white organdie dress with blue sable, Princess de la Tour d'Auvergne, Countess de Castellane, Romy Schneider and Maurice Chevalier. The Knights of Malta were there too, but not in their uniforms. Pope John XXIII had just died and they were in mourning, 'which spoiled the effect', remarked one po-faced journalist. The theatre was decorated with thousands of flowers donated by the rose gardens of the Loire Valley. Car keys were given away with each over-priced programme, and one lucky key opened the door of a Renault R4 displayed in the foyer. The record Callas and Prêtre had made the month before was also on sale in the foyer.

The concert itself could not have been other than a success. From the gods to the stalls the audience went wild. Callas could have sung anything and they would still have clapped, just as they clapped Maurice Chevalier when he took his seat.

But what of her voice? Olivier Merlin writing in *Le Monde* probably made the fairest comment, since other accounts tended to be biased or something other than straight-forward musical criticism. 'In the programme she chose', wrote Merlin, 'Maria Callas carefully avoided the dizzying *tessiture* of the Bellini of *Norma,* the Donizetti of *Lucia* and the Verdi of *Trovatore* or *Aida,* preferring the less well-known repertoire of the Italian romantic period or easier arias which were on everyone's lips at the end of the last century. She was thus able to draw on her charm, produce half-hints and veil or mask her timbre so that only a few strident high notes pierced a vocal display performed with consummate musicianship and with that wealth of colours and different inflexions for which her recordings have become famous.'

Olivier Merlin had more to say about the splendour of Callas, and it is with this image of her, slimmer, taller and more beautiful than ever, radiant before her Parisian audience which called her back again and again for fifteen curtains, that we close this period of her life. After the Théâtre des Champs Elysées concert and a final concert in Copenhagen, Callas once again retreated into the shadows. Six appearances in a year. From 1959 to 1963 she gradually fell silent.

Her swan song was all that remained.

Norma in the Paris production by Zeffirelli (opposite)

Chapter Six

THE DEATH OF THE SWAN
(1964-1965)

1964. Suddenly a miracle: Callas rediscovered. For three years her tall silhouette had slowly faded into a back-stage limbo; then she made a sudden comeback and once again brought us face to face with genius. At the height of her powers again – though no longer the same as in 1953-58 – she emerged from the shadows. And no tragic actress has ever seemed greater than Callas then.

Many factors contributed to her comeback. First, a supreme effort of the will to prove to others and to herself that she could still sing the women whose music rang in her ears: Traviata, Leonora, Tosca. Then there was the part played by the handful of men already mentioned who by their encouragement, hope and persistence managed to rekindle in her a taste for adventure. These were men who still believed in her with all their heart because they loved her for what she was – Michel Glotz, Georges Prêtre, Jacques Bourgeois and David Webster, then general administrator of Covent Garden.

But the real miracle was her recovery of her voice. Since 1959 Maria Callas had undergone two serious crises: the most dangerous, in the middle of 1962, had left her without a voice for more than six months, and when it recovered it was only a shadow of its former glorious self. Her closest friends could not conceal their pessimism. Her 1963 concerts, her unacknowledged development as a mezzo, seemed to be the last moments of her career. At the age of forty, it seemed, she would retire and live out a royal exile between Paris and Monte Carlo with Onassis and his friends – like those crowned heads who have turned a Portuguese beach into the last refuge of the Almanach de Gotha. She would be remembered as great, and her records, including the pirate recordings which people were beginning to collect, would help preserve the memory of her.

With one of the poodles of which she was so fond

But at the end of 1963 no one could doubt that she was better. The terrible sinus trouble of the previous year had gradually cleared up and when Glotz and Nicola Rescigno arranged a new series of recordings for her in December she seemed to be on exceptional form again. In a repertoire which was not typical – Mozart and Weber – she achieved all the dramatic intensity one might have expected of her, sustained by an almost perfectly even timbre and quite miraculous musicianship. It was the same in her arias from *Otello* and *Don Carlos* (she sang both Eboli and Elisabeth de Valois). This record, issued in August 1964, was to show those only too eager to believe it that Callas was still there.

But it is with her Covent Garden performances of *Tosca* that we return to the great world of grand opera. Callas's remark that she did not really like the part of *Tosca* has been quoted several times, yet she is always associated with the figure of Tosca, the singer and lover. We can listen for hours to her different performances of *Tosca*: the 1950 *Tosca*, the earliest surviving version, where her call 'Mario! Mario!' comes tenderly from the heart, or the 1964 *Tosca* with Georges Prêtre where Callas's first 'Mario! Mario!' as she enters Sant'Andrea della Valle is already an expression of fierce jealousy. In between there is a steady progression from the pure, noble 1952 *Tosca* (Mexico City again) or the radiant *Tosca* of 1953, the first commercial recording. The milestones of a life of love and art which became as much ours as hers, as we trembled with her with hope, at Scarpia's death, and horror, at Mario's murder.

It was David Webster who decided to get Callas to sing her first *Tosca* since 1958 in his opera house. Callas had forgotten about Tosca for six years. Webster had also considered *Traviata* and *Trovatore* but Violetta and Leonora were roles which might now have posed problems for Callas which she could easily avoid if she interpreted Floria Tosca in the right way, as a tragic actress sparing of her means and dramatically supercharged. She finally agreed to a series of performances of *Tosca* in London at the beginning of 1964. It was in a way to be a new début, a stupendous reunion with the public, a real comeback, since her last appearances on stage had been her La Scala *Medea* in May and June 1962. A production to match these lofty aspirations was called for and it was Zeffirelli who was responsible for the fantastic success of what were to be almost her last appearances.

With the designer Renzo Mongiardino, Zeffirelli created a production which even today, in 1978, is one of the most magnificent *Tosca*s one could ever hope see. He had loved Puccini's opera for years but had waited to find the ideal Tosca. And who better than Callas to sing the role of a singer consumed by love and jealousy, ready to kill for love and then to die for it? In this opera tailor-made for Callas Zeffirelli imagined a contrast between a grandiose, neo-classical Rome and a woman bursting with femininity, youth and desire. 'I wanted her played as an exuberant, warm-hearted, rather sloppy, casual woman, a kind of Magnani of her time,' explained Zeffirelli.'She was not to be sophisticated and elegant. How I hate the posey-lady, grand diva Tosca.' So Callas made her entrance one January evening in London, radiant in a peach-coloured dress, a bunch of brightly-coloured flowers in her hand. 'Even though she is in a church, she begins to talk about making love with Cavaradossi,' remarked Zeffirelli.

There are a hundred or even hundreds of photographs of the 1964 *Tosca* and the 1965 revival. Looking through them is like watching a vivid, passionate film, brought even more sharply into focus by Tito Gobbi's stunning performance as a dangerous, smooth-talking Scarpia. They form a series of breath-taking stills. '*Ed ora fra noi parliam da buoni amici. . .*' 'And now let us be friends, what is troubling you?' Gobbi asks Callas, a sharp-eyed wolf, an eagle with talons instead of fingers. Callas, her anxious eyes belying her words, her right hand resting on the back of her seat, cannot feign indifference. 'Nothing is troubling me.' She turns away, raises her right hand, holds her left and her whole

Zeffirelli's London Tosca: *'in a way a new debut'. Tito Gobbi was the dangerous smooth-talking Scarpia*

body sways unsteadily. 'The fan?' suggests her tormentor. Maria, still hoping to throw him off the scent, *'Fu sciocca gelosia.'* 'Stupid jealousy.' But she trembles. Transfixed, we follow this terrible dialogue, more moving than the finest verses of Racine or Shakespeare. Callas and Gobbi face to face.

Later in the Farnese Palace she stands, her arms stretched out, crucified in space by Scarpia who is almost on his knees. *'Non toccarmi, demonio, t'odio, t'odio. . .'*, she protests, her whole body like a long strangled cry. Music brings these images to life, with her voice floating dreamily far away, *'Vissi d'arte vissi d'amore'.* She puts down the glass she is holding and her fingers freeze. She *feels* the knife before she sees it. *'Civitavecchia?'* asks Scarpia. As the price for a worthless safe conduct to Civitavecchia, will she agree to be his? Yes, she replies, *'Si!'* Her hand closes on the knife. *'Questo è il bacio di Tosca!'* We know that Scarpia is dead.

In all our memories of opera, there will never again be memories such as these.

The performance on 21 January was recorded. Callas's voice is perfectly controlled, capable of the most exquisite sense of desolation in *'Vissi d'arte'*, and the cry of a savage beast ready to kill or be killed when she stabs Scarpia. *'Come la Tosca nel teatro'* – 'Like Callas at the opera'. There are some unsteady high notes, especially at the beginning of Act I, and signs of fatigue in her middle register which seems less interesting and slightly veiled in the duet in Act III. But otherwise she is once again the goddess stolen from us by – by what? Illness, her voice, Onassis and all the rest.

The evening was an incredible success with a standing ovation for Callas's return. The press and critics piled superlative on superlative for six evenings, until 5 February. All signs of excessive vibrato in her upper register had vanished according to the London critic Peter Heyworth, as had the grating notes which had recently disfigured her voice; her voice had not been so good for years. On 9 February Act II was filmed for television, bringing the images to life – a last legacy from Maria to all those who loved her so passionately, an unsurpassable performance of a role she had almost had to be forced to take.

The Callas machine now seemed to be in working order again and we can watch her gradual progress – in London, Paris, New York, Paris again and London – towards supreme beauty, then tragedy and silence.

In Paris between February and April 1964 Maria recorded excerpts from early Verdi works with Nicola Rescigno in the Salle Wagram. *Attila, I Lombardi alla Prima Crociata* and *I Vespri Siciliani,* as well as two arias from *Un Ballo in Maschera,* including a spine-chilling '*Ecco l'orrido campo'* (Amelia's scene beneath the gallows at midnight), and an undistinguished '*Ritorna vincitor'* from *Aida.* Callas was back. A few weeks later she recorded more arias from *I Lombardi* and *Un Ballo in Maschera* and extracts from *Trovatore,* but she had misgivings and for the time being EMI did not issue the recording.

Callas was now preparing for a return to Paris Opéra where she was eagerly awaited. On 22 May 1964 she was to sing an entire opera there for the first time and of course it had to be *Norma.* So far she had only appeared in Paris twice at gala performances of selected pieces, privileged evenings for the privileged. In *Norma,* thanks to Georges Prêtre and Zeffirelli, again responsible for a memorable production, Callas was strikingly beautiful. In the first act she stood on a rock, crowned with a laurel wreath, a mantle of red velvet draped across her white dress, addressing the Gallic warriors – a statue lost and then found. In the second act, wearing a flowing low-cut white dress with transparent veils floating behind her, her hair coiled back, she looked eighteen or twenty, a delicate, touching figure. In the third act, dressed in black, she embraced her children with fierce tenderness. Charles Craig was Pollione except for two performances when Franco Corelli sang the part superbly well. He was also a marvellous friend to Callas, helping and supporting her in their duets when his young, strong tenor might have created problems for a partner whose voice still hung in the balance. Fiorenza Cossotto as Adalgisa was not so considerate however. At the peak of her vocal form and a singer of powerful means, then as now, she made no allowances, though for the first performances Callas managed to hold her own.

However her voice was no longer what it had been at the time of her London *Tosca.* It varied from evening to evening and sometimes faltered. The French critic Claude Samuel wrote that her first '*Casta diva'* made him wince, but that from Act II onwards she was sublime. However at the fourth performance, he reported, she missed many of her high notes, making the audience shudder a dozen or so times between eight o'clock and midnight, and giving them two particularly violent shocks during the fourth act. But Harold Rosenthal in *Opera* magazine, discussing her fifth performance with Corelli on 10 June, felt that after a disappointing beginning Callas had never sung the fourth act so well since her 1952 *Norma*. The general public was dazzled and applauded wildly, and overall the Callas-Zeffirelli *Norma* is to be remembered as a magnificent success – even if her voice was beginning to crack.

Another important step was her recording of *Carmen* between 6 and 20 July 1964, again a happy occasion. Callas had recovered her vocal equilibrium and was guided step by step, note by note, by Georges Prêtre; foreseeing the pitfalls and understanding the potential glories of her voice he helped her to make one of her most fascinating commercial recordings.

Callas had never sung the part of Carmen before, though legend has it that she knew the score by heart as a child. Over the past few years she had given admirably spirited performances of the *Habanera* and *Séguedille* at concerts and on record, but singing the whole opera was a different matter. *Carmen* was another Glotz-Prêtre initiative. The young artistic director and conductor, both full of ambition for Maria, seemed to have replaced the old men who had mounted a watchful and jealous guard round her for so long. And the adventure appealed to Maria, partly because of the way her voice was developing: she was now beginning to move towards mezzo roles, with arias like those of Eboli and la Cenerentola. Though the distinction between mezzo and soprano is relatively recent – in the nineteenth century the roles of Norma and Adalgisa, for example, were interchangeable and Giuditta Pasta and Giulia Grisi could sing either – Bizet's music was certainly well suited to the timbre of her voice now. In addition Carmen's character appealed to Callas – the cigarette girl, violent and in love, tantalizing and dangerous, marked out by fate to die by Don José's knife in a near-perfect suicide. The part had everything about it to attract her. Once before she had been accused of singing Rosina in *Il Barbiere* as if she were Carmen; now she really would be Carmen! During an eight-day Aegean cruise to study the score and the libretto in depth Callas became Carmen.

EMI, which invested in *Carmen* one of the largest sums ever spent in France on an opera recording, particularly of a French opera, mounted a large-scale publicity campaign to launch it. The cast also included Nicolai Gedda (one of the finest and most musicianly tenors of his time, a marvellous Faust and Orfeo and as recently as 1977 a superb Riccardo in *Un Ballo in Maschera),* Robert Massard as Escamillo, and a very young Andréa Guiot as Micaela. The recording sessions were held in the Salle Wagram between two boxing matches and a firemen's or old boys' ball in sweltering heat. The Paris newspapers followed Callas's movements closely, but increasingly they were interested less in the star of café society than in the singer. Her Paris *Norma* seemed to have encouraged a more serious approach, since she was after all the greatest soprano in the world.

For Callas was still the greatest soprano in the world. Her Carmen,

Callas and Zeffirelli; the greatest soprano in the world with the man who helped make so many of her appearances so successful

Tosca

166

issued at the end of the year, is amazing. Apart from anything else there is her diction, a strange and individual Italian-Greek-American intonation which gives each word she utters a harsh, exotic sound. When Don José forbids her to speak because he is Don José, a man and a corporal of dragoons, her retort is a challenge, '*Je ne te parle pas . . . je pense. Il n'est pas interdit de penser!*' (I'm not talking to you . . . I'm thinking! That's not forbidden!') A declaration of freedom by the first woman in opera to declare herself free. With frightening lucidity Callas as Carmen accepts her destiny – death: '*La mort, la mort, la mort. . .*' Even before she reads it in the cards, she knows what her fate will be and she does not recoil from it. In Act IV when she tells José that she no longer loves him, she is stating her true passion – death – in a declaration of unsurpassed beauty.

Vocally her performance is admirable, her middle register no longer blurred, her high notes still hard but under control and her bottom notes sung from the depths of her dark gypsy soul.

Carmen, another milestone as Callas's career drew to its end, and a total success. After two weeks recording she returned to Greece and her life with Onassis for a period of rest and calm. On the *Christina* or on Skorpios, the island Onassis had bought in the Ionian, she rested, played the piano and made the most of this happy interlude when she had recovered her voice and was confident that she could still sing.

There were more plans, some of which materialized. An exchange between the London *Tosca* and the Paris *Norma* was suggested. Then there were old dreams – a recording of *Macbeth,* a second recording of *Traviata* – but nothing ever came of them. We can only imagine what the Callas-Carmen of 1964 would have made of Lady Macbeth.

But now we reach another milestone: eight performances of *Tosca* in Paris between 19 February and 10 March 1965, so successful that Callas agreed to sing a ninth on 13 March. The London production and cast were brought over lock, stock and barrel, with Zeffirelli, Gobbi and Renato Cioni. Paris was eager to hear *Tosca* and ready to love it – and Paris was right. Vocally Callas was in almost as good form as in London, and her Paris Tosca was dazzling. As in London the confrontation between Scarpia and Tosca, with Gobbi living up to his reputation as a fine actor and singer, was again the highlight. *France-Soir* also noted that Callas sang in Paris for far less than anywhere else in the world.

A few weeks before she sang *Tosca* at Paris Opéra Callas made her second commercial recording of it at the Salle Wagram, with Carlo Bergonzi, and with Gobbi and Georges Prêtre again. Tosca's harsh cries in Act II have a wounding power, and we cannot help loving these two records, this rending and heart-rending voice. But a writer in the French magazine *Lyrica* recently commented that her voice 'is debased and her interpretation, previously so instinctive and full of genius, is now calculated and too heavily emphatic, like over-made-up eyes.' Whatever their faults these records are evidence of her unsurpassed art. Despite their weaknesses we can listen to them again and again, enthusiastically though not unconditionally, recognizing the differences between them and her sublime 1953 recording.

According to the critics, her New York appearances were also sublime. She pressed on regardless, making the most of her life and voice while there was still time. After London and Paris the Metropolitan was finally to hear the Zeffirelli-Callas *Tosca,* with Gobbi, and with Corelli and Richard Tucker appearing alternately as Mario. Callas received a twenty-five-minute ovation when the curtain fell. All New York was there, led by Jacqueline Kennedy.

The 19 March performance, conducted by Fausto Cleva, was recorded and surprisingly, Callas sounds more reserved, less instinctive and more musical than in the commercial recording of the previous December; by comparison it seems perhaps over-done. Yet her outcry against Scarpia, '*Assassino!*' and her challenge '*Quanto?*' '*Il prezzo!*' are the work of a tragic actress who knew how to 'speak' her text as no other singer, even Callas herself in earlier days, had ever dared. With the help of Corelli, whose victory cry on hearing the outcome of the battle of Marengo receives a round of applause, the records made on 19 March 1965 are a stunning vocal display and utterly convincing. Apart from two unsuccessful high Cs and a '*Vissi d'arte*' which ends rather badly, Callas is very natural and remains perfectly in control of her voice throughout. She seems more carried away by her singing, more sure of herself as she 'speaks' her role than four months earlier.

Preparing for an appearance as Tosca

Her May performances of *Norma* in Paris marked the beginning of the end. For a year Callas had marshalled all her forces and her voice, almost intact apart from a few cracks, was still the instrument we knew before. But suddenly in Paris, in spring 1965, everything went wrong.

Callas returned from New York tired. In a few weeks she had lost another ten pounds, Meneghini was still indulging in legal quibbles and Onassis was away from Paris. Things looked bad: her doctors diagnosed a serious lowering of blood pressure and advised her not to sing. But she knew what would happen if she failed to appear as promised. A few days before in Catania Mario del Monaco had broken off a performance of *Carmen* in mid-stream, and his indisposition was regarded as quite normal and acceptable. If Renata Tebaldi called off a performance at the Metropolitan, public and press were full of understanding. But if 'la' Callas cancelled, it was a scandal or a show of temperament. Besides, Maria loved Paris and did not want to let down Georges Auric, director of the Opéra, or Georges Prêtre who had as much confidence in her as she in him. She decided to sing, regardless of the effect on her voice – and life. She was only to appear six more times on stage.

On 14 May, an hour before the first performance, she was alone in her dressing-room with her dresser when she suddenly felt she could not go on. Stagefright gripped her. Stuffed full of injections and medicines, forty-two years old, she was about to face an opera audience which like her suspected nothing and only remembered her performances of *Tosca* in February. She decided she would sing but asked for an announcement to be made beforehand, saying she was unwell. The audience was asked to be indulgent. As the first act of Zeffirelli's production of the previous year began everyone feared the worst; but with her old friend Giulietta

Norma, in one of her final appearances in Paris

Simionato as Adalgisa, she was superb. Side by side, hands linked, Callas and Simionato triumphed together. Though 'Casta diva' was sung *mezza voce* the critics all applauded what they heard.

Three days later, during a television broadcast, Maria still seemed serene and self-confident and everyone wondered why she had apologized for her voice when she seemed in such good form. But her Paris *Norma* was doomed. As everyone waited with bated breath Callas held on, then cracked. For the third performance on 21 May Fiorenza Cossotto replaced Simionato. Callas was feeling worse. She just got through the first act and then asked for a coramine injection during the interval. The opera continued smoothly but Callas was so exhausted that she had to lie down during the last interval. Cossotto tried to steal the show, and sang all their duets at full voice, wearing out Callas who could not keep up. On 25 May she was better, but now the question was would she be able to sing? She sang. Triumphantly she got through the evening again.

Now only the last performance on 29 May remained. Nothing went right. Perhaps even before she went on stage Callas knew she would not be able to complete the performance. She certainly feared the worst, as all her fellow-artists sensed: according to one it was unbearable to watch her physical, mental and vocal agony. In her dressing-room, full of roses and the Lanvin perfume she loved, she suddenly seemed to feel better. She got up, finished dressing, slipped on her dark mantle over her white tunic, no longer afraid: Prêtre, Ivo Vinco, young Gianfranco Cecchale as Pollione were with her. The first act, then the second, passed without incident. Callas was like another person watching herself singing. In the third act came her duet with Adalgisa and Cossotto, singing at the top of her voice, sweeping everything before her, was challenging her, testing her to see whether she could keep up. Suddenly Callas could not go on: she fell silent. She spent the rest of the act in a walking coma and collapsed in the wings as soon as she left the stage. Unconscious she was carried to her dressing-room where she was given an injection. The curtain never went up for the fourth act. Slowly the audience left the theatre: only one solitary voice called out from the balcony for a refund.

An hour and a half later, Callas supported by two men, left Paris Opéra for ever. This time she was suffering from severe nervous exhaustion. The press recognized it and was very kind. Her blood pressure very low, she left to rest on board the *Christina*; Onassis joined her and she spent the weeks before her next performances – *Tosca* at Covent Garden again – trying to recover. She ate normally, exercised her voice a little and hoped her blood pressure would settle down. But these were her last days and no one could doubt it.

She was due to arrive in London on 28 June but her doctor examined her the day before in Paris and insisted that it would be madness for her to travel to London in this state, let alone give four performances there. The telephone lines between Paris and London hummed. The Covent Garden management were in a panic. The performances had sold out as soon as the box office opened, and Prêtre, Gobbi and Cioni were waiting to begin rehearsals.

Maria made a deal. She would go to London, but would only sing once. As soon as the news broke the English press, which had always behaved so well towards her before, turned on her. They did not seem to realize that the days of Callas's temperament were past, that she had suffered a complete breakdown when she left Paris Opéra on 29 May.

Callas arrived in London, as promised, two days before the date fixed for her only appearance there. Marie Collier replaced her on the first night – the touching singer who fell to her death one stormy night '*Come la Tosca nel teatro!*' Before the performance, a Canadian businessman who had the room next to hers at the Savoy told the *Daily Express,* Callas sang through the night. According to him, she sounded in good voice. But on the evening of 5 July her beloved London audience (though to be fair to London it was only the first-night audience of socialites prepared to pay £100 for an orchestra stall because it is for charity and tax-deductible too) sat as if turned to stone when Tosca made her entrance in Sant'Andrea della Valle, though on previous occasions applause had greeted her first cry of '*Mario!*' from the wings. She sang and the critics gave favourable reviews of her performance, though her voice was not very powerful.

After the final curtain fell Callas took her bows first with Tito Gobbi, Renato Cioni and Georges Prêtre, then alone. A car was waiting to take her to the Savoy. Maria Callas never sang another opera on stage anywhere in the world.

'Come la Tosca nel teatro. . .'

Chapter Seven

TU, IN QUESTA TOMBA (1966-1977)

Much, perhaps too much, has been said about Callas's last years and silence. Anyone who ever got near her has an anecdote to tell. People who interviewed her for twenty minutes on television or spoke to her during a public discussion, suddenly turn out to have been intimate friends and all want to talk about her, to tell their own story through her.

I shall only add what is relevant to her last years and perhaps try to understand her better now that it is all over. By the end her emotional, professional and financial affairs were an inextricable tangle and everyone believes that he or she alone knows the truth about her. As I do not wish to contradict any of these versions of the truth, though each may run counter to someone else's sincerely held view, I shall preface what follows, in best novelist's tradition – and after all this life story is like a novel – with the disclaimer that 'any resemblance to any person living or dead is purely coincidental.'

I shall seek to understand how and why we reached this point – we, her audience, making her sing on until the end, until she fell silent. To understand her silence too, as the curtains fell and doors slid shut like blocks of stone slipping into place to seal the tomb of an Egyptian goddess, Aida walled up alive in a pyramid of silence without Radamès. Callas imprisoned in her apartment on Avenue Georges Mandel, looked after to the end by Bruna and Ferruccio.

By now her voice was a ruined instrument sometimes capable of the most beautiful sounds, but quite unreliable. The sad truth was that Maria Callas no longer had confidence in her voice. Sometimes it would soar melodiously in the music of Bellini or Puccini, but then it would fail. A cracked note, a strident or hoarse sound bearing little resemblance to the vibrant voice so reviled by some but capable of moving us to tears, or those resounding low notes, ringing like bronze from the depth of her throat. Sometimes she still sang her Cs or Ds, but she missed some and could not risk appearing on stage.

Worse, Maria no longer had confidence in herself. She was terrified that the stage-fright she had experienced before her last performances of Norma would return, leaving her paralysed by fear, unable to go on. 'It is not my voice which is sick, it is my nerves,' she confessed one day, without meaning to be coy. After her *Norma* in Paris and her one performance of *Tosca* in London she knew she could not hold out. Day by day her health became more shaky. She was doped with vitamins, coramine, black coffee, injections and pills to keep her going. She would smile apologetically and admit, 'Yes, I'm more fragile than I look.' How then could she hope to make a fresh start?

But for eight years, until 1974, Maria kept going. She still hoped to sing, at the opera, at concerts, on records or in a film, and she did sing again in 1973, giving a series of concerts which were a resounding success. Music and singing were still her main concern. She read music, played the piano and in 1971 and 1972 gave her famous master classes in Philadelphia and at the Juilliard School of Music in New York, remembered with emotion by everyone who attended them as far more than a mere course of lessons. In 1973 she even produced an opera.

In 1965 Maria's matrimonial affairs were finally settled. After the court hearing in Brescia Meneghini had regretted his original generosity and decided to take action against her. During the summer of 1965 a Milan court at last gave a ruling which Maria hoped would be final. Both partners were held responsible for the break-up: Maria was blamed for her liaison with Onassis, which went beyond the limits of friendship, but Meneghini was also held guilty of causing Maria considerable losses by giving damaging interviews about her. His claim that Maria was solely responsible for their separation was rejected, though he continued to protest – with an air of injured innocence – that he had always behaved like a perfect gentleman. Exit, once and for all, Meneghini.

However, Maria's life with Onassis sometimes proved difficult. Onassis admired and idolized her. He recognized her beauty and talent and was proud that they belonged to him: he had bought them. Maria loved him madly, desperately, like a woman who knows that she cannot love in any other way, that she can only love the wrong man with a blind passion which will destroy him, her and their love. Jealous, passionate and in love, she was unbearable. She was Onassis's slave and his alone, though not Prince Calaf's little Liù in *Turandot* – but more like Turandot, a princess in love who chooses to become a slave. She invented a whole system of rites and priorities to be observed, friendships to be forbidden, hatreds to be upheld. The question of marriage was left open. Perhaps Onassis would have married Maria if she had not demanded more each day, while at the same time giving all. 'We were doomed, but oh how rich we were . . .' Callas remarked on television one day, looking back with a wry, nostalgic smile. She and Onassis continued to live side by side, a few doors apart in Avenue Foch; or one in Paris, the other in some far corner of the earth.

Maria even went into business with Onassis, and they discussed producing films and buying ships together. Sometimes it all turned out badly, like the Vergottis affair – a sad story of broken friendship with a Greek financier whom Maria had regarded as a father-figure. Onassis and Vergottis had joint interests and decided to buy a cargo boat, the *Artemision II*, together. As Maria had some money to invest Onassis suggested she should join them, the arrangement being that she would acquire 25 per cent of the shares for £60,000 and Onassis would give her another 26 per cent, thus giving her the majority holding. But Vergottis, who held these shares, took offence at a rather curt telephone call from Maria and with a tired old man's stubborness refused to give her what she was entitled to, simply because it was she who had paid. Onassis and

Callas were obliged to take the matter to court, where Vergottis had a platform for his slanderous remarks and indiscreet questions, a chance to make Maria confess everything she had always refused to admit, to sully her reputation in a fit of destructive rage. Finally in 1967 and in 1968, on appeal, the court ruled against Vergottis, but the whole affair left a bitter taste. Love and money – it was all part of life with Onassis, known to the press in all its minute detail.

Suddenly it came to an end: in the early autumn of 1968 it was announced that the Greek shipowner had married the widow of a murdered president.

From now on Maria lived alone with her dreams, her memories and herself. But Maria would not admit defeat. She listened to many proposals, she made plans, and she dreamed up schemes.

First she planned to make a film. Ever since her first cruise on the *Christina* – when Carl Foreman had wanted her to play the main female part in *The Guns of Navarone* – she had had the thought of a film at the back of her mind. With her face, figure and beauty, many producers had thought of her too: one suggestion was a film of the Bible. Joseph Losey and Visconti had more realistic ideas. The former, who was working on *Boom!*, based on a play by Tennessee Williams, wanted Callas to take the part of the star, living among her diamonds and memories on an island in the middle of the Mediterranean, who is visited by the angel of death. Callas would have been superb, devoured by her jewels and burned by the fire of a last love, but she refused and Elizabeth Taylor took the part, with Richard Burton and Noel Coward in one of his last appearances. Maria was afraid: 'I could not begin my film career by playing an old actress.'

Visconti planned to make a film of Puccini's life and hoped Maria would play Maria Jeritza, the Czech soprano whose path crossed Puccini's. The plan came to nothing and Maria did not even have to refuse. She was still incapable of saying yes or no, and would delay answering questions until others were forced to take her decisions for her – as Rudolph Bing had done in 1958.

Indecision was also the keynote in her plans for a possible stage comeback, if only for a farewell performance (though this idea appalled her). Until 1967 Michel Glotz tried to make her change her decision not to sing any more, but she put so many difficulties, proposals and counter-proposals in his way that none of his schemes ever saw the light of day. She seemed terrified of no longer being a legend or of failing to live up to her image. She seemed to lack both willpower and courage.

First a real comeback was planned in a large-scale new production of *Medea* for Paris Opéra. Alexis Minotis was to have produced it, and Callas would have appeared for the last time in one of her great roles, in a last reconstruction of Corinth. Approaches were made, and letters exchanged – but that was all. Plans for a Visconti production of *Traviata* also for Paris Opéra got further and everyone was optimistic, but once again they foundered. Visconti and Callas demanded a budget and an amount of rehearsal time which Paris Opéra was unable to provide. 'I

Violetta in 1955, Maria Callas sang this role 63 times in eight years

only made one condition,' she explained in 1970, 'twenty to thirty days of rehearsals for orchestra and chorus. I could not have this, so the scheme fell by the wayside. . . .' Not through her fault of course. But in the late sixties no opera house in the world could afford thirty days of rehearsal for chorus and orchestra for *Traviata*. And she knew it well.

Would she have been up to it? In the late sixties could she still have sung *Traviata*, in Paris or in Dallas, where Lawrence Kelly and Nicola Rescigno were hoping she would return to sing Violetta again? Or *Trovatore* and *Norma* in San Francisco as had been suggested, again with an offer of inadequate rehearsal time? Or at the Met? Callas had made up her quarrel with Rudolph Bing and was eager to sing again in New York – if dates could be arranged. And of course when it came to dates, to choosing a month and a day she gave up. Nothing suited her. None of Lawrence Kelly's plans, Kurt Herbert Adler's (no longer an enemy), Bing's or anybody's would do.

Caught between her eagerness to make a comeback and her apparent inability to make up her mind, she clearly felt the need for someone to help and encourage her. But she had broken with Michel Glotz and the people who now surrounded her perhaps only encouraged her in her unwillingness to commit herself, assuring her that she of all people must only accept the best. Some suicidal impulse seemed to be driving her towards absolute silence. In fact she was resigned and uncertain. Once again she did not dare. She totally lacked confidence and she could no longer control her voice.

The abortive plans to make film versions of *Tosca* and *Traviata* show the force of her inertia. First *Tosca*. After Zeffirelli's London production, Maria toyed with the idea of making a film of it. Since all we have are bad copies of two versions of Act II of *Tosca*, filmed in Paris and at Covent Garden, and a few minutes of Norma, filmed in Paris (three minutes to be precise, since that was all the musicians' union would allow the orchestra), the thought of a film of Callas in one of her greatest roles is something to dream about – Callas in Zeffirelli's great production filmed by Zeffirelli himself. Karajan, thanks to Michel Glotz now reconciled with Maria, was also to be involved in the scheme. As regards the sound track, there were three possibilities – to use the 1953 *Tosca*, or Prêtre's 1964 version or to record the whole opera again with Karajan. Needless to say Maria could not decide. Franco Zeffirelli had many other plans but was particularly keen on this one and so he waited. Then he too began to have doubts and finally he got tired of waiting. There was no film of *Tosca*.

The scenario was almost identical for *Traviata*. Maria was keen, everyone encouraged her and she now got on well with Karajan who was again to take part. They would meet to discuss their plans for a second recording of *Traviata* (which Maria never got round to) as well as for the film. But Maria could not commit herself. She wanted a contract which allowed her to make all the decisions, almost down to the tiniest details of casting or photography. This time Karajan got annoyed and there was no more talk of *Traviata*. Like Zeffirelli's *Tosca* it is only a dream. In an attempt to save the situation Callas, at the last minute, suggested that Giulini should replace Karajan, but Giulini had not even been consulted and it was too late.

One of these plans did come to fruition – Pasolini's *Medea*. Here for the first time Callas, alive and in colour, stunningly beautiful, left us an image of herself to flesh out her legend.

Pier Paolo Pasolini's idea was simple. He had already made a film of *Oedipus Rex,* set against the landscape of the tragedy. He had seen and loved Callas in the great opera houses of the world and he believed that he could make a film in which Callas and Medea, actress and character, became one with the parched, brutal landscape. There was to be practically no dialogue, but sequences constructed like scenes from opera – scenes of cruelty going far beyond reality. There would be no singing either. Maria would remain silent almost throughout.

Franco Rossellini the main producer and Pierre Kalfon in France gave the scheme their full support. Pasolini, another doomed figure, reread Mircea Eliade and Jung. His intention was not to reproduce Euripides, but to return to the sources of tragedy in the poetic unconscious of a Mediterranean world preserved in legend. Jason and Corinth, representing order and authority (nearby Athens was to symbolize universal reason), are challenged by the dark, alien, secret religion of Medea, but challenged in vain since by comparison with their power her crime is negligible. She is a woman who still wants to believe, while men prefer the new technology and bourgeois marriage to the mysteries of more sacred nuptials.

Surprisingly, since apparently she did not like Pasolini's earlier work much, Callas agreed to take the part. She had seen *Theorem* and claimed to have been shocked by its excessive use of full-frontal nude shots. Her taste in films was fairly basic: 'There are so many terrible things in the world already . . . I go to the cinema to be entertained.' But now that her voice was gone, it was a chance for her to show her face and to leave an impression of what had been one of her greatest roles, without music, but with the same intensity as before. She was also very fond of Pasolini who kept her amused and made her laugh; and Callas liked to be amused. The press shamelessly hinted at romance between them, though the suggestion was patently absurd. Maria went so far as to deny it. But Pasolini did respect Callas and she liked to be respected.

The film was shot in 1969 in Asia Minor and Italy. Maria adapted well to what was expected of her. Turkey and Aleppo, Pisa, the lagoons of Grado on the Adriatric, the outskirts of Rome, each landscape out of context was more desolate than the last and Maria gave more and more of herself. One day she fainted from exhaustion after filming all day in the blazing sun. She was almost burned alive on another occasion when, standing in for her stand-in, she had to pass through a wall of fire somewhere in the middle of Turkey. Once again everyone admired her professional dedication, her careful study of each moment of her role and enthusiasm. Dozens of journalists from all over the world followed the filming. Maria now agreed to all interviews. She seemed to have accepted

Pasolini's Medea

her role as a star – in the past tense – and all the risks it involved.

When she spoke in the film the ancient Greek words sounded on her lips like a long unbroken cry of violence, a rugged, archaic language. Her face was made up to look completely natural and, with her beautiful arms and shoulders, she looked like a living statue burnt by the sun, parched by terror. In marvellous costumes designed by Piero Tosi who had worked with her before at La Scala, she was a barbarous princess, sometimes distraught, sometimes statuesque. Certainly in making this film she felt she was completing her own legend. It is absurd that there is nothing left as evidence of her acting in opera, except the two versions of Act II of *Tosca* from Paris and London, especially if one remembers that Geraldine Farrar, a famous Carmen from the golden days of the Met, played the part of Carmen in the days of silent cinema. In the film of *Medea* Callas gave herself wholeheartedly so that a living image of her might survive.

The film's première on 28 January 1970 was one of those ostentatious Parisian galas, so glowingly described by *France-Soir*. Subsequently the film had an honourable career in art cinemas. Maria went back home and closed the door. In vain Visconti offered her any part – goddess or bourgeoise, aristocrat or tragedienne – if only she would make a film for him, but she always refused. She had dared to do it once and that was enough.

However, two years later, Maria did emerge from her isolation – not for a film this time but for a return to the world of singing, her former glory and *raison d'être*. She decided to bequeath a little of her knowledge and give her admirers an insight into how Callas was what she was. In 1971 and 1972 she agreed to give a series of master classes in the United States before a live audience. These classes gave the audience and those who followed what went on a unique chance to see Callas at work and understand her better.

The first series of classes ended after the second lesson because in February 1971 the Curtis Institute of Music in Philadelphia could not provide students advanced enough to interest Callas, and so the experiment was a failure. But she tried again a few months later and the lessons she gave at the Juilliard School of Music, New York, were a valuable legacy for a whole generation of new singers.

At the Juilliard – one of the most famous music schools in the world – Callas gave two series of classes in October-November 1971 and in February-March 1972. This time the pupils had been carefully chosen by the staff and by Maria herself who auditioned over 300 candidates, admitting only a handful of the best. For students at the school the classes were part of their course, but pupils from outside had to pay $240 for twelve classes. Season tickets were available for the audience. In fact so few of Callas's admirers knew about the classes that the first course, especially at the beginning, took place before a half-empty hall of a thousand places. Later, since the Juilliard School would only sell tickets for the whole course, there were some gate-crashers, and some keen Callas fans managed to get in on forged tickets. In the hall the tenor

Placido Domingo and Rudolph Bing, the pianist Alexis Weissenberg and Lilian Gish might find themselves sitting side by side.

These classes were a marvellous show. Callas the teacher was no longer a prima donna, but she *was* still very much Callas. The classes were held every Monday and Thursday afternoon and lasted for two hours from 5.30 to 7.30. Callas worked on five or six arias with as many students at each session, always with the same tremendous enthusiasm. She explained, argued, sang and listened. She brought not just the music to life, but the entire role, revealing every aspect of a character in a few minutes as skilfully as she had in a single band of a record when working in Paris. It was a dazzling display of adaptability, versatility and deep understanding. She would sing a few bars of each aria, tenor, mezzo or bass, as well as the whole range of soprano roles. Her audience could sense in her the energy and vigour she used to bring to her characters on stage. It was sheer genius. Humble Adriana Lecouvreur becoming even more humble, Rigoletto growling like a wild beast, Marguerite in *Faust,* her eyes and voice sparkling with innocent eagerness at the sight of the jewels. Dressed in a dark skirt and white top, her hair loose, and wearing her spectacles at last, Maria would for a few seconds become a Cilea heroine, a Verdi baritone, a French prima donna. Each example was a relevation to those who listened and followed her advice. In fifteen or twenty minutes of individual tuition she could transform a singer, inspire him with her own passion, and make him forget all the bad habits he had picked up from traditional teaching and suddenly long to get out there and perform.

'You must vibrate,' declared Callas. The girl stopped singing and stared at her blankly. 'Vibrate like a violin.' Callas took a step forward and sang a few notes from *La Bohème*. It was enough. Everyone understood – and gasped. A moment of genius, but no one was allowed to clap. They could only admire this miracle in silence. But at other times Callas's voice would rise proudly, then break. As in her Paris *Norma,* there was nothing left – a phrase of five or six notes, velvety as ever, would float across the room and then disappear without warning. But the fact that Callas had agreed to give these classes and appear before an audience showed that she wanted to do more.

Certainly she now felt far more confident. Like an invalid recovering from a serious illness, assuring herself that everything is still possible. But all that remained were the last broken fragments of her voice, its last faltering notes, no longer even a swan song.

Her venture into opera production was less successful. She had been invited to produce *I Vespri Siciliani* with di Stefano in Turin, the opera in which she had made her début at La Scala twenty-one years before. Feeling daring at this point in her life, she agreed. As soon as she reached Turin she quarrelled with Gavazzeni, the conductor, and then went on to direct the singers, including Raina Kabaiwanska, still a moving Tosca today, and Gianni Raimondi, in an undistinguished production which did little to enhance her reputation. The first night, in April 1973, had only a lukewarm reception.

Callas with di Stefano and Almeida during the recording session held in London in 1972

On the other hand her attempted return to recording and above all her 1973-74 concerts showed that so far as the general public were concerned Callas was still a star who could draw the crowds. Even in her lifetime this proud, hieratic figure with the broken voice was becoming a legend in the history of singing.

Her last record was made in London at the end of 1972 but never issued. Callas had begun to see di Stefano again, the fiery di Stefano of her youth, and all the memories they shared – disagreements, tantrums and triumphs alike – suddenly seemed to her happy ones. A London impresario, Gorlinsky, suggested they should make a record of duets together. Maria and di Stefano had a strange relationship based on tremendous affection and a mixture of professional, emotional, and business considerations. When she rediscovered di Stefano it brought back to her everything they had done together, the records they had made for the La Scala collection. She longed to start again, to try and go on together.

A young conductor, Antonio de Almeida, now musical director at Nice, specializing in Offenbach and rare French and Italian operas, conducted the London Symphony Orchestra. The recording sessions were held in the ancient church of St. Giles Cripplegate near the Barbican in the City of London. For two weeks Almeida attempted the impossible: to resurrect a voice. The duets were classics – *Don Carlos, La Forza del Destino, Otello, I Vespri Siciliani, L'Elisir d'Amore* and *Aida*. But by now Callas's voice was affected by terrible vibrato which distorted everything she did, while di Stefano had completely lost the ability to sing *piano* and could really only sing at the top of his voice. Maria also heard the news of her father's death at this time and was, as can be imagined, in a bad state psychologically. In the end she herself decided that the record, made by skilful editing of many arias recorded several times, should not be released. None of the people who took part in the session kept tapes of Maria's last attempt to leave us something of her voice.

On the other hand there are a hundred pirate recordings of her concerts the following year, each more painful than the last. Painful, but evocative. Maria still went on trying to recover what was lost. Di Stefano was with her, an ever-present reminder of the past, and for the first time she felt almost happy with him. They travelled together and faced the public together on their grand tour of 1973-74, another sad story of farewells and departures, a long series of concerts in eight countries spread over seven months and then extended to the Far East. It was a long drawn-out demonstration of the death of Maria Callas's voice. Without the necessary vocal means or technical resources and no longer daring to rely entirely on her dramatic powers, Maria wavered. With di Stefano at her side, his voice too no more than a memory, she attempted *La Gioconda* or 'O mio babbino caro' from *Gianni Schicchi* with touching caution. All too clearly she realized she was no longer up to it, but she went on trying. She uttered sounds which were shadows of everything we might have loved, but suddenly exaggerated with all their faults to the point of caricature.

When singing duets with di Stefano she sometimes seized his hand and clung to it, their fingers locked together to give each other courage. Somehow they got through their duets from *Don Carlos, I Vespri Siciliani* and *Cavalleria Rusticana*. As the tour went on from Hamburg to Dusseldorf, Munich to London, they showed the same weaknesses each time, but each time they were greeted with enthusiasm by audiences which applauded each piece wildly. The tour was a phenomenal success, in Europe and America and then in Japan where it ended. Hand in hand, Callas and di Stefano received the applause and took their bows, overcome with emotion. But what everyone was applauding was not an aria or a voice, but a legend, *the* legend. Most of those who were carried away by their feelings in concert halls in Germany or America had never heard the real Callas, except on record. But in the presence of a myth, particularly when the myth was still the most beautiful woman in the world, who could say no?

On the stage of the Festival Hall in London on 26 November 1973 Maria dressed in black was like a trembling reflection of our earliest memories. Her '*Suicidio*' sung by a voice now harsh and guttural was a tarnished, but living, image of the first *Gioconda* she had sung in Verona twenty-six years before. Every sound was unstable or strained, yet easily recognizable – as Maria, Norma or Tosca, that voice for which we would give everything. The tour went on, and in Madrid, Paris, Milan, then Philadelphia, Boston, Chicago, Miami Beach, or Montreal there were always the same moments of intense emotion before a voice which no longer existed. It was the same thing in Korea and Japan in October 1974, the same reawakening of buried memories, the same wild ovation for the singers. The end was near. Seoul, Tokyo, Fukuoka, Tokyo again, Osaka, Hiroshima, Sapporo – a string of towns, theatres and auditoriums. On 2 November 1974 Maria Callas sang for the last time in public in the Hokkaido Koseinenkin Kaikan in Sapporo. What, we may well ask, was the Hokkaido Koseinenkin Kaikan? And which of us has ever been to Sapporo?

Callas had finished singing.

We tiptoe through her apartment in Avenue Georges Mandel, past the tasteful curtains, the silk sofas, the antique furniture all too clearly revealing the hand of the interior decorator. Silence. A maid Bruna and a chauffeur-butler Ferruccio looked after Maria. With the few friends that remained, for many had left – left or died, but more often left – and others had been driven away. Or rather, she had seen them less and less often and then not at all. The list of those who disappeared like this is long: Michel Glotz, Zeffirelli, even di Stefano. A misunderstanding, a missed appointment, a quarrel, sometimes over money for money was very important to Maria, or simple lethargy. What was too much for some was not enough for Maria. Silently the velvet curtains fell. The telephone rang less often.

She lived in a waking dream among what remained. She refused the tangible evidence both of the present and of the past as it really was,

Paris 1973

181

remembering it as it should have been. She lived an illusion, invented reality. 'There are no great conductors any more. Only Serafin and Giulini knew how to conduct opera'. But Serafin was dead, and Giulini did not conduct operas any more. 'There are no tenors any more: how can you do Bellini?' After a concert given by some superb mezzo, peeved that the superb mezzo had not been perfect throughout she would remark to a friend 'What can you expect, one has to make do with what one can get now.' She might not say so, but 'now' meant now she was no longer singing. Everything used to be so wonderful before. 'Do you remember the orchestra of the San Carlo in Naples? How marvellous it was!' But the orchestra of the San Carlo was a hotch-potch, and Maria knew it.

She rejected the past as it had been, the present as it was. She lived on memories. From all over the world people sent her recordings of her concerts or performances in such and such an opera house, pirates to end all pirates. She would listen to them unwearyingly and make other people listen too. A new *Norma* or *Puritani*. 'Do you remember when. . .' Her friends gathered round to listen. The violin underlining the inflexions of Amina's voice so beautifully as she murmurs that even her tears cannot reawaken lost love – our love. Against the background hiss her voice would soar in pain or madness. The tape turning on the deck might come from Berlin or Tokyo, Seattle or Nice, it might be a concert from Dallas, an opera from New York, a *Lucia* from La Scala, which someone had recorded in the theatre or from the radio, making two copies, one to keep, the other to send Maria as a tribute. Only Maria and the fanatical collector would ever know this *Lucia,* this *Puritani,* but it did not matter so long as the memory was there.

Sometimes her friends would leave quietly, because Maria was afraid of them, afraid she would be pushed forward or used. 'It is very difficult to be friends with a star,' she one day told someone who longed for this friendship. She never wanted to get involved, so she would warn people off, afraid they would discover. . . what? She would try to escape, calling off a dinner or a tea at the last moment. Bruna would telephone. Or someone would telephone Bruna and be told, 'I was just going to call you. Madame has a terrible migraine. . .' In these, the last days of her voice, Maria would take refuge in paralysing perfectionism as an excuse for refusing a record or concert. 'There are no tenors or conductors any more'; so what was the use of putting on a new *Traviata?* Or the record she would not allow to be released. 'Can't you hear the harp. It's too loud. We must start again!' Only they never did start again and the record never was released.

One brief episode explains it all. One day Maurice Béjart wanted to produce *Traviata* for Callas. Alone on the stage Violetta would dream of her love. Alfredo and his affection might never have existed. For Violetta Valery, courtesan, money and success were the only realities. Maria let Béjart talk about his plan, she decided she liked him, but he put on his *Traviata* without her, and in a different way. Another curtain fell.

There were fewer people there now. A gifted pianist, a leading opera

'Addio del passato. . .'

critic, a theatre administrator, the director of a recording company. And society figures, people with money and famous names, all the outward signs of success for the little Greek emigrant. The days when Callas had denied being a woman of the world were long past. These were the people who took her out to dinner. The others had disappeared.

'My mother used to pray I would get cancer of the throat,' Maria said bitterly. The family had dispersed – her father, the only one she really loved, was dead and her mother and sister were plotting against her. Onassis was dead. Visconti was dead. Lawrence Kelly was dead. Madame von Z, her closest friend, was dead. She lived in Sunset Boulevard with photographs of the past on the piano – Maria in white as Ifigenia or La Vestale. Sometimes a singer came to see her – Leontyne Price, a friend of hers, Monserrat Caballé or Sylvia Sass. Maria was pleased by these attentions. And she was pleased yet embarrassed by the young people in the street who recognized her and gave her flowers. One day one of them opened her car door and placed a spray of roses on the seat beside her and Maria was frightened.

She was kind to Monserrat Caballé. 'I like her,' she declared after she had left. Caballé admired her and listened to her a great deal. Callas gave Sylvia Sass, the young Hungarian soprano who had just triumphed at Aix in *Traviata,* a real lesson. The young singer had come to hear her talk about the part of Violetta and she talked for four hours, happy to meet someone so like her at last. 'A young Callas', they called Sylvia Sass, who later racked her voice singing Lady Macbeth at La Scala at the age of twenty-six or twenty-seven.

But these visits became rare. How could people know that Maria wished for visits although they frightened her? She still seemed to hope for something to rouse her from the torpor into which she was gradually drifting with her piano, her roses and her acquaintances. How could they know? Someone who claimed to be her friend, and really was her friend, was amazed afterwards. 'It's true. I hadn't seen her for over a year!'

'Quanto hai penato, anima mia'

The curtains had nearly all fallen now. A tape turned on the deck – the London *Tosca* of her last season but one. Maria lay stretched out on a sofa. 'How long have you loved me?' No one dared speak. 'She lived in a dream, like a child'. She was fifty-four and had nothing left, except medicines to raise her blood pressure, coramine to keep her going and strong black coffee. She still had occasional bursts of temper: 'Opera is not what it was. All these producers trying to make a name for themselves at all costs. In my day there were no producers. It was a matter between the conductor and singers!' Jorge Lavelli's production of *Faust* in Paris with sets like the cast-iron framework of some great Victorian exhibition hall made her furious. She had railed against theatre directors and impresarios in the same way in earlier days. In her beautiful voice, rolling her 'r's, she invented problems out there where everything still went on without her, while she had nothing left.

Nothing – except that out there in the street, in the world, everyone knew who she was and what she stood for. This was the real miracle. At a time when opera had fallen into abeyance, a forgotten glory shared by

183

the select few, Callas had rediscovered the road to opera. Her name alone was enough to interest people, make them ask questions, want to know more. What was *Norma*, *Traviata* or *Tosca*? At sixteen I used to queue outside Paris Opéra from six in the moring waiting for the box office to open. With a handful of madmen – not enthusiasts, madmen – who arrived early to buy seats at the top of the gods, the cheapest seats from which one could see. A little group, always the same people, the old lady with her camp stool and the young man holding forth – could it have been me? Then Callas arrived and swept everything before her. This was the Callas miracle, so how could anyone say there was nothing left?

Once there were a hundred or five hundred of us. Now there are ten or a hundred thousand. We seek out her records and photographs. First we made do with commercial records – those we could find since not all were available. We would send for *La Somnambula* from London or *Butterfly* from America. Then we began to lok for pirate recordings – the early classics, Giulini's *Traviata*, Karajan's *Lucia*, *Nabucco*, *Macbeth* and *I Vespri*. Then other pirates released in small numbers by obscure firms – the Mexico City *Toscas*, *Il Trovatore*, *Rigoletto*. Dear Mr Smith of New York, who recently closed up shop, we shall no longer receive your flowery letters telling us of your treasures! We exchanged addresses, records, tapes and photos. Callas was imprisoned all alone her apartment in the XVIe arrondissement. But we were all around her, embalming her alive.

16 September 1977 in Avenue Georges Mandel was simply the last movement of a slow symphony, a triumphant burial march. Suddenly Maria Callas met Violetta, Mimi, Tosca, Norma and Gioconda face to face.

She woke late and said she felt well. The previous day she had gone for a short walk, played with her dog, played the piano, perhaps seen a film – an undemanding film, since 'there are so many terrible things in the world'. That morning she had her breakfast and perhaps forgot to take her usual medicines, but she often forgot towards the end. She stayed in bed.

Suddenly as she so often did she felt unwell – her blood pressure was very low. Bruna found the coramine as usual, then went away. Maria was alone in her bedroom with its heavy Venetian furniture. She rose and took a few steps towards the bathroom. Bruna head the sound of a fall. Maria had fallen in the bedroom near a little table beside the bathroom door. 'I felt ill.' She grimaced and Ferruccio arrived to help Bruna carry her back to bed. Suddenly a terrible pain in her left side – Violetta's last moments.

Panic-stricken Bruna and Ferruccio telephoned Maria's doctor, but he was out. Then another, who refused to come. Finally they found an emergency doctor who agreed to call. Bruna made some very strong black coffee to rouse Maria. She drank a little and felt better. When Bruna and Ferruccio looked back Maria Callas was dead.

Two hours later, laid out on the embroidered sheet, Maria Callas had never been younger or more beautiful.

LIST OF CALLAS'S ROLES

All the roles Callas sang on stage are included in this list, together with dates, places and number of performances, the conductor and other principal singers.

For ease of comparison, any commercial recordings she made of these roles are also included.

YEAR	MONTH	NUMBER	PLACE	CONDUCTOR	PRINCIPAL SINGERS
			AIDA – 33		
1948	September	4	Turin	Serafin	Turini, Nicolai
	October	3	Rovigo	Berrettoni	Turini, Pirazzini
1949	July	1	Buenos Aires	Serafin	Vela, Barbieri
1950	February	2	Brescia	Erede	Del Monaco, Protti, Pini
	April	3	Milan	Capuana	Del Monaco, Barbieri, De Falchi
	April/May	4	Naples	Serafin	Picchi, Stignani, Savarese
	May/June	3	Mexico	Picco	Kurt Baum, Simionato, Robert Weede
	October	1	Rome	Bellezza	Picchi, Stignani, De Falchi
1951	February	1	Reggio Calabria	F. Del Cupolo	Soler, Pirazzini, Manca-Serra
	July	3	Mexico	Fabritiis	Del Monaco, Dominguez, Taddei
1953	June	4	Covent Garden	Barbirolli	Kurt Baum, Simionato, Jess Walters, Joan Sutherland
	July	4	Verona	Serafin	Del Monaco, Nicolai, Protti
1955	August		*Recording*	Serafin	Tucker, Barbieri, G bi
			ALCESTE – 4		
1954	April	4	Milan	Giulini	R. Gavarini, Panerai, Silveri
			ANDREA CHENIER – 6		
1955	January	4	Milan	Votto	Del Monaco, Protti
	February	2	Milan	Votto	M. Ortica, Taddei
			ANNA BOLENA – 12		
1957	April/May	7	Milan	Gavazzeni	G. Raimondi, Rossi-Lemeni, Simionato
1958	April	5	Milan	Votto	G. Raimondi, Siepi, Simionato
			ARMIDA – 3		
1952	April/May	3	Florence	Serafin	F. Albanese, Zilliani
			UN BALLO IN MASCHERA – 5		
1956	September		*Recording*	Votto	Di Stefano, Gobbi, Barbieri
1957	December	5	Milan	Gavazzeni	Di Stefano, Bastianini, Simionato
			IL BARBIERE DI SIVIGLIA – 5		
1956	February/March	5	Milan	Giulini	Alva, Gobbi, Rossi-Lemeni
1957	February		*Recording*	Galliera	Alva, Gobbi, Zaccaria
			DON CARLOS – 5		
1954	April	5	Milan	Votto	Ortica, Mascherini, Stignani, Rossi-Lemeni
			DIE ENTFÜHRUNG AUS DEM SERAIL – 4		
1952	April	4	Milan	Perlea	Prandelli, T. Menotti, Munteanu
			FEDORA – 6		
1956	May/June	6	Milan	Gavazzeni	Corelli, Zanolli
			FORZA DEL DESTINO – 6		
1948	April	4	Trieste	Parenti	Vetecchi, B. Franci, Siepi, Canali
1954	May	2	Ravenna	Ghione	Del Monaco, Protti, Modesti, Capecchi
1954	August		*Recording*	Serafin	Tucker, Tagliabue, Rossi-Lemeni, Capecchi, Nicolai
			LA GIOCONDA – 13		
1947	August	5	Verona	Serafin	Nicolai, Tucker, Tagliabue
1952	July	2	Verona	Votto	Nicolai, Poggi, Inghilleri

185

YEAR	MONTH	NUMBER	PLACE	CONDUCTOR	PRINCIPAL SINGERS
1952	September		*Recording*	Votto	Barbieri, Poggi, Silveri
1952-1953	December/January/February	6	Milan	Votto	Stignani, Di Stefano, Tagliabue
1959	September		*Recording*	Votto	Cossotto, P. Miranda Ferraro, Cappuccilli

IFIGENIA IN TAURIDE – 4

YEAR	MONTH	NUMBER	PLACE	CONDUCTOR	PRINCIPAL SINGERS
1957	June	4	Milan	Nino Sanzogno	F. Albanese, Cossotto

LUCIA DE LAMMERMOOR – 46

YEAR	MONTH	NUMBER	PLACE	CONDUCTOR	PRINCIPAL SINGERS
1952	June	3	Mexico City	Picco	Di Stefano, Campolonghi
1953	January/February	4	Florence	Ghione	Lauri-Volpi, Bastianini
	February		*Recording*	Serafin	Di Stefano, Gobbi
1953	March	2	Genoa	Ghione	Di Stefano, Mascherini
	April	2	Catania	Fabritiis	Turrini, Taddei
	May	3	Rome	Gavazzeni	Poggi, Guelfi
1954	January/February	7	Milan	Karajan	Di Stefano, Panerai
	February	3	Venice	Angelo Questa	L. Infantino, Bastianini
	October	2	Bergamo	Molinari-Pradelli	Tagliavini, Savarese
	November	2	Chicago	Rescigno	Di Stefano, Guelfi
1955	September/October	2	Berlin (Scala)	Karajan	Di Stefano, Panerai
1956	March	3	Naples	Molinari-Pradelli	Raimondi, Panerai
	June	3	Vienna (Scala)	Karajan	Di Stefano, Panerai
	December	4	New York	Cleva	Campora/Tucker, Sordello/F. Valentino
1957	June	1	Rome R.A.I. (Radio)	Serafin	E. Fernandi, Panerai
1958	February	3	New York	Cleva	Bergonzi, Sereni
1959	March		*Recording*	Serafin	Tagliavini, Cappuccilli
	November	2	Dallas	Rescigno	G. Raimondi, Bastianini

MACBETH – 5

YEAR	MONTH	NUMBER	PLACE	CONDUCTOR	PRINCIPAL SINGERS
1952-1953	December/January	5	Milan	De Sabata	Mascherini, Tajo, Penno

MADAMA BUTTERFLY – 3

YEAR	MONTH	NUMBER	PLACE	CONDUCTOR	PRINCIPAL SINGERS
1955	August		*Recording*	Karajan	Gedda, Danieli, Borriello
	November	3	Chicago	Rescigno	Di Stefano, Eunice Alberts, Robert Weede

MEDEA – 31

YEAR	MONTH	NUMBER	PLACE	CONDUCTOR	PRINCIPAL SINGERS
1953	May	3	Florence	V. Gui	C. Guichandut, Barbieri
1953-1954	December/January	5	Milan	Bernstein	Penno, Barbieri
	March	3	Venice	V. Gui	R. Gavarini, G. Tucci
1955	January	4	Rome	Santini	Albanese, Tucci, Christoff
1957	September		*Recording*	Serafin	Picchi, Scotto
1958	November	2	Dallas	Rescigno	Vickers, Berganza
1959	June	5	London	Rescigno	Vickers, Cossotto
	November	2	Dallas	Rescigno	Vickers, N. Merriman
1961	August	2	Epidaurus	Rescigno	Vickers, Kiki Morfoniou
	December	3	Milan	T. Schippers	Vickers, Simionato, Ghiaurov
1962	May	2	Milan	T. Schippers	Vickers, Simionato, Ghiaurov

MEFISTOFELE – 3

YEAR	MONTH	NUMBER	PLACE	CONDUCTOR	PRINCIPAL SINGERS
1954	July	3	Verona	Votto	Tagliavini, Di Stefano, Rossi-Lemeni

NABUCCO – 3

YEAR	MONTH	NUMBER	PLACE	CONDUCTOR	PRINCIPAL SINGERS
1949	December	3	Naples	V. Gui	Becchi, A. Pini

NORMA – 89

YEAR	MONTH	NUMBER	PLACE	CONDUCTOR	PRINCIPAL SINGERS
1948	November/December	2	Florence	Serafin	Picchi, Barbieri, Siepi
1949	June	4	Buenos Aires	Serafin	Vela, Barbieri, Rossi-Lemeni
1950	January	3	Venice	Votto	Penno, Nicolai, Pasero
	February/March	5	Rome	Serafin	Masini, Stignani, Neri
	March	4	Catania	Berrettoni	Picchi, Gardino, Stefanoni
	May	2	Mexico	Picco	Baum, Simionato, Moscona

YEAR	MONTH	NUMBER	PLACE	CONDUCTOR	PRINCIPAL SINGERS
1951	February	2	Palermo	Ghione	Gavarini, Nicolai, Neri
	September	1	São Paulo	Serafin	Picchi, Barbieri, Rossi-Lemeni
	September	2	Rio	Votto	Picchi, Nicolai, Christoff
	November	4	Catania	Ghione	Penno, Simionato, Christoff
1952	January/February/April	8	Milan	Ghione	Penno, Stignani, Rossi-Lemeni
	November	5	Covent Garden	V. Gui	Picchi, Stignani
1953	April	4	Rome	Santini	Corelli, Barbieri, Neri
	June	4	Covent Garden	Pritchard	Picchi, Simionato, Neri, Sutherland
	November	4	Trieste	Votto	Corelli, Nicolai, Christoff
			Recording	Serafin	M. Filippeschi, Stignani, Rossi-Lemeni
1954	April-May				
	November	2	Chicago	Rescigno	Picchi, Simionato, Rossi-Lemeni
1955	December/January	9	Milan	Votto	Del Monaco, Simionato, Zaccaria
1956	October/November	5	New York	Cleva	Del Monaco, K. Baum, Barbieri, Siepi
	November	1	Philadelphia	Cleva	Del Monaco, K. Baum, Barbieri, Moscona
1957	January	2	Covent Garden	Pritchard	G. Vertecchi, Stignani, Zaccaria
1958	January	1	Rome	Santini	Corelli, Pirazzini, Neri
1960	August	2	Epidaurus	Serafin	Picchi, Morfoniou, Mazzoli
	September		Recording	Serafin	Corelli, Ludwig, Zaccaria
1964	May/June	8	Paris	Prêtre	Craig, Corelli, Cossotto, Vinco
1965	14-29 May	5	Paris	Prêtre	Cecchele, Simionato, Cossotto, I. Vinco

ORFEO ED EURIDICE – 2

YEAR	MONTH	NUMBER	PLACE	CONDUCTOR	PRINCIPAL SINGERS
1951	June	2	Florence	E. Kleiber	B. Christoff, T. Tygeson

PARSIFAL – 5

YEAR	MONTH	NUMBER	PLACE	CONDUCTOR	PRINCIPAL SINGERS
1949	February/March	4	Rome	Serafin	H. Beirer, Siepi, Cortis
1950	November	1	Rome (R.A.I.)	V. Gui	Baldelli, Christoff, Panerai

IL PIRATA – 7

YEAR	MONTH	NUMBER	PLACE	CONDUCTOR	PRINCIPAL SINGERS
1958	May	5	Milan	Votto	F. Corelli, Bastianini
1959	January	1	New York (Concert)	Rescigno	P. M. Ferraro, Ego
	January	1	Washington (Concert)	Rescigno	Ferraro, Ego

POLIUTO – 5

YEAR	MONTH	NUMBER	PLACE	CONDUCTOR	PRINCIPAL SINGERS
1960	December	5	Milan	Votto	Corelli, Bastianini, Zaccaria

I PURITANI – 16

YEAR	MONTH	NUMBER	PLACE	CONDUCTOR	PRINCIPAL SINGERS
1949	January	3	Venice	Serafin	Pirino, Savarese, B. Christoff
1951	November	4	Catania	Wolf-Ferrari	W. Wenkow, Tagliabue, Christoff
1952	January	2	Florence	Serafin	Conley, Tagliabue, Rossi-Lemeni
	May	3	Rome	Santini	Lauri-Volpi, Silveri, Neri
	May	2	Mexico	Picco	Di Stefano, Campolonghi, Silva
1953	March		Recording	Serafin	Di Stefano, Panerai, Rossi-Lemeni
1955	October/November	2	Chicago	Rescigno	Di Stefano, Bastianini, Rossi-Lemeni

RIGOLETTO – 2

YEAR	MONTH	NUMBER	PLACE	CONDUCTOR	PRINCIPAL SINGERS
1952	June	2	Mexico	Mugnai	Di Stefano, Campolonghi
1955	September		Recording	Serafin	Di Stefano, Gobbi

LA SONNAMBULA – 22

YEAR	MONTH	NUMBER	PLACE	CONDUCTOR	PRINCIPAL SINGERS
1955	March/April	10	Milan	Bernstein	C. Valetti, G. Modesti, E. Ratti
1957	March	6	Milan	Votto	Monti, Zaccaria, Cossotto
	March		Recording	Votto	Monti, Zaccaria, Cossotto
	July	2	Cologne/Scala	Votto	Monti, Zaccaria, Cossotto
	August	4	Edinburgh/Scala	Votto	Monti, Zaccaria, Cossotto

TOSCA – 33

YEAR	MONTH	NUMBER	PLACE	CONDUCTOR	PRINCIPAL SINGERS
1941	July, August/September		Athens		
1950	June	2	Mexico	Mugnai	Filippeschi, Weede
	September	1	Bologna	Questa	Turrini, Azzolini
	September	2	Pisa	Santarelli	Masini, Poli
	October				
1951	September	1	Rio	Votto	Poggi, Silveri

YEAR	MONTH	NUMBER	PLACE	CONDUCTOR	PRINCIPAL SINGERS
1952	June/July	2	Mexico	Picco	Di Stefano, Campolonghi
1953	August		*Recording*	De Sabata	Di Stefano, Gobbi
1954	March	3	Genoa	F. Ghione	Ortica, Guelfi
1956	November	2	New York	Mitropoulos	Campora, London
1958	February/March	3	New York	Mitropoulos	Tucker, W. Cassel/London
	December		Paris	Sebastian	Lance, Gobbi (*Act II*)
1964	January	6	London	Cillario	Cioni, Gobbi
	December		*Recording*	Prêtre	Bergonzi, Gobbi
1965	February/March	9	Paris	Prêtre	Cioni, Gobbi
	March	2	New York	Cleva	Corelli/Tucker, Gobbi
	July	1	Covent Garden	Prêtre	Cioni, Gobbi

LA TRAVIATA – 63

YEAR	MONTH	NUMBER	PLACE	CONDUCTOR	PRINCIPAL SINGERS
1951	January	3	Florence	Serafin	F. Albanese, E. Marcherini
	March	2	Cagliari	Molinari-Pradelli	Campora, Poli
	July	4	Mexico	Fabritiis	C. Valletti, G. Taddei
	September	1	São Paulo	Serafin	Di Stefano, Gobbi
	September	2	Rio	Gaioni	Poggi, Salsedo
	October	2	Bergamo	Giulini	Prandelli, Fabbri
	December	1	Parma	Fabritiis	Pola, Savarese
1952	March		Catania	Molinari-Pradelli	Campora, Mascherini
	June	2	Mexico	Mugnai	Di Stefano, Campolonghi
	August	4	Verona	Molinari-Pradelli	Campora, Mascherini
1953	January	2	Venice	Questa	Albanese, Savarese
	January	3	Rome	Santini	Albanese, Savarese
	September		*Recording*	Santini	Albanese, Savarese
1954	November	2	Chicago	Rescigno	Simoneau, Gobbi
1955	May/June	4	Milan	Giulini	Di Stefano/Prandelli, Bastianini
1956	January/February April/May	17	Milan	Giulini	G. Raimondi, E. Bastianini
1958	February	2	New York	Cleva	Daniele Barioni/Campora, Zanessi
	March	2	Lisbon	Ghione	A. Kraus, M. Sereni
	June	5	London	Rescigno	C. Valetti, Mario Zanasi
	October/November	2	Dallas	Rescigno	Filacuridi, Taddei

TRISTAN UND ISOLDE – 12

YEAR	MONTH	NUMBER	PLACE	CONDUCTOR	PRINCIPAL SINGERS
1947 1948	December/ January	4	Venice	Serafin	Tasso, Barbieri, Christoff
1948	May	3	Genoa	Serafin	Lorenz, Nicolai, Rossi-Lemeni
1950	February	5	Rome	Serafin	Seider, Nicolai, Neri

IL TROVATORE – 20

YEAR	MONTH	NUMBER	PLACE	CONDUCTOR	PRINCIPAL SINGERS
1950	June	3	Mexico	Picco	K. Baum, Simionato, Warren
1951	January	3	Naples	Serafin	Lauri-Volpi, Elmo, Silveri
1953	February/March	5	Milan	Votto	Penno, Stignani, Tagliabue
	June/July	3	London	Erede	Simionato, James Johnston, Jess Walker
	August	1	Verona	Molinari-Pradelli	Danieli, Zambruno, Protti
	December	3	Rome	Santini	Barbieri/Pirazzini, Lauri-Volpi, Silveri
1955	November	2	Chicago	Rescigno	Björling, Stignani, Bastianini
1956	August		*Recording*	Karajan	Barbieri, Di Stefano, Panerai

TURANDOT – 24

YEAR	MONTH	NUMBER	PLACE	CONDUCTOR	PRINCIPAL SINGERS
1948	January/February	5	Venice	N. Sanzogno	Soler, Rizzieri, Carmassi
	March	2	Udine	O. De Fabritiis	Soler, Ottani, Maionica
	July	3	Rome	O. De Fabritiis	G. Masini, Montanari, Flamini
	July/August	4	Verona	Votto	Salvarezza, Rizzieri, Rossi-Lemeni
	August	2	Genoa	Questa	Del Monaco, Montenari, Maionica
1949	February	4	Naples	Perlea	R. Gigli, Montanari, Petri
	May/June	4	Buenos Aires	Serafin	Del Monaco, Arismendi, Rossi-Lemeni
1957	July		*Recording*	Serafin	Fernandi, Schwarzkopf, Zaccaria

IL TURCO IN ITALIA – 9

YEAR	MONTH	NUMBER	PLACE	CONDUCTOR	PRINCIPAL SINGERS
1950	October	4	Rome	Gavazzeni	Valetti, Bruscantini, Stabile
1954	August/September		*Recording*	Gavazzeni	Gedda, Rossi-Lemeni, Stabile
1955	April/May	5	Milan	Gavazzeni	Valetti, Rossi-Lemeni, Stabile

YEAR	MONTH		NUMBER	PLACE	CONDUCTOR	PRINCIPAL SINGERS
					LA VESTALE – 5	
1954	December		5	Milan	Votto	Coreli, E. Sordello, Rossi-Lemeni, E. Stignani
					I VESPRI SICILIANI – 11	
1951	May/June/ December		4	Florence	Kleiber	Bardi-Kokolios, Mascherini, Christoff
1952	January		7	Milan	De Sabata	Conley, Mascherini, Christoff
					DIE WALKÜRE – 6	
1949	January		4	Venice	Serafin	Voyer, Torres, Dominici
	January		2	Palermo	Molinari-Pradelli	Voyer, Neri, Magnani

DISCOGRAPHY

This discography includes Maria Callas's recordings of complete operas only. It does not include her concerts, nor, with a few exceptions, excerpts from operas. Commercial recordings are given with the name of the recording company in italics. All available references, often several, are given for pirate recordings. Towards the end of 1977 and early 1978 the Italian firm CETRA began to release new pressings of many of these recordings, in Italy, at least, under the label 'Cetra Opera Live' (L.O.). These records are of far better quality than all previously available pirates.

TITLE	PLACE	DATE	CONDUCTOR	PRINCIPAL SINGERS	REFERENCES (COMMERCIAL RECORDINGS IN ITALICS)	
				BELLINI		
Norma	Mexico City	23-5-1950	Picco	Baum, Simionato, Moscona		
	Covent Garden	18-11-1952	V. Gui	Stignani, Picchi, Vaghi, Sutherland	OMY	6200
					MRF	11
					BJR	155
					EA	021
		23-4-1954/ 4-5-1954	Serafin		*EMI*	
				Stignani, Filippeschi		
	Rome	29-6-1955	Serafin	Stignani, Del Monaco	Opera Viva JLT 6	
	Scala	7-12-1955	Votto	Simionato, Del Monaco	BJR	147
					LER	103
					CETRA	LO 31/3
	Rome	2-1-1958	Santini	Corelli, Pirazzini, Neri (Act I only)	MORGAN 5801	
		5/12-9-1960	Serafin	Ludwig, Corelli, Zaccaria	*EMI*	
Il Pirata	Carnegie Hall	27-1-1959	Rescigno	P. M. Ferraro, C. Ego	FWR	641
					MRF	51
					BJR	145
					EA	004
I Puritani	Mexico City	29-5-1952	Picco	Di Stefano, Campolonghi	MRF	28
					UORC	191
				–	CETRA	LO 52/3
					EA	028
		24/30-3- 1953	Serafin	Di Stefano, Panerai, Rossi-Lemeni	*EMI*	
Sonnambula	Scala	5-3-1955	Bernstein	Valletti, Modesti, Ratti	ERR	108
					BJR	138
					EA	027
					CETRA	LO 32/3
		3/9-3-1957	Votto	Ratti, Monti, Zaccaria	*EMI*	
				BIZET		
Carmen		6/20-7-1964	Prêtre	Guiot, Gedda, Massard	*EMI*	

TITLE	PLACE	DATE	CONDUCTOR	PRINCIPAL SINGERS	REFERENCES (COMMERCIAL RECORDINGS IN ITALICS)	
			CHERUBINI			
Medea	Scala	10-12-1953	Bernstein	Barbieri, Penno, Modesti	BJR	129
					MRF	102
					MORGAN	5301
					UORC	128
					CETRA	LO 36/3
	Covent Garden	30-6-1959	Rescigno	Vickers, Cossotto, Zaccaria	BJR	105
					ROBIN HOOD	512
		12/19-9-1957	Serafin	Scotto, Pirazzini, Picchi	*EMI* then DGG	
	Dallas	6-11-1958	Rescigno	Berganza, Vickers, Zaccaria	FWR	647
					PENZANCE 41	
					ROBIN HOOD	
						512
	Scala	11-12-1961	Schippers	Vickers, Ghiaurov, Simionato	MRF	102
			DONIZETTI			
Anna Bolena	Scala	14-4-1957	Gavazzeni	G. Raimondi, Simionato, Rossi-Lemeni		
					FWR	646
					BJR	109
					MRF	42
					MORGAN	5703
					CETRA	LO 53/3
Lucia di Lammermoor	Mexico	10-6-1952	Picco	Di Stefano, Campolonghi	FWR	650
		2-1953	Serafin	Di Stefano, Gobbi	*EMI*	
	Berlin (Scala)	29-9-1955	Karajan	Di Stefano, Panerai, Zaccaria	LER	101
					BJR	131
					MORGAN	5401
					CETRA	LO 18/3
	New York	8-12-1956	Cleva	Campora, Sordello, Moscona	ERIM	412
					ESTRO	
	Scala	16/21-3-1959	Serafin	Tagliavini, Cappuccilli	*EMI*	
Poliuto	Scala	7-12-1960	Votto	Corelli, Bastianini, Zaccaria	FWR	644
					RJR	106
					MRF	31
					EA	006
			GIORDANO			
Andrea Chénier	Scala	8-1-1955	Votto	Del Monaco, Protti	OA	1010
					MRF	66
					UORC	286
					EA	012
					CETRA	LO 39/2
			GLUCK			
Alceste	La Scala	4-4-1954	Giulini	Gavarini, Silveri, Panerai, Zaccaria		
					UORC	273
					ERR	136
					CETRA	LO 50/2
Iphigénie en Tauride	Scala	1-6-1957	Nino Sanzogno	Cossotto, Albanese		
					FWR	649
					PENZANCE	12
					MRF	63
					MORGAN	5704
					CETRA	LO 54/2
			LEONCAVALLO			
Pagliacci		25-5/17-6 1954	Serafin	Di Stefano, Gobbi	*EMI*	
			MASCAGNI			
Cavalleria		3/4-8-1953	Serafin	Di Stefano, Panerai	*EMI*	
			PONCHIELLI			
Gioconda	Turin	9-1952	Votto	Barbieri, Amadini, Poggi, Silveri, Neri	*CETRA*	
		5-10-1959	Votto	Cossotto, Camparez, Ferraro, Cappuccilli, Vinco	*EMI*	

TITLE	PLACE	DATE	CONDUCTOR	PRINCIPAL SINGERS	REFERENCES (COMMERCIAL RECORDINGS IN ITALICS)	
			PUCCINI			
La Bohème		20/25-8-1956 3/4-9-1956	Votto	Moffo, Di Stefano, Panerai, Zaccaria	*EMI*	
Madama Butterfly		1/6-8-1955	Karajan	Gedda, Danieli	*EMI*	
Manon Lescaut		18/27-7-1957	Serafin	Di Stefano, Calabrese	*EMI*	
Tosca	Mexico City	8-6-1950	Mugnai	Filippeschi, R. Weede	UORC HRE	184 211
	Rio	24-9-1951	Votto	Poggi, Silveri (Extracts only)	PENZANCE	11
	Mexico City	1-7-1952	Picco	Di Stefano, Campolonghi	BJR MORGAN CETRA	153 5201 LO 41/2
		10/21-8-1953 1964 24-1-1964	De Sabata Prêtre Cillario	Di Stefano, Gobbi Gobbi, Bergonzi Cioni, Gobbi (Act II only)	*EMI* *EMI* LER	107
		15-3-1965	Cleva	Gobbi, Corelli	EA	013
Turandot		9/15-7-1957	Serafin	Schwarzkopf, Fernandi, Zaccaria	*EMI*	
			ROSSINI			
Armida	Florence	25-41952	Serafin	Albanese, Filippeshci, G. Raimondi	FWR PENZANCE MORGAN CETRA	567 54 5202 LO 39/2
Il Barbiere di Siviglia	Scala	16-2-1956	Giulini	Gobbi, Alva	ROBIN HOOD MRF EA CETRA	507 101 015 LO 34/3
	London	7/14-2-1957	Galliera	Alva, Gobbi	*EMI*	
Il Turco in Italia	Scala	31-8/8-9-1954	Gavazzani	Gedda, Stabile, Rossi-Lemeni, Calabrese	*EMI*	
			SPONTINI			
La Vestale	Scala	7-12-1954	Votto	Stignani, Corelli, Rossi-Lemeni	UORC ERR EA CETRA	217 117 009 LO 33/3
			VERDI			
Aida	Mexico City Mexico City	30-5-1950 3-7-1951	Picco De Fabritiis	Simionato, K. Baum, R. Weede Dominguez, Del Monaco, Taddei	UORC BJR MRF EA CETRA	200 104 21 001 LO 40/3
Un Ballo in maschera		10/24-8-1955	Serafin	Barbieri, Tucker, Gobbi	*EMI*	
	Scala	5/12-9-1956	Votto	Ratti, Barbieri, Di Stefano, Gobbi	*EMI*	
		7-12-1957	Gavazzeni	Ratti, Di Stefano, Bastianini, Simionato	BJR MRF MORGAN CETRA	127 83 5709 LO 55/3
La Forza del destino		17/27-8-1954	Serafin	Tucker, Rossi-Lemeni, Elena, Nicolai	*EMI*	
Macbeth	Scala	7-12-1952	De Sabata	Enzo Mascherini, G. Penno, I. Tajo	FWR BJR MRF Opera VIVA EA CETRA	655 117 61 JLT 3 005 LO 10/3

TITLE	PLACE	DATE	CONDUCTOR	PRINCIPAL SINGERS	REFERENCES (COMMERCIAL RECORDINGS IN ITALICS)	
Nabucco	San Carlo	20-12-1949	V. Gui	Gino Bechi, L. Neroni, A. Pini	ERR	114/3
					EA	026
					CETRA	LO 16/3
Rigoletto	Mexico	17-6-1952	Mugnai	Di Stefano, Campologhi	BJR	101
					CETRA	LO 37/3
	Scala	3/16-9-1955	Serafin	Di Stefano, Gobbi	*EMI*	
La Traviata	Mexico City	17-7-1951	De Fabritiis	Valletti, Taddei (Excerpts)	FWR	650
				(Excerpts)	BJR	130
	Mexico City	3-6-1952	Mugnai	Di Stefano, Campolonghi	UORC	181
					BJR	130
		9-1953	Santini	Fr. Albanese, U. Savarese	CETRA	
	Scala	28-5-1955	Giulini	Di Stefano, Bastianini	MRF	87
					CETRA	LO 28/2
	London	20-6-1958	Rescigno	Valletti, Zanasi	FWR	652
					LER	102
Il Trovatore	Mexico	20-6-1950	Picco	Simionato, Baum, Warren	HRE	207
					BJR	102
					FWR	651
	Naples	27-1-1951	Serafin	Lauri-Volpi, C. Elmo, Silveri	FWR	654
					EA	025
					CETRA	LO 2
	Scala	23-2-1953	Votto	Stignani, Penno, Tagliabue	ROBIN HOOD	
						500
					MRF	78
					CETRA	LO 35/3
		3/9-8-1956	Karajan	Di Stefano, Panerai, Barbieri	*EMI*	
I Vespri siciliani	Florence	26-5-1951	Erich Kleiber	Kokolios-Bardi, B. Christoff, E. Mascherini		
					FWR	645
					MRF	46
					PENZANCE	6
					EA	018
					CETRA	LO 6/3
			WAGNER			
Parsifal	R.A.I.	20/21-11-1950	V. Gui	Baldelli, B. Christoff, Panerai, Modesti	FWR	649
					EA	055